A REVIEW AND ANNOTATED BIBLIOGRAPHY OF FAMILY BUSINESS STUDIES

DEDICATED TO OUR FAMILIES

Sanjay Smita

Chander and Yoginer Joshi Sushma and Madan Mohan Sha

Vina Aparna Dinkar

Karen N. Chrisman

James John Chrisman Mildred N. Chrisman

David P. Chrisman John N. Chrisman

Sherrie Chrisman Louise Chrisman

Alicia Alba Ray Alba

Vernon Waller Jeanette Waller

Ronald Waller Shem Miller

Eva Kan

Simon Chuahe Loreta Huan

Flora and Alfonso Lim William and Tita Chua

Ely and Annie Chua Gene and Cherie Chua

Oscar and Jane Chua Natividad and Johnny So

A REVIEW AND ANNOTATED BIBLIOGRAPHY OF FAMILY BUSINESS STUDIES

by

PRAMODITA SHARMA
Ph.D. Candidate, Policy and Environment Area
Faculty of Management
The University of Calgary

JAMES J. CHRISMAN, Ph.D.
Professor of Venture Development
Faculty of Management
The University of Calgary

JESS H. CHUA, Ph.D.
Professor of Finance
Faculty of Management
The University of Calgary

Springer Science+Business Media, LLC

Library of Congress Cataloging-in-Publication Data

A C.I.P. Catalogue record for this book is available from the Library of Congress.

ISBN 978-1-4613-4685-2 ISBN 978-1-4419-8768-6 (eBook)
DOI 10.1007/978-1-4419-8768-6

Printed on acid-free paper.

CONTENTS

PREFACE

Interest in the study of family business has increased very significantly over the last decade. This is evident in the number of articles published about family business and the number of universities that have started family business research and teaching programs.

We originally prepared this review and annotated bibliography for ourselves to learn about the family business literature. Colleagues who saw it encouraged us to publish it as an introduction to the literature. While we cannot claim that all major articles written about the subject of family business are reported here, we have made an effort to include all those of which we are aware.

This review and annotated bibliography is divided into four sections. The first section reviews the research done in this field by identifying the major areas of interest, the contributions, and controversies. It also presents an extensive list of topics for further research. In section 2, we classify the articles annotated according to research topic, summarizing the type of research and key finding of each article annotated. This provides a simple guide to the research published under each topic.

The third section contains the annotated bibliography with the annotations arranged by author in alphabetical order. We categorize each article as an empirical study, a conceptual or theoretical article, a case study, a review article, a consulting report, or a professional advice. For empirical studies, we also report the sample, the method of data collection, and the data analysis performed. The main part of each annotation is a summary of the key points made in the article. The conclusions, conjectures, and opinions presented in each annotation are entirely those of the author(s) of the article, as we interpreted them. We make no attempt to express our opinion as to the relevance of the research topic, the quality of the research, or the justification for the conclusions. Key words are listed at the end of each annotation to provide a quick reference to the dominant themes in the article.

In the fourth section, we present a selected bibliography of articles: papers, books, and dissertations of which we are aware but have not annotated. In the last section we provide a subject index. We hope that this work gives family business owners, managers, consultants, researchers, and educators a comprehensive and easy-to-use guide to the emerging and fascinating field of family business.

Acknowledgments

We would like to thank the Faculty of Management at The University of Calgary for its support throughout the duration of this project. A large part of the funding came from the endowment for family business research set up by an anonymous donor.

1

A REVIEW OF THE FAMILY BUSINESS LITERATURE

Recently, there has been a significant rise in interest about family firms. As evidence, the American Business Index - Global shows that the number of articles related to family business rose from 188, during the 14 year period between January 1971 and December 1985, to 680 for the period from 1986 to 1995.

As interest in a field increases, it is useful to take inventory of the work that has been done and integrate the findings in order to consolidate the existing knowledge. This reflective process is necessary to provide directions for future research and derive maximum benefit from previous research efforts (Low & MacMillan, 1988). The purpose of this review is to provide such a reflection. Other reviews of the family business literature have appeared in the past few years (Handler & Kram, 1988; Hollander & Elman, 1988; Handler, 1989; Friedman, 1991; Marshack, 1993; Wortman, 1994) but they addressed specific topics. Here, we attempt to organize and classify a major portion of the literature.

This review results from our reading of 226 articles in 32 major journals. It is organized as follows: first, we address how the literature defines a family business; second, we organize a large part of the literature using a strategic management framework; third, we look at the literature about the family's influence on the family business; finally, other issues raised in the literature but not discussed in the first three sections form the last section.

DEFINITION OF A FAMILY BUSINESS

The family business literature (Desmon & Brush, 1991; Upton, Vinton, Seaman, & Moore, 1993) does not subscribe to a single definition of family business. We found thirty-four different definitions in our survey; these are presented in Table 1. Various authors have called for a systematic analysis of the commonalities in the definitions (Lansberg, Perrow, & Rogolsky, 1988; Wortman, 1994), but few such analyses have been attempted.

Handler (1989) identifies four dimensions used by writers in the family business literature to define the family firm: degree of ownership and management by family members, interdependent sub-systems, generational transfer, and multiple conditions. She observes that although there is no consensus as to what uniquely defines a family business; there seems to be a general agreement that the dimensions to be considered are the first three.

Table 1

Definitions of Family Business

AUTHOR (YEAR)	DEFINITION
OWNERSHIP-MANAGEMENT FOCUS	
Alcorn (1982)	a profit-making concern that is either a proprietorship, a partnership, or a corporation.....If part of the stock is publicly owned, the family must also operate the business (p.230).
Babicky (1987)	[a] small business started by one or a few individuals who had an idea, worked hard to develop it, and achieved, usually with limited capital, growth while maintaining majority ownership of the enterprise (p.25)
Barnes & Hershon (1976)	[a business in which] controlling ownership is rested in the hands of an individual or of the members of a single family (p.106).
Barry (1975)	an enterprise which, in practice, is controlled by the members of a single family (p.42)
Carsrud (1994)	firm's ownership and policy making are dominated by members of an "emotional kinship group" whether members of that group recognize the fact or not (p.40)
Covin (1994)	a business owned and operated by a family that employs several family members (p.288)
Davis & Tagiuri (1985)	a business in which two or more extended family members influence the direction of the business (quoted in Rothstein, 1992; p.398)
Donckels & Frohlich (1991)	[a business in which] family members own at least 60 percent of the equity (p.152)

Table 1

Definitions of Family Business

Dreux (1990)	economic enterprises that happen to be controlled by one or more families' (p. 226). Control has been considered as 'a degree of influence in organizational governance sufficient to substantially influence or compel action (p.226)
Dyer (1986)	[a business] in which decisions regarding its ownership or management are influenced by a relationship to a family (or families) (p.xiv)
Fiegener, Brown, Prince, & File (1994)	a firm that is both family owned and managed (p.318)
Gallo & Sveen (1991)	a business where a single family owns the majority of stock and has total control (p.181)
Holland & Oliver (1992)	any business in which decisions regarding its ownership or management are influenced by a relationship to a family or families (p.27)
Lansberg, Perrow, & Rogolsky (1988)	a business in which members of a family have legal control over ownership (p.2)
Lansberg & Astrachan (1994)	a company that is owned or controlled by a family and in which one or more relatives is involved with management (p.39)
Leach, et. al. (1990)	a company in which more than 50 percent of the voting shares are controlled by one family, and/or a single family group effectively controls the firm, and/or a significant proportion of the firm's senior management is members from the same family (p.2)

Table 1

Definitions of Family Business

Lyman (1991)	[a business in which] the ownership had to reside completely with family members, at least one owner had to be employed in the business, and one other family member had either to be employed in the business or to help out on a regular basis even if not officially employed (p.304)
Pratt & Davis (1986)	[a business] in which two or more extended family members influence the direction of the business through the exercise of kinship ties, management roles, or ownership rights (Chap.3, p.2)
Stern (1986)	[a business] owned and run by the members of one or two families (p.xxi)
Upton & Sexton (1987)	[a business] that includes two or more relatives and has at least two generations working together in an operating capacity (p.316)
Ward (1990)	a business in which there are two or more family members influencing the business (p.66)
Welsch (1993)	[a business] in which ownership is concentrated, and owners or relatives of owners are involved in the management process (p.40)
GENERATIONAL TRANSFER FOCUS	
Churchill & Hatten (1987)	what is usually meant by family business....is either the occurrence or the anticipation that a younger family member has or will assume control of the business from the elder (p.52)
Ward (1987)	[a business] that will be passed on for the family's next generation to manage and control (p.252)
INTERDEPENDENT SUBSYSTEMS	
Beckhard & Dyer (1983)	[a business in which the subsystems] include (1) the business as an entity, (2) the family as an entity, (3) the founder as an entity, and (4) such linking organizations as the board of directors (p.6)

Table 1

Definitions of Family Business

Davis (1983)	the interaction between two sets of organization, family and business, ... establish[es] the basic character of the family business and defines its uniqueness (p.47)
MULTIPLE CONDITIONS	
Astrachan & Kolenko (1994)	family ownership of more than 50% of the business in private firms or more than 10% of the stock in public companies; more than one family member works in the business or the owner anticipates passing the business to the next generation of family members or the owner identifies the firm as a family business... (p.254)
Donnelley (1964)	when [a business] has been closely identified with at least two generations of a family and when this link has had a mutual influence on company policy and on the interests and objectives of the family (p.94)
Handler (1989)	an organization whose major operating decisions and plans for leadership succession are influenced by family members serving in management or on the board (p.262)
Litz (1995)	ownership and management are concentrated within a family unit, and its members strive to achieve and/or maintain intra-organizational family based relatedness (p.103)
Rosenblatt, deMik, Anderson, & Johnson, (1985)	any business in which majority ownership or control lies within a single family and in which two or more family members are or at some time were directly involved in the business (p.4-5)
Shanker & Astrachan (1995)	**Broad definition:** requires family to have some degree of effective control of strategic direction, and the intention of keeping the business in the family. **Mid-range definition:** All the above + founder or descendant's of the founder should run the business. **Narrow definition:** Multiple generations should be involved in daily operations of the business (p.23)

Some authors use only one of the aforementioned dimensions to define a family business; although their writings do recognize the importance of the others. For example, Barry (1975) defines the family business as "an enterprise which, in practice, is controlled by the members of a single family", but he recognizes that "the problem area is the question of management succession" (p.42). Similarly, Barnes and Hershon (1976) define the family business as one wherein the "controlling ownership is rested in the hands of an individual or the members of a single family" (p.106), yet they describe the transition from one generation to the next "as one of the most agonizing experiences that any (family) business faces"(p.105). If all these dimensions are important in defining the family business, then a definition must incorporate them all to be widely acceptable.

Handler's (1989) attempt provides a conceptual clarification of the dimensions involved in defining the family business. Shanker and Astrachan (1995), on the other hand, direct theirs toward the development of a measurable definition of family business. They suggest three definitions of family business: a broad one in terms of effective family control in the strategic direction of the business; a mid-range one in terms of direct family involvement in day to day operations; and a narrow one in terms of the involvement of multiple generations in day to day operation. Based on these definitions the number of family firms in the U.S. can range from 4.1 million to 20.3 million firms, employ 19.8 million to 77.2 million individuals, and provide 12% to 49% of the GDP of US. This highlights the importance of the definition in empirical research.

Whether future efforts in identifying other dimensions of importance or building typologies for family business based on Handler's dimensions will result in a generally accepted definition is unknown. Meanwhile, we believe that as the search for a universally acceptable definition continues, researchers should explicitly state the definition they use in their studies. This will enable other researchers to reconcile and build on each other's findings. It should also help practitioners determine whether the research findings are applicable to their situation or not.

STRATEGIC MANAGEMENT AS AN ORGANIZING FRAMEWORK

Aside from not having a single definition for what it studies, the field of family business also has no integrating framework. For our purpose here, we use the strategic management process as the organizing framework. Although the family business literature has not focused directly on improving the strategic management of the family business, many of the issues addressed may be classified within this framework. Besides, the basic strategic management process should be similar for both family and non-family firms, except that, in the former, the family influences every step of the process (Harris, Martinez, & Ward, 1994). Therefore, in this section, we organize many of the issues raised in the literature using six areas in the strategic management process: goals and objectives, strategy formulation and content, implementation and design, evaluation and control, general management issues, and organizational evolution and change.

Goals and Objectives

Due to family involvement, the goals and objectives of a family business are likely to be quite different from the firm-value maximization goal assumed for the publicly held and professionally managed firms. However, very few attempts have been made to identify these differences. Some authors believe that the firm's goals could be family or business centred (Singer & Donohu, 1992). Tagiuri & Davis (1992) conducted one of the first systematic studies aimed at gaining an understanding of the goals and objectives of family firms. They asked 624 participants in Harvard's Smaller Company Management Program to rate the importance of seventy-four goals assembled from the goals, purposes, and objectives articulated by a hundred family firm managers for their business. Using factor analysis, they identify six goal factors: to have a company where employees can be happy, productive, and proud; financial security and benefits for the owner; develop new quality products; a vehicle for personal growth, social advancement, and autonomy; good corporate citizenship; and job security. It is interesting to note that none of these goals directly involves the next generation. In fact, only one among the seventy-four items (financial security for the owner's family in the future) explicitly mentions the next generation.

Succession occupies roughly twenty percent of the family business literature. Therefore, it is surprising that successfully transferring the business across generations appears only tangentially among the goals and objectives listed by Tagiuri and Davis for family firms. Family firms may, indeed, consider maintaining control within the family as one of their most important goals, but this is not entirely clear from the evidence presented in the literature. In fact, research on Chinese and African American family firms suggests quite the opposite (Dean, 1992; Wong, McReynolds, & Wong, 1992). In these studies, the researchers find succession unimportant because ethnic businesses tend to be viewed as a base to prepare the children for a professional career rather than as a family legacy.

Two recent studies by File, Prince, and Rankin (1994) and Dunn (1995) confirm that family firms have complex, multiple goals and varying priorities. File, et. al. (1994) find that the 183 family investment management firms in their sample may be classified into four groups: firms uninvolved in issues of family dynamics (31%), firms balancing family and business needs (27%), firms with family concerns as the primary goal (22%), and firms most concerned with adapting to changing conditions (19%). In all of the fifteen Scottish firms interviewed by Dunn (1995), the family firms adhered to the notion of "a job as a birthright of family members". A number of these firms acknowledge that employing family members sometimes leads to suboptimal performance, but are willing to do this to maintain good family relationships. Together, these two studies provide evidence that family considerations and business performance can be competing goals in the family business.

Strategy Formulation and Content

In terms of strategy formulation and content, studies in the literature can be classified into those dealing with the following areas: strategic planning process, culture in the family business, internationalization, functional policies, and social issues. A discussion on each of these areas is provided below.

Strategic Planning Process

Researchers who focus on the strategic planning process used to simply espouse the benefits of strategic planning and offer opinions on how it should be done (e.g., Barry, 1975; Jones, 1982; Ward, 1988). Recently, Harris, Martinez, and Ward (1994) have pointed out the importance of more research about the effects of family influences on strategy formulation and implementation.

Empirical studies to determine whether family and non-family firms differ in their strategic decision making policies provide different conclusions. Lyman (1991) finds differences between family and non-family firms in terms of customer service policies while File, Prince, and Rankin (1994) find them in buying behaviour, hiring practices, and decision making. However, Trostel and Nichols (1982) find no significant differences in management styles or processes, Kahn and Henderson (1992) find none in location preferences, and Daily and Thompson (1994) find none in the strategic postures adopted.

These findings suggest that family and non-family firms likely behave similarly with respect to some strategic issues and differently with respect to others. The findings barely start to address the many subjects we do not understand about the strategic planning process used by the family business. For example: What role does family play in the strategic planning process? How does the family business scan its environment, assess its capabilities, and search or evaluate alternative strategies? How is strategy formulation influenced by family considerations and interests? Are the alternatives considered by the family firm different from those considered by a non-family firm? How are the dynamics and politics of decision making different in the family firm? Does the family business use different criteria to make strategic decisions at the corporate, business, and functional levels of the organization? Which types of family influences are advantageous and which are deleterious to the process?

Culture in the Family Business

Understanding a family firm's culture should help the organization to formulate its strategy and run the business smoothly (Dyer, 1988; Hollander & Bukowitz, 1990; Schien, 1983). Dyer (1988) identifies four distinct cultures in family firms: paternalistic, laissez-faire, participative, and professional. He bases each on a different assumption about human nature. A paternalistic culture assumes that human beings, unless they belong to the family, are basically untrustworthy. The laissez faire and participative cultures believe that people are trustworthy; they give employees more autonomy. The professional culture relies upon professional rules and makes no judgment about human nature.

Dyer (1988) further suggests that the most common culture among first generation family firms is the paternalistic one. In this culture there is a heavy reliance on the leader and the next generation's training is often neglected, frequently leading to a change of culture when the next generation takes over.

Obviously, our understanding of family business culture is at very a early stage. Aside from concepts, we will need more comparative studies of family and non-family firms to help identify the uniqueness of the family business culture.

Internationalization

We found only two studies that deal with internationalizing the family firm (Gallo & Sveen, 1991; Swinth & Vinton, 1993). These two conceptual studies actually reach opposite conclusions regarding the family firm's probability of success in internationalization. Gallo and Sveen (1991) believe that the family business has a strong local orientation and will be slow to make the organizational changes needed to internationalize. Swinth and Vinton (1993), on the other hand, suggest that family firms transcend cultures through shared values such as: trust, loyalty, and long-term business focus. According to those authors, these shared values should enable family firms to bridge the cultural barriers more effectively than publicly held companies. Therefore, they argue, international joint ventures between two family businesses are more likely to succeed. These conflicting conclusions are difficult to reconcile. Together, they do suggest, however, that the family firm's success in internationalizing will depend critically on whether the family based values facilitate or hinder the organizational changes needed to operate successfully in the international setting.

Social issues

The only article that discusses how family ownership affects environmental consciousness is a case study by Post (1993). It suggests that the family firm's local orientation makes the business more likely to engage in environmentally friendly policies. Unfortunately, there is no empirical evidence to prove or disprove this argument.

Strategy Implementation and Design

Research on the organizational structure, systems, and processes that help family firms effectively implement their strategies are discussed in this section. In regards to implementation, the literature has narrowly focused on outside members of the board of directors and organizational structure.

Board of Directors

In the family business, the family and the business are so closely intertwined that the conduct of business is charged with emotion (Alderfer, 1988). Those who believe in the benefits of objectivity and rationality recommend that outside board members be appointed to remedy the situation. As in all of the other areas dealing with family business, the paucity of empirical tests allows no consensus to be reached on this issue. Proponents of the inclusion of outside members argue that outside board members bring many benefits. They provide:

- fresh perspectives and provide new directions (Cabot, 1976; Jain, 1980; Danco, 1981; Heidrick, 1988; Mueller, 1988);
- objective arbitrators (Mace, 1971; Lane, 1989);
- help in the succession process by providing support for the newly elected leader (Harris, 1989);
- more objective analysis of the firm's strengths and weaknesses (Mathile, 1988);
- reduction in the loneliness of the owner-manager (Gumpert & Boyd, 1984; Mathile, 1988);
- catalysts for change (Mueller, 1988);
- sounding boards for the owner-manager (Heidrich, 1988); and
- consultants who are available at all times for a low cost (Nash, 1988).

Thus, Heidrich (1988) describes outside directors as "the biggest bargain in management" (p.277).

In contrast, other authors find outside board members to be of little value to the family firm. Ford (1988) thinks outsiders have minimal knowledge about the firm and its environment. In addition, they are often unavailable to the firm except during board meeting (Ford, 1988). Jonovic (1989) believes that the absence of authority and a definable shareholder interest makes the outside director ineffective, while Alderfer (1988) suggests that outside board members may not be objective because an obligation to the owner-manager comes with the appointment.

These disagreements may be due to differences in size, age and complexity of the business (Harris, 1989; Jonovic, 1989). The owner-manager of a smaller firm may not be in a position to gain from outside board members because knowledge of the business is most important to the firm's operation. The larger firm with professional management teams, effective financial planning and control systems, and formalized strategic planning may benefit more from having outsiders on the board (Jonovic, 1989). For the family firm that is neither large nor complex, other alternatives to the classic board may be more appropriate. These are the family council (Ward, 1987, Lansberg, 1988), the review council (Jonovic, 1989), and the advisory council (Tillman, 1988).

The role and functions of the family business board has been studied by Ward and Handy (1988) using a survey of 147 privately held companies. They conclude that the type of board formed (outside, inside, or token) for an organization depends on the size and type of business, nature of ownership, and the personality and experience of the CEO. In turn, the type of board formed determines the role and functions of the board. What needs to be done with respect to outside board members is to empirically test their effects on performance.

Organization structure

Geeraerts (1984) and Daily and Doeringer (1992) present results that show the family owned and managed business to be less horizontally differentiated, less formalized, and less reliant on internal controls than the professionally managed firm. Harris, Martinez, and Ward (1994) argue that the family firm can make quick decisions and may be more successful in implementing decisions that require a lean and responsive structure. Aside from these results, there is very little that we know about the organization structure of the family business or how family involvement affects the benefits and costs flowing from different types of organizational structures. Clearly, a lot more work is required in this area.

Strategic Evaluation and Control

It is generally accepted that performance must be evaluated vis-a-vis goals and objectives. As discussed earlier, the family business' goals and objectives may be different from those of other firms; therefore, its performance will have to be evaluated differently as well. The available literature has paid scant attention to this issue. The few articles that have addressed this issue directly adopt a rationalist approach and recommend the separation of the family and business in order to improve the financial performance of the family firm (Levinson, 1974).

In a study of 345 firms, Chaganti and Schneer (1994) compare the financial performances of family firms with those of owner-started firms and buy-outs. The results show that owner-started firms have the highest average in return on assets. Family firms have the highest average in annual sales, but in a cross-sectional comparison, this may have no performance implication and simply indicate that they are older and bigger. Kirchoff and Kirchoff (1987) show that although family firms have higher productivity, this does not translate into higher profitability because wages and salaries increase proportionately with revenue. In contrast, a study of family and non-family nursing homes by Kleinsorge (1994) concludes that family owned nursing homes are less efficient than non-family owned ones. If the family business has non-financial goals as well, then these studies only give us a part of the picture.

It is not possible to compare the overall performance of family firms with that of non-family firms or the performances of different family firms without taking into consideration the underlying goals and objectives. Some basic research questions need to be addressed in this area. For example, what are the indicators of success used by family firms? Are there differences in the types and uses of strategic evaluation and control systems between family firms with high and low financial performance? How do family members influence the design and use of strategic evaluation and control systems?

General Management and Ownership Issues

Two topics have received attention in terms of general managerial issues: succession and characteristics of owners.

Succession

Succession constitutes the core of the family business literature. Researchers generally agree that managing the transition from one generation to another is very important and a difficult process. This is recognized by the earliest writers, such as Weber (1947) and Christensen (1953). In more recent writings, Ayers (1990) states that dealing with the issue of succession planning effectively may be the single most lasting gift that one generation can bestow on the other. Peter Davis (quoted in Handler & Kram, 1988) states that "smooth succession is an oxymoron". Lane (1989) suggests that most of the problems of the family business are related to succession. A number of recent literature reviews deal exclusively with this issue: Handler and Kram (1988), Welsch (1993), and Handler (1994). Consequently, we only briefly comment on the main topics discussed in the literature.

Succession in the family business differs from that in the publicly owned and professionally managed one, again, because of family involvement. The issues that exist for both are: continuity in terms of policy and strategy; choosing the successor; defining the future role of the retiring incumbent; and managing the succession planning and implementation processes. With respect to the retiring incumbent's future role, results will be very different in family firms because the retiring incumbent, even with no future active role in managing the business, will remain a member of the family and, often, continue to own a substantial portion of the equity. Additional concerns likely to be unique to the family firm's succession are: the goals and objectives to be achieved by maintaining control in the family; ownership distribution after the succession; and financial arrangement for the retiring incumbent. Beckhard and Dyer (1983) describes these issues in terms of ownership continuity, management continuity, power and asset distribution, and the role of the firm in society.

Despite the number of articles in the literature on succession, there are wide gaps in terms of covering the issues we list above as unique to the family business. We are not aware of an empirical study on the goals and objectives that families hope to achieve by opting for succession within the family instead of a transition to professional management. Ownership distribution and financial arrangements for the retiring family-member manager tend to be viewed mainly from the tax viewpoint. Should the retiring incumbent sell all shares owned at the time of succession or keep them until the successor has established a performance record? How will either affect the motivation of the successor and the overall performance of the family business with respect to its goals and objectives? Should the successor own more shares than the other siblings? What kind of retirement package will help entice the incumbent to let go at the right time instead of hanging on? These and many other questions are waiting to be addressed.

With respect to the issues that we think exist for both family and non-family firms, choosing the successor, continuity of policy and strategy, and succession planning have received attention by researchers.

One of the main objectives of managing a succession process must be to choose the best successor for a firm; however, this objective begs a definition of "best". It appears to us that "best" will depend on the objectives of the family firm. If the firm is most concerned with family harmony, then the successor who will contribute the most toward this end is the best. On the other hand, if the firm's goal is growth and profitability, a different candidate may be ideal. Since the current literature on family firm succession does not explicitly tie prescribed actions and processes to the achievement of clearly stated goals, the prescriptions may not be well-founded.

A second question related to choosing the successor addresses the succession process. Two views prevail in the literature. The first advocates leaving the choice of a successor to a committee (Levinson, 1974). This view follows from the rationalist approach that advocates the separation of the family and the business subsystems to maintain objectivity in business decisions. Other writers (for example, Davis, 1983) recognize that the family and the business are inseparable; thus, they advocate a systems approach to help the owner-manager objectively decide upon the successor.

It is commonly believed that continuity is largely under the control of the current owner-manager (Lansberg, 1988; Malone, 1989). Rutigliano (1986) and Post (1993) observe that successful family firms generate a new strategy for every generation that joins the business. This process helps to provide autonomy to the newly joining family members, thereby facilitating good working relationship. Some suggestions for providing autonomy include starting a new venture or division of the business (Barach, 1984), internationalizing (Gallo & Sveen, 1991), and encouraging the next generation to acquire skills that the current one does not have (Wong, 1993).

The literature on succession planning includes writings that point out its importance and ones that provide prescriptions about how it can be done effectively. Lansberg (1985), Rosenblatt, deMik, Anderson, and Johnson (1985), and Astrachan and Kolenko (1994) observe that although the literature recognizes the importance of succession planning, leadership succession is seldom planned. Tagiuri and Davis (1989) believe that without proper planning, retirement can be a frightening experience for the incumbent. They recommend that the incumbent develop interests outside the company before retirement in order to ease the transition. Successors, on the other hand, have to prepare themselves to deal with the residual conflicts and stress left after the event of succession (Harvey & Evans, 1995). Handler (1992) argues that developing lines of communication between family members is necessary to institutionalize the process of succession in family firms and to reduce the conspiracy (Lansberg, 1988) or resistance (Handler & Kram, 1988) associated with succession. We do not know of an empirical study that demonstrates the positive effects of succession planning on the family firm's performance. Therefore, whether succession planning provides benefits remains to be proven.

The process itself should include at least the following steps: (1) defining the issues; (2) setting the goals and objectives to be achieved through succession; (3) determining the people who should be involved in the process; (4) establishing the planning and implementation processes; (5) agreeing on the criteria for the "best" successor; (6) choosing the successor; (7) training the successor; (8) timing the succession; and (9) re-orienting the retiring incumbent. Some of these issues have received more attention than others.

Succession planning must begin with the current generation's philosophy pertaining to self, the family, the business, and society. This basic philosophy affects the degree and pattern of involvement of both family and non-family members (Barry, 1975; Weiser, Brody, & Quarrey, 1988).

Fiegener, Brown, Prince, and File (1994) note that family firms use a more personal, direct, relationship-centred approach to successor development than non-family firms. This approach emphasizes the importance of the owner-manager in the succession process. A considerable portion of the literature on succession planning focuses on ways that the current owner-manager can effectively plan the process.

Several researchers have expressed their opinions about the mode and timing of the successor's entry into the firm. Ambrose (1983) and Astrachan (1993) suggest that early inclusion of heirs in the business helps to develop their interest in the business, thereby increasing the likelihood of their joining the family business. Davis and Tagiuri (1989) find that life stage clashes between father and son can aggravate the tensions that accompany leadership succession in the family business. If both father and son are going through periods of identity formation or crises, the chances for conflict are greatly increased. For example, children in their 20s are striving for independence and acceptance into the professional world; while fathers in their 40s may be confronting mid-life anxieties and doubts about their achievements. The presence of a son eager to take over the business may be threatening increasing the chances of conflict. Other life-stage combinations can be beneficial. Children in their 30s tend to be attentive students, while parents in their 50s or 70s are constructive teachers eager to pass on their accumulated wisdom (Davis & Tagiuri, 1989; Sonnenfeld & Spence, 1989). Although the specific age at which a particular individual reaches a life-stage can vary, these studies provide an important dimension to our understanding of the succession process. If this life-cycle hypothesis is true, then the timing of a successor's entry into the business and that of the event of succession can be planned to increase the chances of success (Harvey & Evans, 1994a). Dumas (1989) cautions us that we cannot generalize these studies based on male samples to situations involving female owners or successors. She recommends that similar studies be conducted to identify the effects of life-cycle stages on mother-son, father-daughter, and mother-daughter dyads.

As with other areas in the study of family business, the literature on succession is dominated by conceptual articles and those based on consultants' or practitioners' experiences (25 out of 36 articles). In order to validate the effectiveness of the prescriptions made in these articles more empirical studies need to be conducted. Specifically, studies need to be directed toward identifying the factors that differentiate succession in family firms from that in others (Handler, 1989; McCollom, 1990), understanding the factors that contribute to an effective succession, and the impact of succession on firm performance. All such studies should be undertaken in the context of the multiple and possibly competing goals of the family business.

Founder's Characteristics and Management Style

In their literature review, Hollander and Elman (1988) observe that the founder is viewed as the main influence in the family business. They report that "some of the most colourful explorations of the family business have focused on the motivations and characteristics of the founder" (p.148). These articles run parallel to the those in the entrepreneurship literature that study the entrepreneur's characteristics. In our review, however, we observed that they are not as numerous (5 out of 226) as those in the entrepreneurship literature.

In contrast to the energetic, visionary, and heroic founder in the entrepreneurship literature and the popular press, the family business literature paints the founder very differently. Gumpert and Boyd (1984) talk about the loneliness of the founder and Malone and Jenster (1992) focus on the bored and plateaued founder. There is no data to indicate how prevalent these characteristics are or how they influence the business and the successor. The antithetical portrayals of the founder in the two sets of literature may simply be a reflection of the human aging process. The entrepreneurship literature encounters the founder near the start and growth phases of the business while the family business literature meets the person near retirement.

Scholars who study the management style of the founder/owner (Geeraerts, 1984; Birley, 1986; Donckels & Frohlick, 1991) generally report an authoritarian style, with the owner/founder unwilling to share the power. Not only is the leader unwilling to hand over the power, but his continuity becomes important to those around him (Lansberg, 1988). An interesting observation is provided by Post and Robins (1993) in the context of an ailing leader and his inner circle. Members of the inner circle will try to block attempts by the leader to hand over power since the leader's continuity is in their best interest. More studies are needed to identify the role that the members of the leader's inner circle play in the succession process in a family firm.

The final act of the owner-manager is to leave the business. Based on the leader's identification with the organization, and those around him, the departure style of the leader can vary. Sonnenfeld and Spence (1989) identify four departure styles of leaders: monarchs, generals, governors, and ambassadors. Monarchs are successful leaders who find it difficult to let go. Generals are less successful leaders who spend their retirement planning a comeback. Governors have short terms in office, achieve success, leave willingly, and do not maintain contact with the organization. Sonnenfeld and Spence (1989) suggest that the best form of departure style for the family business organization is that of Ambassadors, who lead the organization into moderate levels of growth, and recognize the time to step down. They also maintain contact with the organization and serve as advisors. These are interesting observations based on a large sample. What needs to be done with this classification of departure styles is to determine whether it has any predictive power with respect to the success of the organization after the leader leaves.

Organizational Evolution and Change

How the family business organization evolves and changes has been studied in terms of the organizational life cycle and the transition to professional management. We discuss the literature in each of these areas below.

Life Cycle Stages

Various attempts have been made in the literature to sort out the complexities of the family business using evolutionary models based on developmental stages. These models attempt to describe the temporal changes that occur in the family business. A review by Hollander and Elman (1988) identifies three different approaches adopted by researchers to formulate the developmental models.

The first approach relates the firm's developmental stages to the family's generational progression. Hershon's (1975) study is representative of this approach. He discusses how, as the founding family moves from founder to children to grandchildren, the management pattern must move from close supervision to collaborative management to collective management.

The second approach focuses on the interaction between the firm's needs and the life stages of the individuals crucial to the firm. Danco (1975) focuses on how the founder's behaviour changes at different stages in the firm's life cycle. McGivern (1989) characterizes the interaction in terms of a cycle corresponding to before, during, and after the succession. Davis and Tagiuri (1989) use the combination of the father's and son's life cycle stages to predict the quality of the working relationship.

The third approach expands the players to include the firm, the family, and the key individuals. Using this expanded set of players, Ward (1987) identifies three stages of family business evolution. At the first stage, there is consistency in the needs of the business and the family; the owner-manager makes all the decisions and the family supports the business. At the second stage, both the business and the potential successors are growing; the owner-manager is still in control and the children's growth and development is of prime importance to the family. The last stage is characterized by a conflict between the different needs of business and the family; the business is stagnant and in need of regeneration, the owner-manager is bored or retired, and maintenance of family harmony is the primary family goal. At the different stages, delegation of responsibility and power to non-family members will vary significantly. What is needed to test the validity of these evolutionary models of the family business is a large longitudinal data base which is not yet available.

Transition Toward Professional Management

Another approach taken to study how the family business evolves and changes concentrates on the firm's transition toward professional management. Researchers disagree whether this transition follows a three, four, or five stage process. Navin (1971) suggests a five stage model: initiator, founder, founder's heirs, technician, and professional. Holland and Boulton (1984), Dyer (1986), and Goffe and Scase (1985)propose four stage models consisting of pre-family, family, adaptive family, and post family. Ward's (1987) model uses three: founder, family, and professional. In an empirical study of 41 businesses, Holland and Oliver (1992) find support for only the three stage model.

Other researchers of the transition toward professional management examine why the family business professionalises and delegates authority to non-family managers; growth and complexity are the most commonly cited reasons. Lack of the requisite management skills within the family; preparation for leadership succession; and the need to change the norms and values of the business are others (Matthews, 1984; Dyer, 1989). There may be resistance to the transition because the owner-manager lacks formal training and knowledge of management techniques (Dyer, 1989), fears losing control (Perrigo, 1975), or believes that professionalization is an unnecessary expensive overhead.

Goffe and Scase (1985) and Whisler (1988) believe that quasi-organic management structures are used in many firms making the transition to professional management . In this type of management structure, managers are given considerable autonomy but the proprietor maintains the prerogative of arbitrary intervention. In this difficult transition, outsiders such as board members and auditors can be of considerable help (Whisler, 1988; Schaefer & Davis, 1992). However, in their study of the stages and phases in the evolution of the family business, Holland and Oliver (1992) do not find any strong evidence of conflict as firms move from family to professional management. Any research result could be caused by the peculiarity of the sample or research design, but this study does raise questions about the prevalence of the conflict so often believed to be present as family firms move toward professionalization. Future studies need to determine the frequency with which such conflicts occur in the family business and the mechanisms adopted to overcome these difficulties.

As organizations move toward professionalization, planning and procedures inevitably replace entrepreneurial initiatives and vision (Mintzberg & Waters, 1990).

The challenge for family firms is to maintain the capacity to innovate while increasing in size. Many large corporations are discovering that superior performance may be achieved by decomposition into small units that can be run using an informal, personalized approach (Fox, 1984). The challenge for the family firm will be to find the right mix of management by rules and by personality. Poza (1988) lists some of the factors that may help in determining the right mix as business culture, family values, and the technical and marketing expertise of the firm. We need to better understand the mechanisms used by successful family firms to maintain their capacity to innovate while moving toward professional management.

FAMILY INFLUENCE

No business can escape family influence; even the decisions of the CEO of a publicly held and professionally managed firm is influenced sometimes by the spouse and children. Therefore, it is imperative that we understand the nature of the family influence that makes the family business different. Family influence may be studied within the strategic management framework in terms of how it affects goals, strategy, structure, and performance. Research in this area has not, however, reached this detailed level of investigation.

Early theorists called for rationality in the family business and advocated ways to excise or minimize family influence (Miller & Rice, 1988; Levinson, 1971; Cohn & Lindberg, 1974). This approach has been replaced by the dual systems approach (Lansberg, 1983b; Davis & Tagiuri, 1985; Swartz, 1989) that views the family business as a combination of two subsystems, family and business. Researchers now acknowledge that to understand the family business we must recognize that the two subsystems co-exist and it is their relative powers that make a family business unique (Davis & Stern, 1988; Kepner, 1983; Beckhard & Dyer, 1983b; Hollander 1983; Barnes & Hershon, 1976; Hollander & Elman, 1988; McCollom, 1988; Friedman, 1991). Unlike the rational theorists, the dual systems approach does not focus on finding ways to separate the two subsystems but, instead, focuses on finding ways to operate effectively within this unique form of organization (Hollander & Elman, 1988).

The literature on family influence can be categorized according to the family's involvement in the business, the uniqueness of the family business, and the types of family business. Each of these categories focuses on the family's influence on the business in a different manner and are discussed below.

Family Involvement in the Business

The family's involvement in business has been studied in terms of intergenerational relationships, sibling rivalry, women in the family business, nepotism, and the family type.

Inter-Generational Relationships

The relationship between the owner-manager and members of the next generation is extremely important because successors in the family firm are trained using a personal and direct approach rather than the formalized, detached, and task-centred approach utilized by non-family firms. Fiegener, Brown, Prince, and File (1994) believe that the personal approach is riskier because of the heavy involvement of leaders in mentoring successors. The experience will be excellent if the leader-successor relationship is healthy and affirming. But if this is not the case, the successor may find it extremely difficult to assimilate the lessons of the leader. Others (e.g., Lansberg & Astrachan, 1994; Seymour, 1993) confirm this by finding a positive association between the leader-successor relationship and the quality of the successor training received, thus underscoring the importance of this relationship.

Levinson (1971) observes that the relationship between father and son is ambivalent at best. The father cannot let go and the son wants to prove himself. While a son's independence may be perceived as disloyalty, his compliance may be seen as weakness (Seymour, 1993). On his part, the son may wish to change the parent's methods (Babicky, 1987), while the parent may want his own achievements to stand as enduring monuments (Levinson, 1974). Moreover, factors not totally related to the business such as a parent's dissatisfaction with the child's relationships, divorce, marriage, etc. may affect the relationship between the two generations (Babicky, 1987).

Both the owner-manager and the heir have a considerable stake in the smooth completion of the succession process. The successor should be sensitive to the needs of the founder (Lansberg, 1988) and should exercise patience and diplomacy (Jonovic, 1989); he/she needs to become a student of the organization and learn its intricacies and culture (Horton, 1982). Holland and Boulton (1984) suggest that an individual with high power both in the business and the family is in a position to turn his or her thoughts into action. On the other hand, the individual with low power in both the business and the family is in a precarious position and needs to use considerable interpersonal skills to cultivate support of others in better positions (Holland & Boulton, 1984).

Sibling Rivalry

Primogeniture is the most widely accepted form of transfer of power in the family business but it has become less automatic than it once was (Barnes, 1988; Goldberg & Woolridge, 1993). This shift from primogeniture can lead to tensions that arise from the incongruent hierarchies of family members in the family and the business. It is easy to accept intellectually that the eldest may not always be the best choice (Levinson, 1971; Ayres, 1990; Barnes, 1988; Kaye, 1992) and that sons are not necessarily better suited to take over than daughters (Lyman, Salangicoff, & Hollander, 1985; Salangicoff, 1990); but when the hierarchies of the family are not reflected in the firm, the relationships become very complicated. For a younger sibling, leadership in the business comes with the challenge of managing the different business and family statuses. One way to resolve this problem is to make sure that the younger sibling has established a track record outside the family business (Barnes, 1988). Another is to have each family member establish an independent operation to lead (Levinson, 1971). The effectiveness of these recommendations have not been empirically tested; thus Barnes' and Levinson's assertions should be considered opinions.

In terms of sibling relationships, Friedman (1991) argues that although the competition for parental love and attention always generates sibling rivalry, the parents' response has a major influence on the relationship that develops among their children. When parents indulge in comparisons based on characteristics beyond the control of the siblings, adhere to equality instead of equity as the mode of justice, and interfere in sibling conflicts, they exacerbate sibling rivalry. Children in such situations feel that they must outdo their rivals (brothers or sisters) to win parental attention. Moreover, they do not learn ways to resolve their conflicts. Friedman (1991) recommends open communication about the roots of the siblings' rivalry, establishing empathy by inviting them to imagine their roles reversed, and encouraging them to continually redefine their relationships.

Women in the Family Business

Although the literature has historically focused on the relationship between father and son, the father-daughter dyad has received some attention lately. Dumas (1989) reviews empirical studies on the relationship between father and son and compares them with those on the father-daughter dyad. She suggests that the father-daughter relationship is not only more harmonious than the father-son relationship, but that it is also different in nature. Daughters willingly assume the role of caretaker (both of the father and of the business) and do not compete with their fathers over power and control. An interesting finding of this study is the presence of triangulation - in the struggle for visibility, role management, and identity formation, daughters often compete for power and authority with a third important member (a male non-family manager or the mother).

Various studies report that women are not generally considered for the top job in the family business (Hollander & Bukowitz, 1990; Salangicoff, 1990; Upton & Sexton, 1987). Their position as caretakers of family concerns, however, may provide them with a unique understanding of the family and of the business (Lyman, Salangicoff, & Hollander, 1985). Hollander and Bukowitz (1990) recommend that the family business attempt to build an environment that supports family and economic activities for both male and female participants. Salangicoff (1990) suggests that women acquiring appropriate skills, training, and experience will enhance their chances of joining the family business.

Nepotism

Nepotism is a given in the family business. Bensahel (1975) and Cambreleng (1969) provide some suggestions for dealing with this issue including maintaining open communication with non-family employees, objective evaluation of the nepot's performance, and explicit policies regarding family members joining the firms. The impact that the presence of nepots has on the performance of non-family employees has not received any attention in the literature and needs investigation.

Types of Family

Singer and Donohu (1992) classify families, according to their organizational values, as either a family centred business (business is seen as a way of life) or a business centred family (business is seen as a means of livelihood). Whether families in business can actually be cleanly classified in this manner has not been empirically tested.

Reiss (1982) categorizes families as consensus-sensitive, interpersonal distance-sensitive, and environment-sensitive. The members of a consensus-sensitive family view the environment as hostile and feel a great need to be in agreement with each other. In order to maintain an uninterrupted agreement, members avoid addressing difficult issues that may cause conflict. In the interpersonal-distance-sensitive family, each member has an area of expertise to which only he/she attends. They split the environment into different parts and assigns a particular member to handle each. Members are concerned about demonstrating individual mastery, not about improving joint performance.

Davis (1983) suggests that, under stress, the excessively consensus-sensitive family becomes "enmeshed" while the interpersonal-distance-sensitive family becomes "disengaged". When a family becomes enmeshed, no individual actions is taken. While at the other end, the disengaged family cannot act as an entity. Hoffman (1981) concludes that neither of these two ends of a continuum provides the congenial atmosphere needed to nurture a family business. Davis (1983) and Reiss (1982) suggest that the environment-sensitive family provides the most effective background for the success of a family business.

In her research on three department stores, McCollom (1988) shows that families can behave differently at work and at home. A family enmeshed at home may not be so in the business; therefore, members of the family can achieve stability both at work and at home. This finding prompts her to caution that we must be careful in suggesting that there is one type of system that is best for all family firms as stability may be achieved by using different combinations at home and at work.

Uniqueness of the family business

In family firms, the close interaction between the family and the business leads to unique challenges and strengths. It also causes work-family conflicts and spillover of problems from one environment to the other. Each of these is discussed below.

Unique Strengths and Challenges of the Family Business

The strengths of the family business are generally recognized to be: a loyal and dedicated work force (both family and non-family members), warmer interpersonal relationships, greater sensitivity to local culture, and long term continuity (Donnelley, 1964; Hayes, 1981). The unique problems include: lack of managerial talent since non-family members generally shun working for family firms, lack of discipline and professionalism because of the informal policies and procedures practiced, pressure to maintain tradition, and the impact of family conflicts on business (Burack & Calero, 1981).

In order to be effective, the family business needs to handle two key relationships effectively; those among family members and those between family members and professional managers (Horton, 1986). The literature has devoted considerable attention to the relationship among family members but the role of professional managers in the family business has largely been ignored. Future research needs to be directed toward understanding the mechanisms adopted by the family business to take advantage of its unique strengths and meet its challenges.

Work-Family Conflicts and Spill-overs

The basic sociological differences between the family and the business have been examined by theorists from both the "rational" (Miller & Rice, 1988; Lansberg, 1983b) and the "systems" (Davis, 1983; Swartz, 1989). These differences are: the reasons for existence (nurturing versus providing goods and services); the basic orientation of the two subsystems (emotional versus task); selection, training, and appraisal of individuals (non-market versus market based); criteria for membership (non-voluntary versus voluntary); culture (non-competitive versus competitive); and the rules of behaviour (informal versus formal). Recognizing these differences, both groups of theorists suggest ways to reconcile them. For example, Lansberg (1983b) suggests that all relatives should be given the opportunity to learn but only the most competent ones should be hired. He believes that this will meet the demands of both subsystems.

Kanter (1989) argues that, historically and across cultures, the organization attempts to exact loyalty and commitment from its members and, in the process, strives to exclude or neutralize particularistic ties that compete with loyalty for the organization. Because a family is an insidious source of particularistic loyalties, the organization will attempt to separate the family from the business (Kanter, 1989).

However, in the modern industrial society, separate work and family lives is a myth because the two subsystems are so closely interconnected.

After studying 86 businesses terminated between 1976 and 1981, Ambrose (1983) argues that the demands placed by the business on the time of the founders leaves them with less time to build relationships in the family. This may be one of the reasons why the next generation does not become interested in the business. Spill-overs in terms of time, stress, and worries have been reported in other studies by Willmott (1971), Burke, Weir, and DuWors (1980), and Crouter (1984). After examining the literature in this area, Greenhaus and Beutell (1985) conclude that when the time, strain, and behavioral pressures within the domain of family and work are incompatible, the chances of work-family conflicts are higher. The seriousness of the conflict will vary according to the self-perception of role requirements, role salience, career stage, and the existence of negative sanctions for noncompliance with role demands.

The literature has started to identify the differences between family and business sub-systems and the sources of work-family conflicts. However, it still has to direct research toward finding ways to manage these differences effectively. Comparative studies of the coping mechanisms adopted by different family businesses to meet the challenges of family-work conflicts and spillovers can provide valuable insights.

Types of family business

The family business literature also includes studies of the home-based business and copreneurs. Research on home-based business covers the degree of family involvement in the business (Owens & Winter, 1991; Beach, 1993), the relative importance of family and business characteristics in determining success (Rowe, Haynes, & Bentley, 1993), and differences in the performance of related and unrelated workers (Heck & Walker, 1993). Owen, Carsky, and Dolan (1993) suggest that studies on home-based businesses should also consider family goals and opportunities, differences in work styles, nature of the work, and the work environment.

It is to be expected that family involvement, both formal and informal, is higher in the home-based businesses. Beach (1993) observes that children in a home-based business get socialized into the business at a very young age; however, the long-term effects of this involvement on the children's attitude toward the business is unknown.

Owen and Winter (1991) highlight some of the impacts of a home-based business on family life. They present results showing that the age of the business, income, and the hours worked are positively related to perceived family disruption. They also find women to be less disturbed by a home-based business than men. Rowe, Haynes, and Bentley (1993), on the other hand, study the performances of home-based businesses and conclude that personal characteristics, such as owner's age and education, are better indicators of profitability than the organizational factors, such as size, age of the business, location, and marketing efforts.

In an attempt to understand the relative contribution of related and unrelated workers on the performance of home-based businesses, Heck and Walker (1993) interviewed 508 proprietors of home based businesses. Their results suggest that paid workers, both immediate family and unrelated, contribute positively to success whereas unpaid related workers decrease the output of the business.

Marshack (1993) finds the literature on copreneurs (married couples who jointly own and manage a business) to be very limited. Moreover, the few studies available focus either on the family or the work and not on the holistic unit. The primary interest in this area is to understand the complexity of relationships between these partners. After all, the couple faces all the problems of marriage and dual-careers as well as those faced by a family business. In a comparison of 30 dual career couples with 30 copreneurs, Marshack's (1994) findings show that, compared to dual-career couples, copreneurs are quite traditional in their sex-roles. This finding was not supported, however, in a study of farm families by Rappaport (1995). Full-time partner-wives of farmers help in the farm and their husbands perform a higher number of household tasks than husbands whose wives work off the farm. Notwithstanding the complexity of issues the couple faces and the common adherence to traditional sex roles in the division of household chores and child care, both the wives and husbands generally report high levels of satisfaction with their life styles (Barnett & Barnett, 1988); some even reported that working together enhances their relationship (Nelton, 1986).

OTHER ISSUES STUDIED

In this section we discuss studies on ethnicity, professional advise, and methodological issues.

Ethnicity

Researchers in ethnicity seek to understand differences in the basic philosophies of ethnic families in business. These studies implicitly assume that ethno-cultural background affects the running of the business. The different ethnic groups studied include the Chinese (Chau, 1991; Wong, McReynolds, & Wong, 1992; Wong, 1993), Japanese (Wong, 1993; Fruin, 1980), Latin Americans (Lansberg & Perrow, 1991), Jews (Rothstein, 1992; McGoldrick & Troast, 1993), Italians, African-Americans, Irish, Anglo Saxons (McGoldrick & Troast, 1993; Dean, 1992), and American Indians (Stallings, 1992).

Certain ethnic differences, including patterns of communication, have been cited as having significant effects on the family business. Open communication is encouraged in the Jewish and African-American families but personal relationships are not discussed among the Irish. Conflicts are resolved according to fairness by the Anglo-American family; by open discussion in the Jewish one; by reference to clear values of right and wrong in the Italian one; and allowed to linger in the Irish family.

Jewish families attach great importance to education; Jews, Chinese, and Japanese have the lowest divorce or separation rate; Chinese, Japanese, Italian, and Jewish families all have strong value systems; women are encouraged to participate in the Jewish families and have clearly defined roles in the Italian family. All of these differences are believed to affect how the family business is governed and managed.

Studies of immigrant Chinese and African-American family businesses reveals the interesting finding that succession is not a priority. These businesses are viewed more as a foundation to prepare the children for a professional career than as a family legacy (Dean, 1992; Wong, McReynolds, & Wong 1992). This revelation may be useful in explaining the closure of family businesses among these ethnic groups.

Chau (1991) provides a comparison between the succession approaches of Chinese and Japanese family firms. The Chinese family practices coparcenary and divides the family's assets equally among the male members, while the Japanese family traditionally passes control and ownership of the family's assets to a single male heir. He believes that this difference in succession practice may explain the relative longevity of Japanese businesses. The longevity of the Japanese family business may be further enhanced by careful succession planning and the separation of ownership and management; both practiced since the 17th century (Fruin, 1980).

Professional Advice

In an empirical study aimed at understanding the consulting needs of small businesses, Krentzman and Samaras (1960) report that only about a third of small business managers use the services of consultants. This low number is the results of fears over the fees charged, the possible waste of time, and the leakage of information. Based on these findings, the authors suggest that consultants should adopt a different attitude when consulting for small firms. They must be prepared for a long term relationship, be flexible in their fees, and must first establish a trusting relationship with the small business manager. Recently, Mandelbaum (1994) conducted a similar study with family firm owners. The respondents indicate that they prefer informational seminars, assistance manuals, and reasonably priced professional advise (Mandelbaum, 1994).

The literature recommends that family firms use consultants and outside advisors to bring objectivity into their decision making process. However, it also suggests that the high degree of reciprocal interdependence between the family and the business makes consulting for the family business significantly different from consulting for non-family businesses (Babicky, 1987; Hollander & Elman, 1988; Lane, 1989; Swartz, 1989). Although emotional forces are present in non-family firms (Correll, 1989; Alderfer, 1988), family involvement compounds the emotional undercurrents. Who the important members of the family are may not be obvious. Destructive relationships may have solidified since childhood (Babicky, 1987) and the call for help often comes from the disgruntled and weaker party (Barnes, 1988; Levinson, 1983); but effective consulting requires the cooperation of the owner-manager and other important family members (Lane, 1989).

Consultants act as facilitators to help family members develop skills in dealing with the intricacies of their relationships (Astrachan, 1993; Lane, 1989; Swartz, 1989). They need to be generalists and possess expertise in many areas. Beckhard (quoted in Lane,1989) compares a family business consultant to the family doctor, "who can treat most bumps and bruises but must call in a specialist for more serious matters" (p.14). To accomplish this challenging task, multidisciplinary-teams that use the technique of process consultation have been recommended (Armenakis & Burdg, 1986; Swartz, 1989; Lansberg, 1983b). Furthermore, consulting in family firms is not a one-shot job, but requires a long term commitment on the part of the consultant (Swartz, 1989; Lane, 1989).

In addition to general consulting in family businesses, some expert advise has been offered in the literature to solve specific problems. For example,Alderfer (1988) offers advise on handling the group dynamics that may prevail in family business boards, and Erfurt, Foote, Heirich, and Holtyn (1993), Lichtenstein (1993), and Stier (1993) have suggested mechanisms for smaller family firms to reduce health care costs without losing comprehensive health care. In addition, the literature also offers detailed advise on handling taxes (Hayes & Adams, 1990; Mastromarco,1992; Weiser, Brody, & Quarrey, 1988; Forbes, & Paddock,1982) and raising capital (Dreux,1990). In terms of raising capital, Dreux (1990) suggests that many non-public financing alternatives are available to family firms. Some of these include recapitalization, private equities, joint ventures, employee stock ownership plans, etc.

Methodological Issues

Research about family businesses is very different from other business research because it involves research about families (Handler, 1989). Families have a penchant for privacy (Davis, 1983; Ward, 1987) that often prevents them from releasing information. Faced with this difficulty, researchers may have to use some non-traditional methods to collect data. For example: instead of collecting data directly from family firms, Geeraerts (1984) collected them from the family firms' consultants; Davis and Tagiuri (1989) included an extra questionnaire in their study to be completed by another family member; Handler (1989) and McCollom (1990) suggest the use of research teams; Carsrud (1993) suggests using focus groups; Budge and Janoff (1991) and McCollom (1992a) suggest using narratives and stories to hear the different voices of family and business; and McCollom (1990) argues for clinical methods to capture the dynamics of an extremely complex system and to gain access to the system members' experiences at a deep level.

The difficulty in obtaining data may have forced family business research to rely so extensively on case studies and consultant's accounts. As a result, whether the insights gained are generally applicable is always uncertain. The only way to determine this is to do more large scale and longitudinal studies.

Recent articles stress the need to study the family business from a strategic management or organizational behaviour perspective (Dyer, 1994; Harris, Martinez & Ward, 1994; Wortman, 1994), while others compare the developments in the field with those of entrepreneurs and provide related suggestions for future research directions (e.g., Brockhaus, 1994; Dyer & Handler, 1994; Hoy & Verser, 1994). As mentioned by Dyer (1994), the results of research in organizational behaviour and strategy should be used to enrich our understanding of family businesses.

CONCLUSION

In the last few years, the family business literature has grown very significantly. This particular overview of the literature is largely presented from a strategic management perspective. The literature is divided into four broad areas: (1) definitional issues, (2) strategic management issues, (3) family influences, and (4) other issues. In each area, the major topics, contributions, and controversies have been discussed. What follows is an extensive list of research questions waiting to be answered. We hope that this effort provides a good introduction to the field and helps to determine directions for future research.

SUGGESTED RESEARCH QUESTIONS

Definitional Issues

What is a family business? What are the different types of family business? What are the characteristics of a business that make a family business different from the non-family business?

Strategic Management Issues

Goals and Objectives

How are the goals and objectives of a family business different from those of a non-family business? Do the goals and objectives of the high performance family business differ from those of low performing family firms? How are goals and objectives formulated in high and low performing family businesses? How do their goal formulation processes differ from those of non-family businesses? Why? How should performance be measured with respect to these goals and objectives? Does the family business perform better with respect to the traditional goals and objectives of the non-family business or the unique goals and objectives of the family business?

Strategy Formulation and Content

Does the family business use different criteria to make strategic decisions at the corporate, business, and functional levels of the organization? If so, what are the differences? Are the differences a matter of kind or degree? How are the dynamics and politics of decision-making different in the family business? What are the specific family influences that lead to the differences in dynamics and politics? How much do these differences affect strategic decisions? Which types of family influences are advantageous and which are deleterious to the process? How does the family business scan its environment, assess its capabilities, search or evaluate alternative strategies? Are family firms likely to follow corporate, business, or functional level strategies different from those of non-family firms in the same industry? If so, are these differences justified by differences in resources, skills, or cultures? How do family firms differ in their decisions regarding which market to enter and how to operate in the market? Does the family business utilize strategic alliances? Are these alliance partners generally family or non-family firms? Are ethics and values in the family business similar or dissimilar to those in the non-family business? Is the family business socially responsible? Is it easier to implement social consciousness in these firms than in non-family firms? Are they more successful than non-family firms in meeting environmental concerns? Are family firms more successful in their capacity to adopt innovative strategies? What are the key differences and similarities between family and non-family firms?

Strategy Implementation and Design

Do different types of boards have different impacts on the performance and succession planning of family firms? Which organizational structure is likely to be most effective for the family business? Does the family business have inherent advantages in certain implementation activities? In what ways does the joining of next generation family members require structural changes in family businesses?

Strategic Evaluation, Control, and Performance

Do high and low performing family businesses use different strategic evaluation and control systems? Do they use the same systems in different manners? How important are any differences? How do family members influence the design and use of strategic evaluation and control systems? Is the influence positive or negative?

General Management and Ownership issues

What strategies are used by the family business to provide autonomy to members of the next generation joining the business? What are the effects of life-cycle stages on the relationships between mother and son, father and daughter, mother and daughter? How do these stages impact the succession process? What are the factors that influence the likelihood of a non-problematic succession in the family firms? Does the quality of the succession process have an impact on the performance and success of the business? How does succession in family businesses differ from that in other organizations? How prevalent is the loneliness and/or the plateauing of the founder of a family business? What are the coping mechanisms used by the family business founders who find themselves bored, lonely, or plateaued? What are the impacts of these behaviours on the business and on the succession process? What is the role played by members of the founder's inner circle in succession planning? Does the inner circle influence the departure style adopted by the founder? Is there a difference in the departure style adopted by the bored or plateaued founder? Are there gender or cultural differences in terms of the departure style adopted by the family business owner?

Organizational Evolution and Change

Which of the proposed phases and stages model is most accurate? What affect the number of phases taken by a family business in its transition toward professional management? What are the problems associated with various stages of development in the family firms? How often is the move from family management to professional management ridden with conflicts in family firms? What are the mechanisms used by owners of family firms to achieve a less problematic transition from family management to professional management? As the family firm grows in size and non-family professionals take over management, what are the mechanisms used to maintain the capacity to innovate? Is the transition toward professional management easier if it proceeds in step with a change in leadership?

Family Influence

Family Involvement in the Business

Do father-son dyads handle the relationship with employees differently than the father-daughter dyads? What strategies can parents adopt to encourage a harmonious relationship among siblings? Are there gender differences in terms of the effectiveness of these strategies? When the hierarchies of the family are not reflected in the business, how do family members manage the different status levels of the successor? How do relationships between family members and non-family employees influence relationships among family members and vice-versa? Are the systems adopted in the work place different for different types of families? Is a particular type of family prone to be more successful in business? Does a differentiated work environment work best for all types of families? What mechanisms do family members use to deal with nepots in the organization? Does the presence of nepots in the organization have an impact on the performance of non-family employees?

Uniqueness of the Family Business

Does the degree of perceived work-family conflict vary according to the age of the business, the role requirements, role salience, career stage, and the existence of negative sanctions for noncompliance with role demands? Is there a relationship between effective management of work-family conflicts and business performance? What are the different coping mechanisms adopted by the family business to meet the challenges of family-work conflicts and spillovers?

Types of Family Business

In terms of home-based businesses, how does socialization into the business at an early age affect the children's attitude toward business or the business? How does perceived family disruption influence the home based business' success? What are the advantages and disadvantages of a home-based businesses, as compared to other family businesses? What are the mechanisms adopted by copreneurs to meet the demands of their family and work lives? Are copreneurs generally more satisfied than dual career couples and, if so, why?

Other Issues

Ethnicity

Is there a higher rate of family business continuity and success among any particular ethnic group? If so, what are the factors that lead to their success?

Professional Advice

What are the consulting needs of the family business? Do these needs vary according to the gender or ethnic background of the owner-manager? What are the attitudes of family business managers toward consultants? Do the attitudes of founders toward consultants differ from those of the subsequent generation family members?

Methodological Issues

Are specific methodologies specifically suited to study the family business?

References

Adizes, I. (1979). **Organizational passages - diagnosing and treating life-cycle problems of organizations.** *Organizational Dynamics,* Summer: 3-25.

Alcorn, P.B. (1982). ***Success and survival in the family owned business.*** New York: McGraw Hill.

Alderfer, C.P. (1988). **Understanding and consulting to family business boards.** *Family Business Review,* 1(3): 249-261.

Ambrose, D.M. (1983). **Transfer of the family-owned business.** *Journal of Small Business Management,* 21(1): 49-56.

Anonymous (1983). **Family partnerships.** *Estate Planning, CPA Journal,* May: 71-78.

Anonymous. (1984). **Succession planning in closely held firms: Begin now - the company's future depends on it.** *Small Business Report,* November: 52-58.

Armenakis, A.A. & H.B. Burdg (1986). **Planning for growth.** *Long Range Planning,* 19(3): 93-102.

Astrachan, J.H. (1988). **Family firm and community culture.** *Family Business Review,* 1(2): 165-189.

Astrachan, J.H. (1993). **Preparing the next generation for wealth: A conversation with Howard. H. Stevenson.** *Family Business Review,* 6(1): 75-83.

Astrachan, J.H. & T.A. Kolenko (1994). **A neglected factor explaining family business success: Human resource practices.** *Family Business Review,* 7(3): 251-262.

Ayres, G.A. (1990). **Rough family justice: Equity in family business succession planning.** *Family Business Review,* 3(1): 3-22.

Babicky, J. (1987). **Consulting to the family business.** *Journal of Management Consulting,* 3(4): 25-32.

Barach, J.A. (1984). **Is there a cure for paralysed family boards?** *Sloan Management Review,* 2(1): 3-12.

Barnes, L.B. (1988). **Incongruent hierarchies: Daughters and younger sons as company CEOs.** *Family Business Review,* Spring, 1(1): 9-21.

Barnes, L.B. & S.A. Hershon (1976). **Transferring power in the family business.** *Harvard Business Review,* 53(4): 105-114.

Barnett, F. & S. Barnett (1988). ***Working Together: Entrepreneurial Couples.*** Berkeley: Ten Speed Press.

Barry, B. (1975). **The development of organization structure in the family firm.** *Journal of General Management,* Autumn: 42-60.

Beach, B. (1993). **Family support in home-based family businesses.** *Family Business Review,* 6(4): 371-379,

Beckhard, R. & W.G. Dyer, Jr. (1983a). **Managing change in the family firm - Issues and strategies.** *Sloan Management Review,* 24(3): 59-65.

Beckhard, R. & W.G. Dyer, Jr. (1983b). **Managing continuity in the family owned business.** *Organizational Dynamics,* Summer: 5-12.

Bensahel, J.G. (1975). **Playing fair in family business.** *International Management,* February: 37-38.

Berenbeim, R.E. (1990). **How business families manage the transition from owner to professional management.** *Family Business Review,* 3(1): 69-110.

Berolzheimer, M.G. (1980). **The financial and emotional sides of selling your company.** *Harvard Business Review,* 58(1): 6-11.

Birley, S. (1986). **Succession in family firm: The inheritors view.** *Journal of Small Business Management,* 24(3): 36-43.

Brady, D. & C. Strauch (1990). **Who are the family foundations? Findings from the foundation management survey.** *Family Business Review,* 3(4): 337-346.

Brockhaus Sr., R.H. (1994). **Entrepreneurship and family business: Comparisons, critique, and lessons.** *Entrepreneurship Theory and Practice,* 19(1): 25-38.

Brown, F. H. (1993). **Loss and continuity in family firm.** *Family Business Review,* Summer, 6(2): 111-130.

Budge, G.S. & R.W. Janoff (1991). **Interpreting the discourses of family business.** *Family Business Review,* 4(4): 367-381.

Burack, E.H. & C.M. Calero (1981). **Seven perils of family business.** *Nation's Business,* January: 62-64.

Burke, R.J., T. Weir, & R.E. DuWors, Jr. (1980). **Work demands on administrators and spouse well being.** *Human Relations,* 33(4): 253-278.

Cabot, L.W. (1976). **On an effective board.** *Harvard Business Review,* 54(5): 40-46.

Cambreleng, R.W. (1969). **The case of the nettlesome nepot.** *Harvard Business Review,* 47(2): p.14.

Carsrud, A.L. (1994). **Meanderings of a resurrected psychologist OR lessons learned in creating a family business program.** *Entrepreneurship Theory and Practice,* 19(1): 39-48.

Cates, J.N. & M.B. Sussman (1982). **Family systems and inheritance.** *Marriage and Family Review,* 5: 1-24.

Chaganti, R. & J.A. Schneer (1994). **A study of the impact of owner's mode of entry on venture performance and management patterns.** *Journal of Business Venturing,* 9: 243-260.

Chau, T.T. (1991). **Approaches to succession in East Asian business organizations.** *Family Business Review,* 4(2): 161-179.

Christensen, C. (1953). ***Management succession in small and growing enterprises.*** Boston: Division of Research, Harvard Business School.

Churchill, N.C. & K.J. Hatten (1987). **Non-market based transfers of wealth and power: A Research framework for family businesses.** *American Journal of Small Business Management,* 11(3): 51-64.

Cohn, T. & R.A. Lindberg (1974). ***Survival and growth: Management strategies for the small firm.*** New York: AMACOM, 1974.

Correll, R.W. (1989). **Facing up to moving forward: A third-generation successor's reflections.** *Family Business Review,* 2(1): 17-29.

Covin, T.J. (1994a). **Perceptions of family-owned firms: The impact of gender and educational level.** *Journal of Small Business Management,* 32(3): 29-39.

Covin, T.J. (1994b). **Profiling preference for employment in family-owned firms,** *Family Business Review,* 7(3): 287-296.

Crane, M. (1982). **How to keep families from feuding.** *Inc.,* February: 73-79.

Crouter, A.C. (1984). **Spillover from family to work: The neglected side of work family interface.** *Human Relations,* 37(6): 425-442.

Daily, C.M. & M.J. Dollinger (1992). **An empirical examination of ownership structure in family and professionally managed firms.** *Family Business Review,* 5(2): 117-136.

Daily, C.M. & S.S. Thompson (1994). **Ownership structure, strategic posture, and firm growth: An empirical examination,** *Family Business Review,* 7(3): 237-249.

Danco, L. (1975). ***Beyond Survival: A Business Owner's Guide for Success.*** Cleveland: University Press.

Danco, L. (1981). **From the other side of the bed**. Cleveland: The University Press.

Danco, L.A. & J.L. Ward (1990). **Beyond success: The continuing contribution of the family foundations.** *Family Business Review,* 3(4): 347-355.

Davis, J.A. & R. Tagiuri (1985). **Bivalent attitudes of the family firm.** Paper presented at the Western Academy of Management Meeting.

Davis, J.A. & R. Tagiuri (1989). **The Influence of life-stage on father-son work relationships in family companies.** *Family Business Review,* 2(1): 47-74.

Davis, P. (1983). **Realizing the potential of the family business.** *Organizational Dynamics,* Summer: 47-56.

Davis, P. & D. Stern (1988). **Adaptation, survival, and growth, of the family business: An integrated systems perspective.** *Family Business Review,* 1(1): 69-85.

Davis, S.M. (1968). **Entrepreneurial succession.** *Administrative Science Quarterly,* 13: 402-416.

Dean, S.M. (1992). **Characteristics of African American family-owned businesses in Los Angeles.** *Family Business Review,* 5(4): 373-395.

Desmon, R. & C. Brush (1991). **Family business: The state of the notion.** In N. Upton (ed.) *Proceedings of the 1991 Family Firm Conference.* Jonestown: Family Firm Institute.

Dietrich, N.B. (1985). **Managing a successful transition.** *Small Business Report,* July: 61-64.

Doeringer, P.B., P.I. Moss, & D.G. Terkla (1992). **Capitalism and kinship: Do institutions matter in the labor market?** *Family Business Review,* 5(1): 85-101.

Donckels, R. & E. Frohlick (1991). **Are family businesses really different? European experiences from STRATOS.** *Family Business Review,* 4(2): 149-160.

Donnelley, R. (1964). **The family business.** *Harvard Business Review,* 42(3): 93-105.

Dreux, IV, D.R. (1990). **Financing family businesses: Alternatives to selling out or going public.** *Family Business Review,* 3(3): 225-243.

Dumas, C. (1989). **Understanding of father-daughter and father-son dyads in family-owned businesses.** *Family Business Review,* 2(1): 31-46.

Dunn, B. (1995). **Success themes in Scottish family enterprises: Philosophies and practices through the generations.** *Family Business Review,* 8(1): 17-28.

Dyer, Jr., W.G. (1986). ***Cultural change in family firms: Anticipating and managing business and family traditions.*** San Francisco: Jossey Bass.

Dyer, Jr., W.G. (1988). **Culture and continuity in family firms.** *Family Business Review,* 1(1): 37-50.

Dyer, Jr., W.G. (1989). **Integrating professional management into a family owned business.** *Family Business Review,* 2(3): 221-235.

Dyer, Jr., W.G. (1994). **Potential contributions of Organizational Behavior to the study of family-owned businesses.** *Family Business Review,* 7(2): 109-131.

Dyer Jr., W.G. & W. Handler (1994). **Entrepreneurship and family business: Exploring the connections.** *Entrepreneurship Theory and Practice,* 19(1): 71-83.

Erfurt, J.C., A. Foote, M.A. Heirich & K. Holtyn (1993). **Saving lives and dollars through comprehensive preventive health care.** *Family Business Review,* 6(2): 163-172.

Fiegener, M.K., B.M. Brown, R.A. Prince, & K.M. File (1994). **A comparison of successor development in family and non-family businesses.** *Family Business Review,* 7(4): 313-329.

File, K.M. (1995). **Organizational buyer behavior of the family firm: A review of the literature and set of propositions.** *Family Business Review,* 8(1): 29-40.

File, K.M., R.A. Prince, & M.J. Rankin (1994). **Organizational buying behavior of the family firm.** *Family Business Review,* 7(3): 263-272.

Firnstahl, T.W. (1986). **Letting go.** *Harvard Business Review,* 64(5): 14-18.

Flemons, D.G. & P.M. Cole (1992). **Connecting and separating family and business: A relational approach to consultation.** *Family Business Review,* 5(3): 257-269.

Forbes, W.F. & A.C. Paddock (1982). **'Freeze' assets to lower estate taxes and keep control.** *Harvard Business Review,* 60(6): 16-28.

Ford, R.H., (1988). **Outside directors and the privately owned firm: Are they necessary?** *Entrepreneurship Theory and Practice,* 13(1): 49-57.

Fox, H.W. (1984). **Managing the transition to professional direction.** *Management Review,* December: 42-45.

Francis, A. (1991). **Families, firms, and finance capital: The development of U.K. industrial firms with particular reference to their ownership and control.** *Family Business Review,* 4(2): 231-261.

Friedman, S.D. (1991). **Sibling relationships and inter-generational succession in family firms.** *Family Business Review,* 4(1): 3-20.

Fruin, W.M. (1980). **The family as a firm and the firm as a family in Japan: The case of Kikkoman Shoyo Co. ltd..** *Journal of Family History,* Winter: 432-449.

Gallo, M.A. & J. Sveen (1991). **Internationalizing the family business: Facilitating and restraining factors**. *Family Business Review,* 4(2): 181-190.

Geeraerts, G. (1984). **The effect of ownership on the organization structure in small firms.** *Administrative Science Quarterly,* 29: 232-237.

Gersick, K.E., I. Lansberg, & J.A. Davis (1990). **The impact of family dynamics on structure and process in family foundations.** *Family Business Review,* 3(4): 357-374.

Gilbert, N. (1989). **Can a family business survive mergermania and divorce?** *Management Review,* January: 38-42.

Gillis-Danovan, J. & C. Moynihan-Bradt (1990). **The power of invisible women in the family business.** *Family Business Review,* 3(2): 153-167.

Goffee, R. & R. Scasse (1985). **Proprietorial control in family firms - Some functions of 'Quasi-Organic' management systems.** *Journal of Management Studies,* 22(1): 53-68.

Goldberg, S.D. & B. Woolridge (1993). **Self confidence and managerial autonomy: Successor characteristics critical to succession in family firms.** *Family Business Review,* 6(1): 55-73.

Greenhaus, J.H. & N.J. Beutell (1985). **Sources of conflict between work and family roles.** *Academy of Management Review,* 10(1): 76-88.

Grisanti, D.A. (1982). **The agony of selling out to relatives.** *Harvard Business Review,* 60(6): 6-14.

Gumpert, D.E. & D.P. Boyd (1984). **The loneliness of small business owner.** *Harvard Business Review,* 62(6): 18-24.

Gundry, L.K. & H.P. Welsch (1994). **Differences in familial influence among women-owned businesses.** *Family Business Review,* 7(3): 273-286.

Guzzo, R.A. & S. Abbott (1990). **Family firms as Utopian organizations.** *Family Business Review,* 3(1): 23-33.

Hall, P.D. (1988). **A historical overview of family firms in US.** *Family Business Review,* 1(1): 51-68.

Hamilton, S. (1992). **A second family business: Patterns in wealth management.** *Family Business Review,* 5(2): 181-188.

Handler, W.C. (1989). **Methodological issues and considerations in studying family businesses.** *Family Business Review,* 2(3): 257-276.

Handler, W.C. (1992). **The succession experience of the next generation.** *Family Business Review,* 5(3): 283-307.

Handler, W.C. (1994). **Succession in family businesses: A review of the research.** *Family Business Review,* 7(2): 133-157.

Handler, W.C. & K.E. Kram (1988). **Succession in family firms: The problem of resistance.** *Family Business Review,* 1(4): 361-381.

Hansen, R.W., A.C. Hallett, S. Fredricks, J.K. Healey, & R.L. Payton (1990). **Continuing in the family foundation.** *Family Business Review,* 3(4): 405-420.

Harris, T.B. (1989). **Some comments on family boards.** *Family Business Review,* 2(2): 150-152.

Harris, D., J.L. Martinez, & J.L. Ward (1994). **Is strategy different for the family-owned businesses.** *Family Business Review,* 7(2): 159-176.

Harvey, M. & R.E. Evans (1994a). **The impact of timing and mode of entry on successor development and successful succession.** *Family Business Review,* 7(3): 221-236.

Harvey, M. & R.E. Evans (1994b). **Family business and multiple levels of conflict.** *Family Business Review,* 7(4): 331-348.

Harvey, M. & R.E. Evans (1995). **Life after succession in the family business: Is it really the end of problems?** *Family Business Review,* 8(1): 3-16.

Hayes, J.L. (1981). **All in the family.** *Management Review,* July: 4.

Hayes, J.T. & R.M. Adams (1990). **Taxation and statutory considerations in the formation of family foundations.** *Family Business Review,* 3(4): 383-394.

Heck, R.K.Z. & R. Walker (1993). **Family-owned home-businesses: Their employees and unpaid helpers.** *Family Business Review,* 6(4): 397-415.

Heidrick, G.W. (1988). **Selecting outside directors.** *Family Business Review,* 1(3): 271-285.

Hershon, S.A. (1975). ***The Problem of Management Succession in Family Businesses.*** Doctoral Dissertation, Harvard Business School.

Hinsz, V.B. (1990). **Family farmers' reactions to their work: A job diagnostic survey.** *Family Business Review,* 3(1): 35-44.

Hirschhorn, L. & T. Gilmore (1980). **The application of family therapy concepts to influencing organization behavior.** *Administrative Science Quarterly,* 25: 18-37.

Hisrich, R.D. & D.J. Cahill (1995). **Buried at the crossroads at midnight with an oak stake through its heart: An entrepreneurial replication of Ross and Staw's extended temporal escalation model.** *Family Business Review,* 8(1): 41-54.

Hoffman, L. (1981). ***Foundations of family therapy.*** New York: Basic Books.

Holland, P.G. & W.R. Boulton (1984). **Balancing the family and the business in a family business.** *Business Horizons,* 27(2): 16-21.

Holland, P.G. & J.E. Oliver (1992). **An empirical examination of the stages of development of family businesses.** *Journal of Business and Entrepreneurship,* 4(3): 27-38.

Hollander, B.S. (1983). **Family-owned business as a system: A case study of the interaction of family, task, and marketplace components.** Doctoral dissertation, University of Pittsburgh.

Hollander, B.S. & N.S. Elman (1988). **Family-owned businesses: An emerging field of inquiry.** *Family Business Review,* 1(2): 145-164.

Hollander, B.S. & W.R. Bukowitz (1990). **Women, family culture, and family business.** *Family Business Review,* 3(2): 139-151.

Horton, T.P. (1982). **The baton of succession.** *Management Review,* July: 2-3.

Horton, T.P. (1986). **Managing in a family way.** *Management Review,* February: 3.

Hoy, F. & T.G. Verser (1994). **Emerging business, emerging field: Entrepreneurship and the family firm.** *Entrepreneurship Theory and Practice,* 19(1): 9-23.

Jain, S.K. (1980). **Look to outsiders to strengthen business boards.** *Harvard Business Review,* 58(4): 162-170.

Jones, W.D. (1982). **Characteristics of planning in small firms.** *Journal of Small Business Management,* 20(3): 15-19.

Jonovic, D.L. (1989). **Outside review in a wider context: An alternative to the classic board.** *Family Business Review,* 2(2): 125-140.

Kahn, J.A. & D.A. Henderson (1992). **Location preferences of family firms: Strategic decision making or "Home Sweet Home"?** *Family Business Review,* 5(3): 271-282.

Kanter, R. (1989). **Work and family in US: A critical review and agenda for research and policy.** *Family Business Review,* 2(1): 77-114.

Kaye, K. (1991). **Penetrating the cycle of sustained conflict.** *Family Business Review,* 4(1): 21-44.

Kaye, K. (1992). **The kid brother.** *Family Business Review,* 5(3): 237-256.

Kepner, E. (1983). **The family and the firm: A co-evolutionary perspective.** *Organizational Dynamics,* Summer: 57-70.

Kirchhoff, B.A. & J.J. Kirchhoff (1987). **Family contributions to productivity and profitability in small businesses.** *Journal of Small Business Management,* 25(4): 25-31.

Kleinsorge, I.K. (1994). **Financial and efficiency differences in family-owned and non-family-owned nursing homes: An Oregon study.** *Family Business Review,* 7(1): 73-86.

Krentzman, H.C. & J.N. Samaras (1960). **Can small businesses use consultants?** *Harvard Business Review,* 38: 126-136.

Kuratko, D.F., H.B. Foss, & L.L. VanAlst (1994). **IRS Estate freeze rules: Implications for family business succession planning.** *Family Business Review,* 7(1): 61-71.

Landes, D.S. (1993). **Bleichoders and Rothschilds: The problem of continuity in the family firm.** *Family Business Review,* 6(1): 85-101.

Lane, S.H. (1989). **An organizational development / team-building approach to consultation with family businesses.** *Family Business Review,* 2(1): 5-16.

Lansberg, I. (1983a). **Conversation with Richard Beckhard.** *Organizational Dynamics,* Summer: 29-38.

Lansberg, I. (1983b). **Managing human resources in family firms: The problem of institutional overlap.** *Organizational Dynamics,* Summer: 39-46.

Lansberg, I. (1988). **The succession conspiracy.** *Family Business Review,* 1(2): 119-143.

Lansberg, I. & J.H. Astrachan (1994). **Influence of family relationships on succession planning and training: The importance of mediating factors.** *Family Business Review,* 7(1): 39-59.

Lansberg, I. & E. Perrow (1991). **Understanding and working with leading family businesses in Latin America.** *Family Business Review,* Summer, 4(2): 127-147.

Lansberg, I., E. Perrow, & S. Rogolsky (1988). **Family business as an emerging field.** *Family Business Review,* 1(1): 1-8.

Leach, P., W.K. Smith, A. Hart, T. Morris, J. Ainsworth, E. Beterlsen, S. Iraqi, & V. Pasari (1990). **Managing the family business in the U.K.: Stoy Hayward Survey in conjunction with the London Business School** London: Stoy Harward.

Levinson, H. (1971). **Conflicts that plague family businesses.** *Harvard Business Review,* 49(2): 90-98.

Levinson, H. (1983). **Consulting with family businesses: What to look for, what to look out for.** *Organizational Dynamics,* Summer: 71-80.

Levinson, R.E. (1974). **How to make your family business more profitable.** *Journal of Small Business Management,* 12(4): 35-41.

Lichtenstein, J.H. (1993). **Factors affecting the provision and cost of health insurance in small family businesses.** *Family Business Review,* 4(2): 173-178.

Liebtag, B. (1984). **Problems tracked in transition from owner to professional management.** *Journal of Accountancy,* October: 38-40.

Litz, R.A. (1995). **The family business: Toward definitional clarity.** *Proceedings of The Academy of Management:* 100-104.

Longnecker, J.G. & J.E. Schoen (1978). **Management succession in the family firm.** *Journal of Small Business Management,* 16(3): 1-6.

Lossberg, J.T. & R.M. Adams (1990). **The role of the non-family administrator in family foundations.** *Family Business Review,* 3(4): 375-382.

Low, M.B. & I.C. MacMillan (1988). **Entrepreneurship: Past Research and future challenges.** *Journal of Management,* 14(2): 139-161.

Lundberg, C.C. (1994). **Unravelling communications among family members.** *Family Business Review,* 7(1): 29-37.

Lyman, A.R. (1988). **Life in the family circle.** *Family Business Review,* 1(4): 383-398.

Lyman, A.R. (1991). **Customer service: Does family ownership make a difference?** *Family Business Review,* 4(3): 303-324.

Lyman, A., M. Salangicoff, & B. Hollander (1985). **Women in family business: An untapped resource.** *SAM Advanced Management Journal,* Winter: 46-49.

Mace, M.L. (1971). ***Directors: Myth and Reality***. Boston: Harvard Business School.

Malone, S.C. (1989). **Selected correlates of business continuity planning in the family business.** *Family Business Review,* 2(4): 341-353.

Malone, S.C. & P.V. Jenster (1992). **The problem of plateaued owner manager.** *Family Business Review,* 5(1): 25-41.

Mandelbaum, L. (1994). **Small business succession: The educational potential.** *Family Business Review,* 7(4): 369-376.

Marcus, G.E. (1991). **Law in development of dynastic families among American business elites: The domestication of capital and the capitalization of family.** *Family Business Review,* 4(1): 75-111.

Marshack, K.J. (1993). **Coentrepreneurial couples: A literature review on boundaries and transitions among copreneurs.** *Family Business Review,* 6(4): 355-369.

Marshack, K.J. (1994). **Copreneurs and Dual-Career Couples: Are they different?** *Entrepreneurship Theory and Practice,* 19(1): 49-69.

Mastromarco, D.R. (1992). **The family owned business in tax policy debates.** *Family Business Review,* 5(2): 191-200.

Mathile, C.L. (1988). **A business owner's perspective on outside boards.** *Family Business Review,* 1(3): 231-237.

Matthews, G.H. (1984). **Run your business or build an organization?** *Harvard Business Review,* 62(2): 34-44.

Matthews, G.H., D.P. Vasudevan, S.L. Barton, & R. Apana (1994). **Capital structure decision making in privately held firms: Beyond the finance paradigm.** *Family Business Review,* 7(4): 349-367.

McCollom, M. (1988). **Integration in the family firm: When the family system replaces controls and culture.** *Family Business Review,* 1(4): 399-417.

McCollom, M. (1990). **Problems and prospects in clinical research on family firms.** *Family Business Review,* 3(3): 245-262.

McCollom, M. (1992a). **Organizational stories in a family-owned business.** *Family Business Review,* 5(1): 3-24.

McCollom, M. (1992b). **The ownership trust and succession paralysis in the family business.** *Family Business Review,* 5(2): 145-160.

McGivern, C. (1989). **The dynamics of management succession: A model of chief executive succession in the small family firm.** *Family Business Review,* 2(4): 401-411.

McGoldrick, M. & J.G. Troast (1993). **Ethnicity, families, and family businesses: Implications for practitioners.** *Family Business Review,* 6(2): 283-300.

McWhinney, W. (1984). **The use of family systems theory and therapy in working with family-managed businesses.** Paper presented at the meeting of the Western Academy of Management, Vancouver, B.C.

Miller, E.J. & A.K. Rice (1988). **The family business in contemporary society.** *Family Business Review,* 1(2): 193-210.

Mintzberg, H. & J.A. Waters (1990). **Tracking strategy in an entrepreneurial firm.** *Family Business Review,* 3(3): 285-315.

Mueller, R.K. (1988). **Differential directorship: Special sensitivities and roles for serving the family business board.** *Family Business Review,* 1(3): 239-247.

Murdock, M. & C.W. Murdock (1991). **A legal perspective on shareholder relationships in family businesses: The scope of fiduciary duties.** *Family Business Review,* 4(3): 287-301.

Nash, J.M. (1988). **Boards of privately held companies: Their responsibility and structure.** *Family Business Review,* 1(3): 263-369.

Navin, T.R. (1971). **Passing on the mantle.** *Business Horizons,* 14(5): 83-93.

Nelton, S. (1986). ***In love and in business: How entrepreneurial couples are changing the rules of business and marriage.*** New York: Wiley.

Owen, A.J., M.L. Carsky, & E.M. Dolan (1993). **Home-based employment: Historical and current considerations.** *Family Business Review,* 6(4): 437-451.

Owen, A.J. & M. Winter (1991). **Research note: The impact of home-based business on family life.** *Family Business Review,* 4(4): 425-432.

Peiser, R.B. & L.M. Wooten (1983). **Life cycle changes in small family businesses.** *Business Horizons,* 26(3): 58-65.

Perrigo, A.E.B. (1975). **Delegation and succession in the small firms.** *Personnel Management,* May: 35-37.

Pettker, J.D. & A.D. Cross (1989). **The new anti-freeze law: A meltdown for the family firm?** *Family Business Review,* 2(2): 153-172.

Ponthieu, L.D. & H.L. Caudill (1993). **Who's the boss? Responsibility and decision making in copreneurial ventures.** *Family Business Review,* 6(1): 3-17.

Post, J.E. (1993). **The greening of the Boston Park Plaza hotel.** *Family Business Review,* 6(2): 131-148.

Post, J.M. & R.S. Robins (1993). **The captive king and his captive court: The psychopolitical dynamics of the disabled leader and his inner circle.** *Family Business Review,* 6(2): 203-221.

Poza, E.J. (1988). **Managerial practices that support interpreneurship and continued growth.** *Family Business Review,* 1(4): 339-359.

Pratt, J.H. & J.A. Davis (1986). **Measurement and evaluation of population of family-owned businesses.** *U.S. Small Business Administration Report No. 9202-ASE-85*. Washington, D.C.: Government Printing Office.

Prince, R.A. (1990). **Family business mediation: A conflict resolution model.** *Family Business Review,* 3(3): 209-223.

Rappaport, A. (1995). **Farm women as full-time partners: Some evidence of sharing traditional gender-based tasks.** *Family Business Review,* 8(1): 55-63.

Reiss, D. (1982). **The working family: A researcher's view of health in household.** *American Journal of Psychiatry*, November: 1412-1420.

Rogal, K.H. (1989). **Obligation or opportunity: How can could-be heirs assess their position?** *Family Business Review,* 2(3): 237-255.

Rosenblatt, P.C. (1991). **The interplay of family system and business system in family farms during economic recession.** *Family Business Review,* 4(1): 45-57.

Rosenblatt, P.C., L. deMik, R.M. Anderson, & P.A. Johnson (1985). ***The family in business: Understanding and dealing with the challenges entrepreneurial families face***. San Francisco: Jossey-Bass.

Rothstein, J. (1992). **Don't judge a book by it's cover: A reconstruction of eight assumptions about Jewish family businesses.** *Family Business Review,* 5(4): 397-411.

Rowe, B.R., G.W. Haynes, & M.T. Bentley (1993). **Economic outcomes in family-owned home-based businesses.** *Family Business Review,* 6(4): 383-396.

Russell, C.S., C.L. Griffin, C.S. Flinchbough, M.J. Martin, & R.B. Atilano (1985). **Coping strategies associated with inter-generational transfer of the family farm.** *Rural Sociology,* 50(3): 361-376.

Rutigliano, A.J. (1986). **Family businesses need help from outside.** *Management Review,* February: 26-27.

Salganicoff, M. (1990). **Women in family business: Challenges and opportunities.** *Family Business Review,* 3(3): 125-137.

Salomon, R. (1977). **Second thoughts on going public.** *Harvard Business Review,* 55(5): 126-131.

Salomon, S. & V. Lockhart (1980). **Land ownership and the position of elderly in farm families.** *Human Organization,* 39(4): 324-331.

Schaefer, R. & J.A. Davis (1992). **Evaluation of auditor's going-concern risk in family business.** *Family Business Review,* 5(1): 63-75.

Schein, E.H. (1983). **The role of the founder in creating organization culture.** *Organizational Dynamics,* 5(1): 13-28.

Schipani, C.A. & G.J. Siedel (1988). **Legal liability: The board of directors.** *Family Business Review,* 1(3): 279-285.

Schwartz, E.L. (1954). **Will your business die with you?** *Harvard Business Review,* 32(5): 110-122.

Schwartz, M.A. & L.B. Barnes (1991). **Outside boards and family businesses: Another look.** *Family Business Review,* 4(3): 269-285.

Scott, M. & R. Bruce (1986). **Five stages of growth in small business.** *Long Range Planning,* 20(3): 45-52.

Scranton, P. (1992). **Learning manufacture: Education and shop floor schooling in the family firm.** *Family Business Review,* 5(3): 323-342.

Seymour, K.C. (1993). **Inter-generational relationships in the family firm: The effect on leadership succession.** *Family Business Review,* 6(3): 263-281.

Shanker, M.C. & J. Astrachan (1995). **Myths and realities: Family businesses' contribution to the U.S. economy.** *Annual proceedings of United States Association of Small Business amd Entrepreneurship*: 21-31.

Siegel, G., D.S. Shannon, C.J. Stahl, & P.R. Melchert (1986). **Marketing consulting services to small businesses.** *Journal of Accountancy,* October: 160-170.

Singer, J. & C. Donohu (1992). **Strategic management planning for the successful family business.** *Journal of Business and Entrepreneurship,* 4(3): 39-51.

Sonnenfeld, J.A. & P.L. Spence (1989). **The parting patriarch of a family firm.** *Family Business Review,* 2(4): 355-375.

Stallings, S.L.A. (1992). **The emergence of American-Indian enterprise.** *Family Business Review,* 5(4): 413-416.

Stern, M.H. (1986). ***Inside the family held business.*** New York: Harcourt Brace.

Stier, S. (1993). **Wellness in the family business.** *Family Business Review,* 6(2): 149-159.

Stokes, J.F. (1980). **Involving new directors in small company management.** *Harvard Business Review,* 58(4): 170-174.

Swagger Jr., G. (1991). **Assessing the successor generation in family businesses.** *Family Business Review,* 4(4): 397-411.

Swartz, S. (1989). **The challenges of multi-disciplinary consulting to family-owned businesses.** *Family Business Review,* 2(4): 329-339.

Swinth, R.L. & K.L. Vinton (1993). **Do family owned businesses have a strategic advantage in international joint ventures?** *Family Business Review,* 6(1): 19-30.

Tagiuri, R. & J.A. Davis (1992). **On the goals of successful family companies.** *Family Business Review,* 5(1): 263-281.

Tillman, F.A. (1988). **Commentary on legal liability: Organizing the advisory council.** *Family Business Review,* 1(3): 287-288.

Trostel, A.O. & M.L. Nichols (1982). **Privately held companies and publicly held companies: A comparison of strategic choices and management processes.** *Academy of Management Journal,* 25(1): 47-62.

Trow, D.B. (1961). **Executive succession in small companies.** *Administrative Science Quarterly,* 6: 228-239.

Upton, N., & D.L. Sexton (1987). **Family business succession: The female perspective.** *Proceedings of 32nd annual world conference of the ICSB*: 313-318.

Upton, N., K. Vinton, S. Seaman, & C. Moore (1993). **Family business consultants - Who we are, what we do, and how we do it?** *Family Business Review,* 6(3): 301-311.

Verdin, J.A. (1986). **Improving sales performance in a family owned business.** *American Journal of Small Business,* 10(4): 49-61.

Vetter, E.W. (1984). **Succession planning: Mastering the basics.** *Human Resource Planning,* 7(2): 99-104.

Walker, E.J. (1976). **'Til' business us do part.** *Harvard Business Review,* 54(1): 94-101.

Walsch, F. (1994). **Healthy family functioning: Conceptual and research developments.** *Family Business Review,* 7(2): 175-198.

Ward, J. L. (1987). ***Keeping the family business healthy: How to plan for continuing growth, profitability, and family leadership***. San Francisco: Jossey-Bass.

Ward, J.L. (1988). **The special role of strategic planning for family businesses.** *Family Business Review,* 1(2): 105-117.

Ward, J.L. (1990a). **The succession process: 15 guidelines.** *Small Business Forum,* 8(3): 57-62.

Ward, J.L. (1990b). **What is a family business? And how can we help?** *Small Business Forum,* 8(3): 63-71.

Ward, J.L. & J.L. Handy (1988). **A survey of board practices.** *Family Business Review,* 1(3): 289-308.

Weber, M. (1947). ***The theory of social and economic organization.*** New York: Oxford University Press.

Weiser, J., F. Brody, & M. Quarrey (1988). **Family businesses and employee ownership.** *Family Business Review,* 1(1): 23-35.

Welsch, J. (1991). **Family enterprises in the UK, the Federal Republic of Germany, and Spain: A transnational comparison.** *Family Business Review,* 4(2): 231-261.

Welsch, J. (1993). **The impact of family ownership and involvement on the process of management succession.** *Family Business Review,* 6(1): 31-54.

Whisler, T.L. (1988). **The role of the board in the threshold firm.** *Family Business Review,* 1(3): 309-321.

Whiteside, M.F. & F.H. Brown (1991). **Drawbacks of a dual systems approach to family firms: Can we expand out thinking?** *Family Business Review,* 4(4): 383-395.

Williams, R.O. (1992). **Successful ownership in business families.** *Family Business Review,* 5(2): 161-172.

Willmott, P. (1971). **Family, work, and leisure conflicts among male employees.** *Human Relations,* 24(6): 575-584.

Winter, M. & M. Fitzgerald (1993). **Continuing the family-owned home-based businesses: Evidence from a panel study.** *Family Business Review,* 6(4): 417-426.

Wong, B., S. McReynolds, & W. Wong (1992). **Chinese family firms in the San Francisco bay areas.** *Family Business Review,* 5(4): 355-372.

Wong, S.L. (1993). **The Chinese family: A model.** *Family Business Review,* 6(3): 327-340.

Wortman Jr., M.S. (1994). **Theoretical foundations for family-owned business: A conceptual and research based paradigm.** *Family Business Review,* 7(1): 3-27.

Ylvisaker, P.N. (1990). **Family foundations: High risk, high reward.** *Family Business Review,* 3(4): 331-335.

2

A CLASSIFICATION OF THE ARTICLES ANNOTATED

In this section we present two tables classifying the articles annotated in section 3. The first table shows the numbers and types of studies under each main research topic in the literature. The second contains the authors, dates of publication, key findings, and types of studies.

Table 2

Number and Classification of the Annotated Articles According to Research Topic

Topic Area	Empirical	Theoretical	Experiential	Total
DEFINITION	**1**	**2**	**-**	**3**
STRATEGIC MANAGEMENT	**52**	**42**	**13**	**107**
Goals and objectives	3	-	-	3
Strategy formulation and content				
Strategic planning process	9	2	2	13
Culture in the family business	3	1	1	5
Internationalization	-	1	1	2
Social issues	1	-	-	1
Strategy implementation and design				
Board of directors	5	8	1	14
Organizational structure	2	-	-	2
Strategic evaluation, control, and performance	6	1	-	7
General management and ownership				
Succession	11	20	5	36
Founder characteristics and management style	3	1	1	5
Organizational evolution and change				
Life cycle stages	6	4	-	10
Transition toward professional management	3	4	2	9

Topic Area	Empirical	Theoretical	Experiential	Total
FAMILY INFLUENCE	**33**	**28**	**7**	**68**
Family involvement in the business				
Inter-generational and sibling relationships	9	1	4	14
Women in the family business	5	2	-	7
Nepotism	2	1	-	3
Types of family	1	8	-	9
Uniqueness of the family business				
Unique strengths and challenges	2	6	-	8
Work-family conflicts and spill-overs	4	3	1	8
Types of family business	10	7	2	19
OTHER ISSUES	**15**	**12**	**21**	**48**
Ethnicity	7	1	2	10
Professional advise	6	3	19	28
Methodological issues	2	8	-	10
GRAND TOTALS	**100**	**85**	**41**	**226**

Table 3

Classification and Key Findings of Annotated Articles

Author (Year)	Key Findings (Type of Study)
DEFINITION (2 articles)	
Litz (1995)	Structure and intention based approaches are combined to clarify the definition of a family business. (Conceptual)
Shanker & Astrachan (1995)	Depending on the definition, family business numbers 4.1 million to 20.3 million, employs 15% - 59% of the total workforce, creates 19 - 78% of new jobs, and represents 12% - 49% of GDP of USA. (Empirical)
STRATEGIC MANAGEMENT (107 articles)	
Goals and objectives (3 articles)	
Dunn (1995)	Family firms differ from non-family firms in terms of their philosophies, practices, and definitions of success. In general, these firms are over-staffed, sub-optimal in performance, and stress good family relationships. (Empirical)
File, Prince, Rankin (1994)	Family firms may be classified into four categories according to their objectives. The guiding objective heavily influences decision making, hiring practices, and buying behaviour. (Empirical)
Tagiuri & Davis (1992)	The six most important goals of family firms are: to have a company where employees can be happy, productive, and proud; financial security and benefits for the owner; to develop new and quality products; personal growth, social advancement, and autonomy; to be a good corporate citizen; and job security. (Empirical)

Strategy formulation and content (21 articles)	
Strategic planning process	
Barry (1975)	Family business owners have four options: continue both ownership and management, retain ownership but let management go, abandon ownership but retain management, and evolve into a more bureaucratic firm. (Empirical)
Daily & Thompson (1994)	Family firms are no different from entrepreneurial, owner-managed, or professionally managed firms in terms of strategic posture or growth. (Empirical)
Doeringer, Moss, & Terkla (1992)	The fishing industry practices two systems of employment and pay: kinship and capitalist. A capitalist system resembles standard competitive firms. A kinship system is based on work guarantees and labour adjustments, and was found to be highly effective. (Empirical)
Donckels & Frohlick (1991)	In comparison to non-family firms, family firms are more stable, pay higher wages, and have a more conservative attitude toward business. (Empirical)
File (1995)	Family firms differ from non-family firms in five areas that influence purchasing: patterns of influence, organizational climate, buying processes, buying motives, and buying strategies. Propositions related to each of these areas are suggested. (Experiential)
Harris, Martinez, & Ward (1994)	The processes for formulating and implementing strategy are discussed. There are critical differences in these processes for family and non-family firms. (Conceptual)
Jones (1982)	The study compares family firms that engage in strategic planning with those that do not. Planning firms scan the environment, identify future opportunities through research, and involve organizational members in planning. These firms are more successful than non-planning firms. (Empirical)
Kahn & Henderson (1992)	Family firms do not seek locations that improve the family's quality of life. Instead, both family and non-family firms choose locations close to market and customers. (Empirical)
Lyman (1991)	Compared with the managers of non-family-owned firms, family business managers use a more personal approach, trust their employees more, and rely less on formal written policies. (Empirical)

Singer & Donohu (1992)	A clear understanding of the organization's business process technology and family-organizational values is helpful in planning the continuity of the business. The firm's operating strategies should be consistent with its chosen position. (Experiential)
Trostel & Nichols (1982)	Privately held companies have higher sales growth than publicly held ones, place greater emphasis on asset utilization, and have a stronger inclination to employ accounting policies that reduce taxable income. No significant differences are found in terms of degree of formalization in planning, education of managers, or ratio of administrative and professional personnel to sales. (Empirical)
Ward (1988)	The strategic planning process should include an assessment of: the family's commitment to business; business health; business alternatives; family and personal goals, interests, and capabilities. (Empirical)
Ward (1990b)	Family business is a business wherein two or more family members influence the business. Family and non-family firms differ in their strategies in terms of top management, reinvestment, innovation, and accountability. Due to the unique characteristics of the family business, the business, estate, and succession plans should be formulated simultaneously. (Conceptual)
Culture in the family business	
Astrachan (1988)	The family business at odds with the local culture will have lower levels of productivity and business harmony. (Experiential)
Dyer, Jr. (1988)	Four types of cultures of family businesses are identified: paternalistic, laissez faire, participative, and professional. For a successful transition, owners must analyze their firms' cultures and plan a change in culture if necessary. (Empirical)
Hollander & Bukowitz (1990)	A family's culture produces the rules, roles, structures, and triangles that are unquestioned. The family business must attempt to build a business community that supports family and economic activities for both male and female participants. (Conceptual)
Landes (1993)	The family firm must guard the identities of both the family and the firm or the organization will lose its identity. (Empirical)

Schien (1983)	To have effective succession, founders must have knowledge about the organizational culture. The article discusses the differences between founders and managers. (Empirical)
Internationalization	
Gallo & Sveen (1991)	Five factors that affect a company's ability to change are: strategy and objectives, organizational structure and systems, company culture, the development stage of the company, and the family's international characteristics. Family firms are generally slower to move into international markets. In order to enter global markets, these firms do not need to give up their family orientation but they have to broaden their local orientation and attitude. (Experiential)
Swinth & Vinton (1993)	International joint ventures between family businesses are more likely to succeed because these firms share values that enable them to bridge cultural barriers more effectively than publicly held companies. Family firms focus on long term profit, business continuity, and family support while non-family firms concentrate on short-term objectives, return to shareholders, and minimizing risks. In international joint ventures, the objectives of the firms affect their compatibility. (Conceptual)
Social issues	
Post (1993)	Together, the commitment of the top management team, the communication and creative thinking, and the reward system determine whether the spirit of ownership meshes with environmental responsibility. (Empirical)
Strategy implementation and design (16 articles)	
Board of directors	
Alderfer (1988)	The group dynamics in the board of directors may bring diversity or divisiveness. Group consultation may be used to manage the sub-group dynamics that may develop within the family firm's board. (Conceptual)
Barach (1984)	When key members of the board do not agree on important issues, the suggested strategies include: inaction, resolving key interpersonal conflicts, waiting for the departure of combatants, one part of family buying the other, and restructuring the firm to resolve crises. (Conceptual)
Ford (1988)	Outside directors are perceived as more effective than insiders. (Empirical)

Heidrick (1988)	Outside directors are described as the biggest bargain in management. They act as sounding boards for owners, help to increase self discipline, strengthen corporate leadership, and provide interim leadership when the CEO is out of action. The characteristics to look for in outside directors, their functions, and their compensation are discussed. (Conceptual)
Jain (1980)	Outside directors can help small companies develop public relations by mediating a wide range of internal issues, and by providing expertise in different areas. The article also discusses the roles and responsibilities of outside directors as well as where to find them. (Empirical)
Jonovic (1989)	The classic board may not be suitable for the family business. Instead, a review council (advisory board) with broader membership and mandate may be more useful. (Conceptual)
Mathile (1988)	Outsiders can be helpful in a closely-held company by providing objective opinions and companionship to the owner-manager. The ideal candidate is a risk-taking peer who has functional strengths required by the company, is compatible with the owner-manager, and possesses a high degree of honesty and integrity. (Conceptual)
Mueller (1988)	The outside director brings distinct advantages by: providing objectivity, acting as an arbitrator, helping to prioritize important issues, providing credibility to the firm, acting as a catalyst for change, and watching out for the interests of all stakeholders in the business. The outside director on a family firm's board receives both psychological and material rewards. (Conceptual)
Nash (1988)	The duties and responsibilities of board members are discussed. Outside board members enhance credibility and provide objectivity in decision-making. The advisory board recommended in the literature may not be effective because it has neither power nor legal authority. (Conceptual)
Schwartz & Barnes (1991)	Outside board members provide unbiased views and help establish networks. However, they do not help the day-to-day operation of the organization or help resolve family tensions. (Empirical)
Schipani & Siedel (1988)	Directors have care and fiduciary responsibilities. Mechanisms to protect directors are: liability insurance, appointment as advisors instead of directors, and agreement to indemnify directors for litigation expenses. (Experiential)

Stokes (1980)	The ratio of outsiders to insiders on family business boards should be such that the insiders are able to provide information to outsiders on an on-going basis. The insiders can be valuable sources of information, are more likely to be aware of the problems in the organization, and can act as two-way conduits. (Conceptual)
Ward & Handy (1988)	48% of firms in the sample have outsiders as directors. Outsiders are useful for advice, counsel, and accountability of management. Only 2% of the respondents report that the board is useful in succession planning. (Empirical)
Whisler (1988)	Outside directors help a company move toward professional management. These directors play three roles: perceptor, technical advisor, and arbitrator. (Empirical)
Organizational structure	
Daily & Dollinger (1992)	Non-family firms are larger, older, more likely to pursue growth, and more reliant on internal controls. The results show no statistically significant difference in the financial performances of family and non-family firms. (Empirical)
Geeraerts (1984)	Firms controlled by professional managers are more horizontally differentiated, more formalized, and have higher internal specialization than family managed firms. (Empirical)
Strategic evaluation, control and performance (7 articles)	
Chaganti & Schneer (1994)	Firm performance and management pattern are affected by the owner-manager's mode of entry: buy-out (BO), family firm (FF), or owner started (OS). The authors suggest different management approaches for OSs, FFs, and BOs. (Empirical)
Heck & Walker (1993)	Workers in the family-owned home business may be paid, unpaid, or contracted. They may also be family, related, or unrelated. Paid family workers, contracted family workers, paid unrelated workers, and contracted unrelated workers have the highest output. (Empirical)
Kirchoff & Kirchoff (1987)	Family members are more productive than non-family members. However, profitability does not increase because wages and salaries increase as a percentage of revenue. (Empirical)

Kleinsorge (1994)	Family owned nursing homes are less efficient in providing care, have lower occupancy rates, lower assets and higher liabilities, and spend less on patient care and more on salaries than non-family owned nursing homes. (Empirical)
Levinson (1974)	The family business can increase profitability by cashing in on flexibility, keeping emotions outside the business, making business plans, and making employment in family businesses more attractive to non-family members. (Conceptual)
Rowe, Haynes & Bentley (1993)	The profitability of a home-based business depends more on personal and family characteristics than on business related variables. (Empirical)
Verdin (1986)	Setting challenging goals and providing regular feedback helps improve a small firm's sales. (Empirical)
General management and ownership (41 articles)	
Succession	
Anonymous (1984)	The CEO of a family business should prepare an annual report listing both the business and personal perspectives on business issues. This can be a critical source of reference during succession planning. (Conceptual)
Astrachan (1993)	In preparing children for the family business, they should be trusted with decision-making and involved in charitable trusts at an early age. Moreover, team work and creative criticism should be encouraged among siblings. (Experiential)
Astrachan & Kolenko (1994)	Family firms use employee manuals, job descriptions, employee reviews, and compensation plans, but have no written entry requirements or succession plans. (Empirical)
Ayers (1990)	It is virtually impossible to achieve absolute economic equality among children. The goal of succession should be rough family justice based on equity rather than equality. (Conceptual)
Beckhard & Dyer (1983a)	Some crucial factors and trigger events that need to be considered during succession planning are discussed. (Conceptual)
Beckhard & Dyer (1983b)	Founder's priorities, conditions in the firm, and family dynamics must be considered when managing continuity in family firms. (Conceptual)

Cates & Sussman (1982)	Family inheritance began with primogeniture. Today, variants of families have led to different inheritance patterns. (Conceptual)
Chau (1991)	Successions in China (coparcenary) and Japan (primogeniture) differ. Coparcenary divides the family assets equally among male descendants while primogeniture gives all of the family assets to the eldest son. Primogeniture contributes to the longevity of Japanese family firms while coparcenary leads to the low survival rates among Chinese ones. (Conceptual)
Churchill & Hatten (1987)	A family business goes through four stages: owner-manager, training and development of the new generation, partnership between generations, and actual transfer of power. (Conceptual)
Davis (1968)	Three patterns of entrepreneurial succession are observed: strong father/weak son, conservative father/progressive son, and branches of a family. Each pattern has its distinct challenges. (Empirical)
Fiegener, Brown, Prince, & File (1994)	Family firms use a more personal, direct, and relationship-centred approach to develop their successors. (Empirical)
Friedman (1991)	Sibling rivalry is inevitable because of competition for parental love and attention. Inter-sibling comparisons, mode of justice (equity or equality), and parental role in conflict resolution determine sibling relationships. Legitimizing rivalry as an acceptable expression for individual differences and building trust among siblings can improve their relationship. (Conceptual)
Goldberg & Woolridge (1993)	Effective successors score significantly higher on self-confidence and managerial autonomy. Success in succession does not depend on birth order of the successor. Owners who lack confidence in the successor's ability or willingness to control are more reluctant to let go. (Empirical)
Handler (1994)	Research on succession follow five streams: succession as a process involving distinct stages, role of founder, perspectives of next generation family members, multiple levels of analysis, and characteristics of effective succession. (Conceptual)

Handler & Kram (1988)	Focusing on multilevel forces of resistance to succession can help us understand the problems of succession. There are individual, group, organizational, and environmental factors that aid or impede the succession process. (Conceptual)
Harvey & Evans (1994a)	A successor's development is heavily influenced by his/her mode and timing of entry into the family business. The appropriate timing and degree of a successor's involvement in the family business should be dictated by the life stages of the siblings and the business. (Conceptual)
Harvey & Evans (1995)	Successors need to implement a pro-active conflict management process to deal effectively with the residual conflicts and stress left after succession in the family firm. (Conceptual)
Horton (1982)	For effective succession, the successor should be open to learning, develop trust, demonstrate objectivity, and attempt to settle the uncertainties and fears of others. (Conceptual)
Lansberg (1983a)	Succession in family firms is both an economic as well as an emotional issue. Family involvement in planning is desirable but may not always be possible. Advisors need to be aware of the whole system and underlying dynamics. Male-female advisory teams are highly desirable in consulting for family businesses. (Experiential)
Lansberg (1988)	Most stakeholders are ambivalent toward succession planning and would like to see the present owner-manager continue in his position for various reasons. Some intervention strategies can be used to help different stakeholders face succession planning. (Experiential)
Lansberg & Astrachan (1994)	Management succession planning and training are affected by: family adaptability and cohesion, the family's commitment to the business, and the relationship between the owner-manager and the successor. (Empirical)
Levinson (1974)	The chance that a succession will fail increases if the successor is chosen by incumbents because they subconsciously seek immortality, want their achievements to stand as enduring monuments, and subconsciously want to demonstrate that no one can succeed them. Using a committee to choose the successor improves the chance of success. (Conceptual)

Longnecker & Schoen (1978)	Succession is a process rather than an event. Family successors are gradually prepared for leadership roles in family businesses. The stages involved in a father-son succession are: pre-business, introductory, introductory functional, functional, advanced functional, early succession, and mature succession. (Conceptual)
Malone (1989)	Level of strategic planning, perceived family harmony, presence of outsiders on the board of directors, and an internal locus of control of the owner-manager increase with higher level of continuity planning. The level of continuity planning is not correlated with size or age of owners. (Empirical)
Mandelbaum (1994)	Lack of time was the most important barrier to succession planning stated. Informational seminars were the most desired form of educational assistance required. (Empirical)
McGivern (1989)	Five main variables influencing the succession process are: stage of organizational development, motivation of owner-manager, extent of family domination, organizational climate, and business environment. (Empirical)
Rutigliano (1986)	A larger number of heirs exacerbates the problems of succession. Generating a new strategy for every new generation coming into the business and the presence of outsiders on the board can help the transition from one generation to the next. (Conceptual)
Schaefer & Davis (1992)	The auditors of a family business must point out how plans and procedures can increase the family firm's chances for survival. (Experiential)
Schwartz (1954)	Succession documents must be drafted correctly to avoid undesirable consequences such as liquidation, unnecessary estate or income taxes, etc. (Conceptual)
Scranton (1992)	In the late 19th and early 20th centuries the successor was trained through shop floor experience (5-8 years) and direct participation. The apprenticeship helped sons to learn about the organization's culture and helped fathers to assess the prowess and potential of their sons. With the passage of time direct apprenticeship has been replaced by more complex formats for entrepreneurial preparation. (Experiential)
Seymour (1993)	Successor training does, but succession planning does not, improve the working relationship between the owner-manager and the successor. (Empirical)

Swagger (1991)	The succession process must take into account the relationship among potential successors. Relationships can vary from fused and enmeshed to highly differentiated. Differentiation has three dimensions that affect both inter- and intra-generational relationships: bonding versus rivalry, autonomy versus dependency, and leadership versus paralysis. (Conceptual)
Trow (1961)	Succession planning improves the subsequent profitability of the firm. Succession is delayed if the owner-manager's son is perceived to be incompetent. In the absence of succession planning, subsequent profitability depends on the successor's abilities. (Empirical)
Vetter (1984)	Succession planning is a process by which an organization identifies candidates to succeed to a given position, should that position become vacant. Qualitative analysis can be useful in understanding the process of succession planning. (Conceptual)
Welsch (1993)	Results show no significant difference between the large industrial family business and non-family firms in terms of the rational, political, or bureaucratic dimensions of management succession. Observed differences are subtle. For example, family firms attach more importance to academic education and personality when selecting managers. (Empirical)
Ward (1990a)	Succession is a time consuming process that involves careful planning and may take from 15-20 years. The founder must: present a career in family business as an option and not an obligation to potential successors; designate areas of responsibility and explicitly state criteria for performance evaluation; teach the historical, cultural, and strategic foundations of the business to the successor; insist on outside experience; and provide non-family mentors to train the successor. (Conceptual)
Founder Characteristics and Management Style	
Brown (1993)	Death of a family member can have a significant influence on a family business. The degree of loss varies with timing, position of the deceased, and legacies of loss. Family members need to keep lines of communication open and develop plans for dealing with the loss of the founder. (Experiential)

Gumpert & Boyd (1984)	Small business ownership is closely associated with loneliness. Remedies include rearranging the work environment, participating in peer group activities, and being attentive to family and friends. (Empirical)
Malone & Jenster (1992)	The owner manager of a family firm may become plateaued because of boredom from doing the same work for two to three decades. The plateaued manager does not derive any satisfaction from business activities and may seek fulfilment through increased involvement in other activities. Ways to avoid plateauing are: taking a break from the business, appointing a board of directors, hiring new employees, and trying out strategic experiments. (Conceptual)
Post & Robins (1993)	When the leader is taken ill, four factors that determine the relationship between the leader and his inner circle are: factors associated with the disease, leader's reaction to his illness, social and political environment, and medical management of the leader. (Empirical)
Sonnenfeld & Spence (1989)	CEOs exhibit four different departure styles: monarchs, generals, governors, and ambassadors. Monarchs and generals are more attached to their stature as CEO and remain in close contact with the organization. Ambassadors and governors are more satisfied with their achievements and maintain a distance after their retirement. The challenge for the departing leader is to plan an ambassador-like departure and ensure objective involvement in the succession process. (Empirical)
Organizational evolution and change (19 articles)	
Life cycle stages	
Adizes (1979)	Four components of an organization can be used to identify the different stages in the life cycle of a firm: production, entrepreneurship, administration, and integration. The article outlines the most likely problems at each stage and the tools that may help to deal with them. (Conceptual)
Barnes & Hershon (1976)	Power transfer in the family firm is examined using inside and outside perspectives. The three stages through which a company passes are discussed: entrepreneurial, specialized functions, and divisional operations. (Empirical)

Berenbeim (1990)	The transition of a business toward professional management goes through three stages: coalition to establish the firm, ascendancy to owner's authority, and founder's departure from active involvement in the business. (Empirical)
Francis (1991)	Stages of control through which a family firm is likely to pass are: members of families, transition to professional management, and control by financial institutions. (Empirical)
Hall (1988)	The article traces the development of family firms from the 18th century. Since early times, different strategies have been used to keep family property intact. Diversification, changing scale of operation, and opposition to dynasticism work against the survival of family firms. (Conceptual)
Holland & Boulton (1984)	Family firms vary in terms of size and ownership-management structure. Based on the degree of family involvement, family firms can be classified as pre-family, family, adaptive family, or post family. An individual's managerial orientation depends upon his/her power in the family and in the business. (Empirical)
Holland & Oliver (1992)	The study supports a three stage model of development for the family business. The three stages are: control by owner manager, control shared by family members, and a professionally managed firm. The transition from family to professional management may not be as conflict ridden as is generally believed. (Empirical)
Navin (1971)	Most companies seem to pass through five stages of development: initiator, founder, founder's heirs, technicians, and professional managers. (Empirical)
Peiser & Wooten (1983)	A small business passes through three life cycle stages: survival, success, and take-off toward a larger organization. As the business goes through life cycle changes, the family undergoes changes too. A life cycle crisis occurs when the goals of two generations collide. It is helpful to delineate areas of responsibility and define procedures and mechanisms for conflict resolution clearly. Project-oriented industries may provide a ripe ground for smoothing the problems of transition as the younger generation can be given responsibility for a project, thereby helping them to gain experience. (Conceptual)

Scott & Bruce (1986)	The small business passes through five distinct stages of growth: inception, survival, growth, expansion, and maturity. Each stage has its own characteristics and useful strategies. This five stage model of growth may be used as a diagnostic tool to analyze the firm. (Conceptual)
Transition toward professional management	
Dyer Jr. (1989)	The family business may professionalize by evolution or revolution. Evolutionary methods are useful when the family wishes to maintain present strategies and make the switch in incremental steps. These methods involve professionalizing both family and non-family members. Revolutionary methods involve bringing in outside management. (Conceptual)
Firnstahl (1986)	Delegating authority and responsibility can be a difficult process for the owner-manager. Delegation can be accomplished by recruiting the best people and setting aside time to train and evaluate them. (Experiential)
Fox (1984)	As the business expands, the owner may retain full ownership and keep the business small, adopt bureaucratic processes, or withdraw. (Conceptual)
Goffee & Scasse (1985)	The proprietor who is reluctant to delegate control may pass control to the executives but retain the prerogative to intervene arbitrarily. (Empirical)
Liebtag (1984)	The most critical factor in transforming the family business into a professional company is the timely withdrawal of the founder from active management. (Empirical)
Matthews (1984)	To facilitate delegation, the owner must define goals succinctly, select people for the task, ask for suggestions, agree on an approach, schedule progress checkpoints, and encourage delegates to summarize the process and recommend improvement. (Experiential)
Mintzberg & Winters (1990)	Over its long life, Steinberg Inc. went through an entrepreneurial mode wherein the owner was fully in charge and a planning mode wherein procedures replaced vision and strategy-making became an extrapolation of the status quo. (Empirical)

Perrigo (1975)	Delegation is difficult for owner-managers because of their fear that subordinates may not perform the jobs as well and because of their inflated views of their own performance. They must keep in mind that they need to delegate in order to do more important things for the firm. (Conceptual)
Poza (1988)	Interpreneurship is revitalization prior to succession. The article discusses the impediments to revitalization, measures to set the stage for it, and intervention strategies. (Conceptual)
FAMILY INFLUENCE (68 articles)	
Family involvement in the business (33 articles)	
Inter-generational and sibling relationships	
Ambrose (1983)	To increase the chance of effectively transferring the business to the next generation, the children should be involved when they are young. (Empirical)
Barnes (1988)	When a younger daughter or son takes over, the family business must deal with the incongruent hierarchies. Only day-to-day actions and behaviours can bring the two hierarchies into line with each other. (Empirical)
Birley (1986)	Family business owners tend to be authoritarian. Whether children return to the family business appears to be a function of gender but not of sibling position. (Empirical)
Correll (1989)	The next generation members in the family firm must struggle to balance emotionality and rationality. (Experiential)
Covin (1994a)	The survey results indicate that students perceive family firms to be as competitive as non-family firms and lack of formalization to be the major weakness of family firms. Gender does not affect the perceptions. Graduate students view careers in family firms less favorably than undergraduates. (Empirical)
Covin (1994b)	Students who prefer a career in family firms differ significantly in background and job characteristics from those who do not. (Empirical)
Crane (1982)	The roles, authority, and responsibilities of the next generation family members should be clearly defined. (Experiential)
Davis & Tagiuri (1989)	The quality of the working relationship between father and son is affected by respective life cycle stages. (Empirical)

Dietrich (1985)	When a next generation family member joins the family business, he/she must deal with personnel problems, reorganizing, management training, and establishing communication channels. Being a woman adds to these challenges. (Experiential)
Dumas (1989)	There are similarities and differences in problems faced by male and female inheritors in the family business. Sons have a desire for autonomy. Daughters take a more submissive role as caretakers and need help with empowerment. (Empirical)
Handler (1992)	The quality of succession in the family firm is affected by individual and relational influences. (Empirical)
Kaye (1992)	The younger sibling who is brought up in a more affluent environment may become an outsider, trapped in the business, defensive, and/or carried by the family. The family must confront this possibility realistically. (Empirical)
Rogal (1989)	Before making the decision to join the family business, the potential heir should analyze self, career alternatives, and options. (Experiential)
Williams (1992)	The spirit of ownership can be inculcated in the next generation through role modelling, formation of an informal family investment partnership, and effective family communications. (Conceptual)
Women in the family business	
Gillis-Danovan & Moynihan-Bradt (1990)	Women have varying degrees of visibility in the family business but may have considerable power and influence. This power is often exercised through other people. (Conceptual)
Gundry & Welsch (1994)	Family involvement in female-owned business influences various dimensions of the business and the women's long term career plans. (Empirical)
Lyman (1988)	The network of women associated with family firms tends to be limited to the family. Non-family business women consciously attempted to separate their work and family lives. (Empirical)

Lyman, Salangicoff, & Hollander (1985)	Because of their unique position as caretakers of family concerns, women hear about the family business and may know it inside out. In addition to this knowledge, they must acquire business skills and develop networks with other working women to manage the business effectively. (Conceptual)
Rappaport (1995)	Full-time partner wives of farm owners assume the role of helpers. Their husbands do more house work than those whose wives work off the farm. (Empirical)
Salganicoff (1990)	Women should get appropriate training and work in other organizations before joining the family business. They should be encouraged to obtain early know-how and feeling for the business. (Empirical)
Upton & Sexton (1987)	Daughters tend to hold stereotypical female positions in family businesses. (Empirical)
Nepotism	
Bensahel (1975)	An incompetent relative may be sent off to assignments where he/she can do minimum harm. A competent one can be provided with an environment congenial for growth. (Conceptual)
Cambreleng (1969)	Clear policies and open communications are useful in dealing with nepots in family firms. (Empirical)
Ewing (1965)	Nepotism is not as prevalent as believed. Executives do not support it but do not dismiss it blindly either. Advantages and likely problems of nepotism are discussed. (Empirical)
Types of Family	
Davis (1983)	There are three types of families: consensus-seeking, interpersonal-distance sensitive, and environment sensitive. The environmentally sensitive family that balances individual and family needs will be most successful. (Conceptual)
Davis & Stern (1988)	To successfully adapt to family and business needs, the family business must tackle: boundary definition, emotional containment, task system adjustment, and the legitimizing process. (Conceptual)
Flemons & Cole (1992)	There are inherent differences between family and business relationships. Creative new rules should be found that incorporate the elements of both relationships. (Conceptual)

Harvey & Evans (1994b)	The three stakeholders in the family business are: the business, the family, and the external stakeholders. The intensity of a conflict varies depending on whether one, two, or three of the stakeholders are involved. The mechanisms used for conflict resolution need to vary according to the intensity of the conflict. (Conceptual)
Hayes & Adams (1990)	A family foundation is a charitable foundation that derives its financial support from the family and less than one-third of its support from the general public. Individuals may claim income, estate, and gift-tax deductions for contributions to private foundations. Income realized by the foundation is usually tax-exempt. (Experiential)
Kanter (1989)	Historically, there has always been a strong interrelationship between work and family life. The modern industrial society tries to separate the two. Instead of this, organizations should strive to incorporate the two in useful ways. (Conceptual)
Lansberg (1983b)	The family and the business differ in terms of reasons for existence and selection, appraisal, allowances, and training of members. Separation of ownership and management is an effective means for managing basic contradictions. (Conceptual)
McCollom (1988)	The family and the business are interdependent and seek stability through reciprocal adjustments. An enmeshed family may achieve stability by using a differentiated work environment. (Empirical)
Walsch (1994)	Family process research may change assumptions about how the family business functions. A better understanding of how the healthy family functions is helpful for family business studies. (Conceptual)
Whiteside & Brown (1991)	Instead of being viewed as two subsystems, the family business should be studied as a holistic system using general systems theory. (Conceptual)

Uniqueness of the family business (16 articles)	
Unique strengths and challenges	
Burack & Calero (1981)	The challenges of the family firm include: dependence on the skills and abilities of founder and family members, the founder's feelings of immortality, obsession with appointing family members, informality in operation, failure to separate the roles of owner and managers, family feuds, and pressure to maintain tradition. (Conceptual)
Donnelley (1964)	The family firm generally has a valuable reputation, has loyal and dedicated family members, and is sensitive to continuity and integrity. Their challenges include dealing with nepotism, lack of managerial talent, and lack of discipline. (Empirical)
Gilbert (1989)	Survival of the family firm has become more difficult because of: a high rate of divorce, an increase in merger activities, an explosion of professionals, business communications, changing values of society, and the reluctance of children to join family firms. (Conceptual)
Hayes (1981)	The advantages of working in a family business are warmer relationships and a greater latitude in decision-making once accepted as an insider. The challenges include less professionalization, unclear lines of authority, and unavailability of stock options to non-family members. (Empirical)
Horton (1986)	The advantages of the family business are: value congruence among family members, willingness to pool resources when necessary, willingness to put in long hours, and togetherness through failure and success. The problems may include the founder's lack of confidence in other family members and conflicts between family members. In order to run a family business effectively, the family must handle properly the relationships among family members and those between family members and professional managers. (Conceptual)
Kepner (1983)	In the family business, the family and firm are subsystems with diffused boundaries. In order to avoid problems associated with this, there should be clear communication about the roles of different members, criteria of competence and performance evaluation, and mode of asset distribution. (Conceptual)

Levinson (1971)	Father-son conflicts and sibling conflicts are common in family businesses. Brothers in a family business should have separate areas of operation. Both family and non-family businesses should try to move toward professional management. (Conceptual)
Miller & Rice (1988)	Difficulties in the family business arise from a difference in the primary tasks of the family and the business. The difficulties include: pressure on family members to join the business, no external criteria of performance evaluation, and a clash between the internal non-competitive culture and external demands. Separation of ownership and management roles is a way to deal with the difficulties. (Conceptual)
Work-family conflicts and spill-overs	
Burke, Weir, & DuWors (1980)	Higher occupational demands lead to lower marital satisfaction, decreased social participation, and increased psychosomatic symptoms among the wives of senior administrators. (Empirical)
Crouter (1984)	Family life influences the morale, stability, and productivity of the work force. Women with young children report high family to work spill-over. (Empirical)
Greenhaus & Beutell (1985)	Work-family conflicts are higher when demands on time, energy, and behaviour requirements of one role conflict with those of another role. Conflict is strongest when there are negative sanctions for non-compliance with role demands. (Conceptual)
Kaye (1991)	Conflicts among family members are fundamentally different from those between unrelated parties because the issues are deeper than what appear on the surface. By charting the course of chronic disagreements an observer can encourage communication between members and help in conflict resolution. (Experiential)
Lundberg (1994)	In the family business, family members communicate both as business colleagues and family members. They play four different roles: a family member, an active role in the firm, a part owner, and a personal role. Miscommunication occurs when the role adopted by a person is misunderstood and when situation cues reflect role conflict and ambiguity. (Conceptual)

Prince (1990)	Three mechanisms for resolving interpersonal conflicts within the family business are: litigation, arbitration, and mediation. Mediation is the only effective method for conflict resolution. (Empirical)
Walker (1976)	It is in everyone's interest for the executive's wife to understand her husband's career goals, for the husband to learn how to share his feelings, and for the company to understand that if the needs of the family are not met, the company may lose the executive. (Conceptual)
Willmott (1971)	Work affects family life as a result of the work hours and the employee bringing work, stress, and worries home. (Empirical)
Types of family business (19 articles)	
Beach (1993)	The family acts as a filter affecting the operation of a home-based business. Children may be involved at four different levels: play, watch and help; assistance with simple tasks; regular unpaid assistance; and regular paid assistance. (Empirical)
Brady & Strauch (1990)	Family foundations differ from other foundations in terms of size (smaller), board composition (more females), limits on board services (fewer), and work demands on staff and trustees (higher). (Empirical)
Danco & Ward (1990)	A family foundation can help the continuity of a family business. The advantages, difficulties, and some basic steps in establishing a family foundation are discussed. (Conceptual)
Gersick, Lansberg, & Davis (1990)	Development over time, measured over generations, is critical to understanding the role of family dynamics in family foundations. (Empirical)
Guzzo & Abbott (1990)	Utopias and family businesses have many similarities in terms of ideals, mechanisms of commitment, and exercise of authority. (Conceptual)
Hansen, Hallett, Fredricks, Healey, & Payton (1990)	Five authors give suggestions about how to maintain continuity in family foundations. These include: adjunct boards, diversity, rotation of board members, long range planning, and regular assessment of the foundation's usefulness. (Conceptual)

Hinsz (1990)	Farm families derive a sense of satisfaction from their work, despite low financial returns and job insecurity. (Empirical)
Lossberg & Adams (1990)	Family foundations provide a special challenge to non-family administrators (NFA). NFAs have a lower turnover rate in families that work well together. In conflict-ridden families these administrators get caught in a political web and even routine tasks are negatively affected. (Experiential)
Marshack (1993)	Co-preneurships is an interaction of love and work. These couples believe that equity rather than equality contributes toward their marital and personal satisfaction. They adhere to traditional sex roles in the household chores and child care. Both wives and husbands reported a high level of satisfaction with the life style. (Conceptual)
Marshack (1994)	Co-preneurs are more traditional in their sex-role orientation than dual-career couples. Both co-preneurs and dual-career couples are satisfied with their marriage and business partners. (Empirical)
McCollom (1992b)	A family trust helps reduce taxes, supports family members with business revenues, and can run the business on a temporary basis until the successor takes over. A badly designed trust however, can limit the effective functioning of the business. (Empirical)
Owen, Carsky & Dolan (1993)	A research framework for the study of home-based businesses is presented. Two sets of variables important in studying the home-based business are the nature of work and the work environment. (Conceptual)
Owen & Winter (1991)	Women perceive less disruption by the home-based business than men. Perceived disruption is increased by the time the business requires of family members and decreased by the use of established managerial practices. Marketing and agricultural workers perceive the most disruption. Business income and age do not influence perceived disruption. (Empirical)
Ponthieu & Caudill (1993)	The relationship between co-preneurs is based on mutual trust, confidence, and a clear division of responsibility. Financial decisions are made jointly by the couple. Although husbands report confidence in their wives, wives do not believe that their spouses trust their decision-making. Men tend to dominate at work but neither partner dominates at home. (Conceptual)

Rosenblatt (1991)	Family goals, such as making room for off-spring to join the family farm and keeping up payments to retired parents, increase the vulnerability of family farms to economic recession. Economic viability can be maintained by careful planning and with expert help. (Empirical)
Russell, Griffin, Flinchbough, Martin, & Atilano (1985)	The coping strategies used by family members during inter-generational farm transfers are: individual coping, discussion, expressions of anger, using professionals, and farm management. The ordering of strategies reflects the basic values of rural Americans: self reliance (individual coping), family (discussion), and community (farm management professionals). Children are found to be more stressed than the parents. (Empirical)
Winter & Fitzgerald (1993)	About 33% of home-based businesses close down after three years, only 20% for economic reasons. Other reasons are health, employment, and family considerations. (Empirical)
Ylvisaker (1990)	The risks, rewards, and ways to improve the effectiveness of foundations are suggested in this article. (Conceptual)
	OTHER ISSUES STUDIED (48 articles)
Ethnicity	**(10 articles)**
Dean (1992)	African-American business owners are preoccupied with business survival and management issues. They do not benefit from community-based associations and report little family-work conflicts. Succession is not a primary concern because the business is used to prepare the children for a professional career. (Empirical)
Fruin (1980)	Since the 17th century, success of the Japanese family business has been based on careful planning of the succession and separation of ownership and management. (Experiential)
Lansberg & Perrow (1991)	Latin American economies are dominated by large family firms (grupos). These grupos are favoured by governments, do not face much competition, generally have highly skilled family members because of a cultural emphasis on quality education, and adopt socially responsibly policies. However, they lack the governance mechanisms needed to handle complex family business issues such as succession planning. (Empirical)

McGoldrick & Troast (1993)	The patterns of interaction, levels of involvement, and modes of management succession and ownership among Irish, African-American, Jews, Italian-Americans, and Anglo-Americans are examined. (Experiential)
Rothstein (1992)	Jewish families have lower rates of marital disruption than the general population. They expect their children to pursue higher education and display strong value systems. (Empirical)
Salomon & Lockhart (1980)	Families that maintain a future orientation and plan for the transfer of holdings are successful in maintaining rich and respectful family relationships. (Empirical)
Stallings (1992)	A major problem for the American-Indian-owned business is raising capital. Sources of capital include: guaranteed loans from the Small Business Administration, economic development grants, and income from reserve-based operations. (Conceptual)
Welsch (1991)	Three previously conducted studies are re-analyzed. A number of demographic data on family businesses are compared. (Empirical)
Wong (1992)	Patterns of family structure, kinship ties, information networks, financial cooperation, and aspiration levels help the first generation Chinese immigrant business survive. The family business is not an attractive career option for the second generation immigrant Chinese when they seek employment in US companies. (Empirical)
Wong (1993)	The Chinese family business passes through different stages of development: emergent, centralized, segmented, and disintegrative. The characteristics of each of these stages are discussed and compared with those of Filipino and Japanese firms. (Empirical)
Professional advice (28 articles)	
Anonymous (1983)	The family partnership can effectively transfer income from one generation to the next. (Experiential)
Armenakis & Brudg (1986)	Process consultation, which involves organizational diagnosis, feedback sessions, work-sessions, and adoption and implementation of plans, is an effective way to consult for family firms. (Experiential)

Babicky (1987)	Consulting for a family business involves dealing with both personal and technical issues. All family members may not be "on board". Destructive relationships may have been solidified since childhood. Consultants should act as facilitators and family members must unanimously agree to all solutions. (Experiential)
Berolzheimer (1980)	Selling a family business is a tough, emotional process that involves careful planning. The owner should carefully select the buyers, develop a strategy for contacting potential buyers, sell for cash, negotiate with two or three buyers, and organize the company so that day-to-day activities can be handled effectively. (Experiential)
Budge (1991)	Consultants can gain significant insights by listening to the stories narrated by family members and by employees of family firms. (Conceptual)
Dreux IV (1990)	Family firms face competing financial interests. They can raise capital by recapitalization, joint ventures, and employee stock ownership plans. (Experiential)
Erfurt, Foote, Heirich, & Holtyn (1993)	Employee assistance and work-life welfare programs can help the small businesses access preventive health care facilities. (Experiential)
Forbes & Paddock (1982)	Asset freezing can help minimize estate taxes, minimize gift taxes over the owner's life, help the current owner maintain control, ensure that control passes to the owner's chosen successor, and provide continuing income and control to the current owner. (Experiential)
Grisanti (1982)	When selling the family business, it is better to hold all negotiations away from the business, give buyers confidence during the negotiation process, obtain valuations of the company from independent sources, entertain a number of buyers, and make all arrangements formal and legal. (Experiential)
Hamilton (1992)	Managing the family's assets becomes more difficult with size. U.S. family firms diversify by investing mainly in publicly traded equities and very little in venture companies. (Empirical)

Hirschhorn & Gilmore (1980)	The mission and administrative structure must change as the organization grows. (Empirical)
Hisrich & Cahill (1995)	Six propositions about how the family business deals with a losing project are derived from a case study of a small family firm. (Experiential)
Krentzman & Samaras (1960)	Only 32% of small businesses have ever used consultants. Two reasons for this are the availability of other sources of help, and the attitudes and fears of the small business manager. Recommendations are made for consulting with small firms. (Empirical)
Kuratke, Foss & VanAlst (1994)	The estate freeze rules of the Internal Revenue Service are examined and alternatives for transferring the ownership of a family business are suggested. (Experiential)
Lane (1989)	Family business consultants need to have a broad knowledge of different areas. A team-building approach to consultation is described. (Experiential)
Levinson (1983)	Three types of family businesses described are family traditional, family conflictful, and entrepreneurial. The entrepreneurial firm is ripe for consultation. If a family wishes to stay together, then differences can be worked out. Otherwise, consultants should find ways to let individuals go their separate ways. (Conceptual)
Lichtenstein (1993)	Health care premiums are higher for smaller firms than for large firms. Smaller firms can contain their costs by increasing deductibles, changing insurance firms, and requiring second opinions before surgery. (Experiential)
Marcus (1991)	Legal arrangements define relationships and specify rights and obligations with more authority than other sources of authority in the family. (Experiential)
Matthews, Vasudevan, Barton, & Apana (1994)	Capital structure decisions are influenced by a firm owner's attitude toward debt. Capital structure decision-making is moderated by an individual's knowledge of the market, financial constraints, and organizational form. (Conceptual)
Mastromarco (1992)	Three federal initiatives useful in inter-generational asset transfer are discussed. These include Section 2036(c), Section 1361, and Chapter 14. (Experiential)

Murdock & Murdock (1991)	When deadlocks develop among equal shareholders, or when minority players feel or claim that they are not treated fairly, litigation occurs. (Experiential)
Pettker & Cross (1989)	The anti-freeze law reduces the tax on estates. It expands the circumstances under which an estate or gift tax will be retroactively imposed on portions of a business that have already been transferred away. (Experiential)
Salomon (1977)	Going public helps the family diversify its assets, ascertain value for estate and inheritance taxes, increase availability of equity capital, and achieve personal satisfaction for family members. However, it also increases pressure from constant exposure to investors, analysts, and competitors, and from having to maintain the stock price. The owner-manager must weigh these demands carefully before going public. (Experiential)
Siegel, Shannon, Stahl, & Melchert (1986)	The CEOs of small businesses report that the most crucial problems they face are in marketing, finance, personnel, operations, and business planning. (Empirical)
Stier (1993)	Poor health among employees leads to increased health insurance premiums, higher medical expenditures, and undesirable employee behaviour. Owners, consultants, and family members can promote wellness programs. (Empirical)
Swartz (1989)	There is a high degree of reciprocal interdependence between family and business in the family business. Multidisciplinary teams are useful in dealing with the challenges of this dual system, but team members should be carefully selected and trained. (Experiential)
Upton, Vinton, Seaman, & Moore (1993)	Consultants to family firms need to understand family dynamics and maintain appropriate communication with all family members. Consulting teams can improve the quality of consulting. (Empirical)
Weiser, Brody, & Quarrey (1988)	Employee stock ownership plans (ESOPs) have benefits and pitfalls, both financial and organizational. When there is no heir interested in the business, ESOPs can help avoid selling the business to outsiders. (Experiential)
Methodological issues (10 articles)	

Brockhaus, Sr. (1994)	Similarities exist in the research histories of entrepreneurship and family business. The author gives recommendations about how to improve the quality and value of family business research. (Conceptual)
Carsrud (1993)	A family business program must be set up to meet the needs of family firm stakeholders. The long term viability of the program will depend on applied research and the ability to provide for these needs. (Conceptual)
Dyer Jr. (1994)	Organizational behaviour research attempts to understand and influence behaviour at the individual, group, and organizational levels. Many of the theories and techniques can be applied to family business. (Conceptual)
Dyer Jr. & Handler (1994)	The family influences entrepreneurial dynamics at four career points. Each nexus has its own research issues. (Conceptual)
Handler (1989)	There are many methodological issues associated with defining the family firm, using process reporting, self-analysis, and alternative methods of research. (Conceptual)
Hollander & Elman (1988)	The family business literature is composed of: the rational approach, the founder, phases and stages models, and the systems approach. The common theme is that family and business are linked and events in one influence those in the other. (Conceptual)
Hoy & Verser (1994)	Overlapping themes in the literatures of family business and entrepreneurship are identified. Areas for future research are suggested. (Conceptual)
McCollom (1990)	Clinical methods offer a distinct advantage for research in family firms because structure, roles, culture, and tasks in these firms are complex. (Empirical)
Lansberg, Perrow, & Rogolsky (1988)	In this introductory article in *Family Business Review*, the authors examine three issues: definition of family business, the prevalence of this form of organization, and the reasons for scholarly neglect. The main reason for scholarly neglect appears to be a general belief that separate research results about family and business are applicable to the family business. (Conceptual)

McCollom (1992a)	Stories narrated by owners center on security and frustration with incompetent employees. Those stories told by employees focus on their relationships with colleagues, frustration with management, and difficulties in dealing with customers. (Empirical)
Wortman (1994)	Empirical work is lacking in the study of family business. In addition, very little conceptual work has been done in the historical, environmental, and organizational components. A large number of studies have focused on the issues of succession and legal studies. (Conceptual)
GRAND TOTAL (226 articles)	

3

THE ANNOTATED BIBLIOGRAPHY

ADIZES, I. (1979). **Organizational passages - diagnosing and treating life-cycle problems of organizations.** *Organizational Dynamics,* Summer: 3-25.

A conceptual article

Key points:

The author uses four elements - 'P' (Production), 'E' (Entrepreneurship), 'A' (Administration), and 'I' (Integration), to describe ten life cycle stages of an organization. He describes the problems faced in each stage and suggests treatments ranging from 'therapy' to 'surgery'. Each stage is described briefly below:

1. The courtship stage (paEi): At this stage there is no organization, only an idea in the entrepreneur's mind, a lot of excitement, and frantic activity.
2. Infant organization (Paei): Producing results becomes more important than the entrepreneurship. The atmosphere in the organization is informal and there are few policies, systems, procedures, or budgets. At this stage, the organization is highly centralized and has no managerial depth; management is busy with short term pressures and misses long term opportunities. The organization survives because of the founder's commitment. Since the organization cannot afford to pay outside agents, an advisory board formed of lawyers, accountants, family, employees, and friends can be helpful.
3. The go-go stage (PaEi): At this stage, the organization's focus is on production, although the entrepreneur continues to shape the vision. Decision-making is quick and intuitive. The atmosphere becomes more formal and the founder's hands-on commitment starts to become dysfunctional. Administrative systems and policies should be set up and founder start to delegate. A strong directive board of directors consisting of non employees can help to improve the organization.
4. The adolescent stage (pAEi): Planning and coordinating meetings grow in importance at the expense of production and entrepreneurship. Cliques form and partners often get divorced at this stage. The organization may become short-run rather than long-run oriented. For a healthy adolescent stage administration should grow at the expense of production not entrepreneurship.
5. The prime organization (PAEi): The organization may become too ponderous and decentralization may be required to maintain an entrepreneurial orientation. Aspirations are reduced and, if held low for a long time, entrepreneurship declines and integration increases.
6. The mature organization (PAeI): The organization starts to enjoy the fruits of earlier efforts. Better interpersonal relationships develop and the climate becomes more formal. The sense of urgency common to earlier stages is lost;

new ideas do not generate much excitement; and less time is spent on R&D and market research.

7. The aristocratic organization (pAeI): At this stage the climate is relatively stale. Although executives have an subconscious fear of competition it is not explicitly expressed. The organization is paralysed by the admiration of its past and great emphasis is placed on style. The organization begins to lose markets and is a prime object for a takeover. Mature and Aristocratic organizations require therapy (not surgery) because they can be rejuvenated and are still cash heavy.
8. The early bureaucracy (_A_i): At this stage the fight for personal survival begins. Instead of fighting competitors, the executives fight amongst themselves and watch each other with suspicion, cliques and coalitions are formed, and, periodically, someone becomes a sacrificial lamb. For those dealing with the organization, things get done if one knows the right person. The end result is bankruptcy, but if the organization is amply financed, it moves on to become a full bureaucracy; however, this stage often requires surgical treatment to identify and replace managers with negative attitudes. Surgery should be used sparingly and performed only once. After surgery, therapeutic treatments must be given.
9. Bureaucracy (_A_ _): At this stage nothing gets done, managers are easy to deal with, they agree a lot but nothing ever happens. Systems, procedures and forms loom high, written work is worshipped, and there is no inclination to change. The organization isolates itself from it's environment.
10. Death (_ _ _ _): There is no P,A,E or I in this stage; organization stops acting and is dissolved.

The author suggests that the developmental stages described above can be broadly classified into two categories:

- *Momentum*: From the courtship stage to the adolescent stage, the underlying philosophy is: 'everything is permitted unless specially forbidden'. Entrepreneurial spirit dominates the organization, function is more important than form, and communications are open. Organizations experience momentum till they reach 'maturity'.
- *Inertia*: From the maturity stage to death, the unwritten rule is: 'everything is forbidden unless specifically permitted'. Administration dominates, form is more important than function, and communications are not open. Organizations in decline stages portray inertia.

Different consulting styles are required for organizations in different life cycle stages.

Key words: Organizational life-cycle stages, Consulting.

ALDERFER, C.P. (1988). **Understanding and consulting to family business boards.** Family Business Review, 1(3), 249-261.

A conceptual article.

Key points:

A board "is a set of individuals who understand that they have agreed to serve as active directors of the corporation, meet together at regular intervals to review the performance of the chief executive, and provide advice and counsel about plans for the future" (p.249). Although it is generally thought that outside directors bring objectivity to decision-making, the author argues that, while these directors may be free of family or firm hierarchial pressures, they are not free of all pressures that influence their judgement.

Just like any other group, the board has its sub-group structures and group dynamics. The sub-group dynamics on boards may bring creative diversity or destructive divisiveness in the board. Outside directors family members vary in their interest in the firm. For the welfare of the firm and the family, the board should be a group in which the interests of both the family and firm are presented in a manner that permits satisfactory negotiation.

The author suggests the use of group consultation to family business boards. The objectives of such consultation are to: improve the way the board operates; enhance the quality of board management relationship; understand how the family relates to the board; and decide whether board deliberations strike a balance between family concerns and interests of the firm.

Key words: Board, Group dynamic forces in a board, Outside directors, Inside directors, Group consultation to family business boards.

AMBROSE, D.M. (1983). **Transfer of the family-owned business.** *Journal of Small Business Management,* 21(1): 49-56.

Sample: 86 businesses terminated between 1976 & 1981 (53 owners and 33 children)
Data collection: Questionnaires
Data analysis: Frequencies, Percentages

Key points:

When business owners are questioned about family members who should be considered for succession, the older generation always mentions immediate family members while the next generation is willing to consider grandchildren or other relatives. Very few founders indicated that providing an opportunity for their children was a significant motivating factor for going into business. The stated reasons for terminations are: children's desire not to continue, government regulations, and business becoming too demanding or unprofitable. Owners below 50 report that their children are too young to assume responsibility of business. The author suggests that if children are not involved before they decide on other career paths, transfer may be unsuccessful. Long established businesses have a higher probability of a successful transfer.

Children with college degrees believe that their parents derive less satisfaction from the business and consider the successful transfer of business to the children unimportant; this belief may discourage them from assuming business responsibility. One reason for the children's lack of interest in the business may be that the owners spend more time working and too little time with their families building relationships or interests in the business. Moreover, education opens new options for children making the confinement, commitment, and obligations of the family business less attractive; however, children without college degrees believe that a successful transfer of the business to the next generation is very important. One way to increase the probability of a successful transfer of the family business to the next generation is to include the children early-on in responsible business positions.

Key words: Termination of family business, Next generation.

ANONYMOUS, (1983). **Family partnerships.** *Estate Planning, CPA Journal,* May: 71-78.

Advise on family business asset transfer through partnership.

Key points:

The family partnership technique offers an opportunity to effectively transfer income from the older to the younger generation. In a well structured partnership, the older members contribute appreciated assets, and the younger members receive the highest cash flow possible. Care should be taken to meet all the requirements necessary for minimization of total taxes (estate, gift, and income); and outright gifts of a partnership interest should be avoided, in favour of the purchase of such interests by younger members. This mechanism of transfer is described in detail in this article.

Key words: Family partnership technique, Inter-generational asset transfer.

ANONYMOUS. (1984). **Succession planning in closely held firms: Begin now - the company's future depends on it.** *Small Business Report,* Nov.: 52-58.

A conceptual article.

Key points:

An annual report by the founder/CEO on the company's status from both the business perspective and personal perspective can be used as a good starting point for succession planning. The annual written report should include :

- *The business perspective*: The financial picture, an administrative profile, operations and technical data, marketing information, purchasing information, systems, and an outside review.
- *The personal perspective*: continuity, liquidity, family needs, and associate relationships.

The report should also address the problems that could arise after retirement, disability, or death of a key position holder.

Key words: Succession planning.

ARMENAKIS, A.A. & H.B. BURDG (1986). **Planning for growth.** *Long Range Planning,* 19(3): 93-102.

Sample: Case study of a chemical company
Data collection: Interviews and work sessions
Data analysis: Qualitative diagnosis

Key points:

Process consultation is an effective intervention technique used by organization development experts to design and implement aggressive growth strategies. Using a case study of a family owned chemical company, the authors describe the objectives, steps to be followed, and advantages of this technique.

The objectives of process consultation are to change the behaviour and interaction of organizational members, promote the accomplishment of tasks, increase individual satisfaction, and ultimately optimize organizational effectiveness.

The four steps of process consultation are:

1. *Organizational diagnosis*: ascertain individual perceptions of key members through in-depth interviews;
2. *Feedback sessions*: inform the group about inadequate management practices and energize them to begin resolving their deficiencies;

3. *Work-sessions*: develop the company's purpose, corporate divisional organization chart, detailed divisional organization chart, and organizational goals and objectives;
4. *Adoption and implementation of the plan*: including job descriptions, training, performance management systems, information systems, and marketing plans.

The advantages of this approach are that it helps build consensus and commitment, facilitates client learning, and impacts organization wide effectiveness.

Key words: Process consulting.

ASTRACHAN, J.H. (1988). **Family firm and community culture.** *Family Business Review,* 1(2): 165-189.

Sample: Case study
Data collection: Interviews, Historical data, Archival data
Data analysis: Percentages

Key points:

The family business that is managed in a manner that is at odds with the local culture will not be successful in the long run. Those that are managed in harmony with the local culture will have a higher level of within-business harmony and long run productivity.

Key words: Organization culture, Continuity.

ASTRACHAN, J.H. (1993). **Preparing the next generation for wealth: A conversation with Howard. H. Stevenson.** *Family Business Review,* 6(1): 75-83.

An interview.

Key points:

Family business owners generally do not talk about wealth, because of their penchant for secrecy and desire for control and partly because the inheritor is looked down upon within the U.S. as not being a self-made man. In order to prepare children/inheritors for success, Stevenson stresses the importance of preparing them for their future job; they should be trusted with decision-making and involved in family charitable trust decisions, etc. This involvement will teach them confidence in dealing with money and help them to understand the values of the community as well as the family. Team work and creative criticism should be encouraged among siblings.

Key words: Next generation, Succession planning.

ASTRACHAN, J.H. & T.A. KOLENKO (1994). **A neglected factor explaining family business success: Human resource practices.** *Family Business Review,* 7(3): 251-262.

Sample: 614 randomly selected family firms
Data collection: Structured telephone interviews
Data analyses: Descriptive statistics, Correlation analysis, t-tests

Key points:

- *The most frequently employed human resource (HR) management practices in family business firms*

The most frequently cited HR management practices are: employee reviews, compensation plans, written employee manuals, and written job descriptions, while written succession planning and formal entry requirements for family members are mentioned less frequently. Family meetings are used more often than written business plans or board meetings.

- *The contributions of HR management practices contribute to family business success and survival*

HR management is positive correlated with personal income, number of full time employees, gross revenue, and access to capital; however, it is not correlated with the generation running the business. The governance scale is positively associated with business success (number of full time employees, gross revenues) and survival (generation running the firm).

- *Are there individual difference variables associated with stronger focus on HR management practices in family firms*

Gender is related to the use of HR management practices. Male owner/CEOs are significantly more likely than females to engage in HR management practices. More highly educated owners are more likely to engage in governance practices.

Key words: Human resource management practices, Succession planning, Success and survival of family firms.

AYRES, G.A. (1990). **Rough family justice: Equity in family business succession planning.** *Family Business Review,* 3(1): 3-22.

A conceptual article.

Key points:

Absolute economic equality among siblings is virtually impossible to achieve. When a family business faces succession issues, systematizing does not work; instead, rough family justice is a more realistic goal. This approach is described as "equity not equality, among members of the family system in a context designed to serve the best interests of the family business" (p.5). The author discusses the important issues that need to be taken into consideration during any transition process, describes different roles that family members may play, and provides some suggestions for smooth transition of business across generations.

Issues that need to be given consideration during the transition process are the needs of the business, the owner-manager, and the next generation; transfer taxes should also figure into the analysis. Family members may have to play different roles in a family business and non-active family members may become minority shareholders; therefore, policies redeeming the stock and dividends must be developed.

In choosing a successor, the owner must try to attain through valued employees, suppliers, customers, professionals, etc., an objective evaluation of all possible leaders before making this decision. Each member of the next generation should be provided with both a challenge and opportunity, within the context of business or out of it.

The authors suggest that to improve the transition process; offspring not involved in the business may be bought out; peer panels, mediation or arbitration may be used to ensure fair treatment; children who are not willing or able to be senior managers can be given a long-term lease on the land where the business is situated, so that non-active members get a passive income from the lease; and stock may be reorganized into voting common stock for active members and non-voting preferred stock for non-active members, with preferred stockholders having a priority over dividends. Other options include converting companies into 'S' corporations, joint investments between active and non-active members, insurance, lifetime gift transfers, and wills and trusts.

In the final analysis, effectively dealing with the issues of succession planning may be the single most lasting gift that one generation can bestow upon the next.

Key words: Rough family justice, Equity in succession, Family-business subsystem.

BABICKY, J. (1987). **Consulting to the family business.** *Journal of Management Consulting,* 3(4): 25-32.

A case study based on a consulting assignment.

Key points:

"A family business is the kind of business started by one or few individuals, who had an idea, worked hard to develop it, and achieved, usually with limited capital, growth while maintaining majority ownership of the enterprise" (p.25). The failure rate is high and the undertaking risky because of competition, high costs, need for a wide diversity of talents, abilities, management skills, and family relationships. Specific problems in family firms are:

- Expectations for the children to learn too fast;
- Children becoming impatient with parents' methods;
- The owner wanting to sell the business while the offsprings are scared because they have never worked elsewhere;
- The owner becoming angry with a child's domestic relationships which, in turn, may be reflected in their day-to-day working relationship;
- The business may be unable to support the offsprings' families comfortably;
- Parents may become jealous of their children's education, youth, benefits, etc. - the very things they worked so hard to provide;
- Parents may be unwilling or unable to recognize their children's abilities;
- Children may not be interested in the business;
- In-laws may introduce rivalries and jealousies;
- Family members may not control the business and those in control may have a different perception of the business;
- Key employees may not know their responsibilities and may not stay long; and
- Some family members may wish to sell while others wish to continue.

Family business consultants face unique challenges such as:

- Important and influential decision-makers may not actually work in the business;
- Destructive relationships may have been solidified since childhood;
- Unusually strong emotional undercurrents;
- Consulting in family business is both a technical and a people problem as, behind every technical problem, there exists a human problem that must be included in any effective solution of the technical problem;
- The consultant must first understand the real problem, then involve the family in goal setting. End goals must be the clients', with the consultant acting only as a facilitator. Family members must unanimously agree to the solution;
- Family should agree on goals, designate a leader, and state the responsibility of each member of the family;
- The choice of successor and the buy-sell arrangements, both with outsiders and among relatives, should be clearly stated; and
- Strategies should be designed to attract outside employees and to retain them.

Key words: Challenges in family firms, Consulting.

BARACH, J.A. (1984). **Is there a cure for paralysed family boards?** *Sloan Management Review,* 2(1): 3-12.

A conceptual article.

Key points:

When the family board or key members of a family are unable to agree or function properly, some strategies for dealing with this are:

- *Inaction* (on rare occasions): if the business does not need a change of strategy, it is emotionally less stressful and may be economically beneficial to maintain the status quo;
- *Resolving key interpersonal conflicts*: the key to conflict resolution is to change attitudes and expectations; thus, when conflict haunts family business, open communication, teamwork, and accommodation are necessary;
- *Wait it out*: sometimes the best strategy is to wait for the departure of the combatant;
- *Bring in outsiders to help resolve the crisis*: outside intervention may bring about changes in the functioning of the board, restructuring, or change of ownership;
- *One part of the family buys out the other*: this may be the most desirable solution to preserve the continuity of the business, but may not be the best to preserve family harmony;
- *Sell out to others*: this is a good solution when owners are approaching retirement, when they desire increased security and lower risk on their capital, when the company cannot be split, when personal or financial reasons prevent one party from buying out the other, or when conflicts cannot be resolved any other way. This option may be less emotionally taxing than selling to family members; and
- *Restructure the firm in order to resolve continuing crises*: for example the firm may be divided into two or more firms, each controlled by different parts of the family. This approach allows the family business to continue, promotes inclusion and autonomy, and reduces potential for conflicts.

Key words: Paralysed family boards.

BARNES, L.B. (1988). **Incongruent hierarchies: Daughters and younger sons as company CEOs.** *Family Business Review,* 1(1): 9-21.

Sample: Several hundred participants in Owner/President Management Program at Harvard Business School (exact number not specified)
Data collection: Taped interviews, Group discussions, Teaching cases.
Data analysis: Not specified.

Key points:

The author examines the tensions that arise as a result of the incongruence between a family member's positions in the family and business hierarchies. Although primogeniture is the most widely accepted form of power transfer in the family business, it has become less automatic than it once was. The position of CEO may now go to a younger son or daughter because of perceived competence; and the lower status sibling may appear simultaneously at the top of the company hierarchy and at the bottom of the family hierarchy. Under these conditions the family dynamics and hierarchies are upset, causing discomfort, tension, and agony for all members of a family.

Daughters or younger sons face a major psychological dilemma and a major shift in expectations, perceptions, and behaviour of family members, friends, and even business colleagues may occur. This identity restructuring is generally initiated by the younger son or daughter, whose competence is proven publicly and loudly, thus forcing members to accept the new status and relationship after a prolonged struggle. Sometimes help for restructuring identity comes from within the family or from within the organization. In other cases, high status friends trusted by all parties may help in the transition process.

Restructuring is not an easy process. The younger son or daughter must recognize that the origins of the problem are structural and only day to day actions and behaviours can bring the two hierarchies into line with each other and change expectations and perceptions.

Key words: Incongruent hierarchies, Younger sons, Daughters in family business, Restructuring identities.

BARNES, L.B. & S.A. HERSHON (1976). **Transferring power in the family business.** *Harvard Business Review,* 53(4): 105-114.

Sample: 35 companies (200 men and women)
Data collection: Multiple interviews
Data analysis: Not specified

Key points:

In considering transition problems it is helpful to examine the perspectives of the family and the business, from both inside and outside the firm. The authors use a two by two matrix (inside and outside the family, inside and outside the business) to describe the four different vantage points from which family and business members may be observed.

The four quadrants formed and the occupants of each quadrant are:

- Family managers: Inside both the family and the business,
- Employees: Outside the family but inside the business,
- Relatives: Inside the family but outside the business,
- Outsiders: Outside both the family and the business.

Most firms pass through a three stage developmental process. The stages are:

1) Entrepreneurial company with direct management;
2) Second level management with specialized functions; and
3) Divisional operations with diverse products and markers.

In between these stages are the transition zones that require time, new interaction patterns, and an awkward period of overlap.

The key assumption for the older generation should be 'the company will live, but I won't'; but it is often avoided by older family members and has to be built into the forced retirement programs of established companies. Forced retirement is often initiated through the intervention of relatives, trusted outsiders, or non-competing employees, who help to find a way to pull out the older family members into a new set of activities. Older managers need to learn how to advise and teach, rather than control and dominate, younger family members should learn new management skills, and relatives should learn how to take third party roles and provide outsider perspectives. The healthiest transitions are those in which both family managers and businesses change patterns simultaneously.

Key words: Succession planning, Family business subsystem.

BARRY, B. (1975). **The development of organization structure in the family firm.** *Journal of General Management,* Autumn: 42-60.

Sample: 25 linked case studies in printing industry in Britain.
Data collection: Not specified in the article
Data analysis: Qualitative analysis

Key points:

A family business owner-manager has four options to maintain business continuity. These are:

- *Continue family ownership and management*: This is a good option when management skills and capital requirements are low, and the business is highly service oriented. For example, in merchant banking, hotels, restaurant, garages, breweries, etc., family management and ownership may be a desirable option. Family business is also a viable option when the business depends on closely guarded secrets in the manufacturing process;
- *Retain ownership but let go of management*: In this case the conflicts between the interests of owners and managers may become a problem;
- *Abandon ownership but retain management control*: This is a good arrangement because the family gets to retain family benefits and access additional resources; however, ownership may become dispersed over generations.
- *Evolve as a more formal bureaucratic concern and lose family control*: If the firm is objectively evaluated and not doing well compared with other firms in its industry, there may be a need to adopt formal means. When the firm is involved in tasks that can be made routine, using mass production, then bureaucratic structures may be beneficial, otherwise (in case of firms involved in creative and craft skills) flexible structures should be maintained.

Key words: Challenges in family firms, Strategic planning.

BEACH, B. (1993). **Family support in home-based family businesses.** *Family Business Review,* 6(4): 371-379,

Sample: 31 individuals (6 family day care providers, 10 shoe stitchers, and 15 families of home workers)
Data collection: Interviews, observation
Data analysis: Qualitative analysis

Key points:

Commonly cited reasons for starting business at home are: low overhead, tax benefits, distaste for conventional work settings, the opportunity to be one's own boss, and the opportunity to respond to both work and family needs in one setting. In this study the data suggest that the family acts as a filter affecting the operation of the home-based business, and this filter has two crucial aspects: ideology and pragmatism.

The study also indicated that children become active in home-based businesses, learning about business culture, developing good work habits and an ability to deal with the public.

The levels of child involvement found are:

1. Play / watch / help.
2. Assistance with simple tasks (elementary school children)

3. Regular assistance (paid or unpaid)
4. Regular paid assistance (teenagers)

Future research needs to focus on the images of home-based businesses that these children carry in their minds, and the related advantages and disadvantages of this form of business.

Key words: Home based business.

BECKHARD, R. & W.G. DYER, JR. (1983a). **Managing change in the family firm - Issues and strategies.** *Sloan Management Review,* 24(3): 59-65.

A conceptual article.

Key points:

The key issues that an owner needs to focus on while deciding the strategy for succession are: ownership continuity or change, executive leadership continuity or change, power and asset distribution, and role of the firm in society.

Events that make it necessary to think about succession include the decision of the founder to step down, death of the founder or another significant member of the family, the entry (or failure to enter) of a family member into the firm or a new position, the decision to merge or sell, and a significant increase in growth or decline in profitability.

Other crucial factors to be considered during succession succession are the economic viability of the firm (reliable ROI or past income), reputation, continuity of key executives, confidence in future top management, relationships between key family members, and the dynamics of family under stress during the period of transition.

Key words: Succession planning.

BECKHARD, R. & W.G. DYER, JR. (1983b). **Managing continuity in the family owned business.** *Organizational Dynamics,* Summer: 5-12.

A conceptual article.

Key points:

Only 30 percent of family businesses survive to the second generation. The founder, key professionals, and family members are involved in the succession process, and each has unique problems and agendas. The mode of adaptation in a family firm is a function of the founder's priorities, conditions in the firm, and family dynamics.

To implement his/her succession plan the founder may use a will or other legal documents with the help of selected family members and/or professional advisors. He or she should recognize the importance of the process of power transfer, design specific transfer mechanisms, and explicitly state the role of the surviving spouse.

Key words: Succession planning.

BENSAHEL, J.G. (1975). **Playing fair in family business.** *International Management,* February: 37-38.

A conceptual article.

Key points:

This article addresses the relationships between relatives and non-family employees in a family firm. One way of dealing with incompetent relatives is to send them to a division in the firm where they can do minimum harm while the competent relatives is allowed to grow on their own without intervention from the owner-manager. A visible effort should be made to disclose off-the-job business related discussions with relatives active in the business to non-family employees. Non-family employees should be made aware that if they are qualified and competent, they have a real chance to succeed. When this policy is followed the chance of unfair favoritism (whether real or imagined) is reduced.

Key words: Nepotism.

BERENBEIM, R.E. (1990). **How business families manage the transition from owner to professional management.** *Family Business Review,* 3(1): 69-110.

Sample: 20 U.S, Latin American, & European companies.
Data collection: Not mentioned
Data analysis: Not mentioned

Key points:

A family firm goes through two basic stages of development:

1. *Coalition*: To establish a company the founder builds a coalition that is formed of supporters such as bankers, highly skilled employees, suppliers and customers. The major developmental task in this stage is to establish the legitimacy of the founder to lead the organization.
2. *Founder ascendant*: In this stage the founder's authority is established and he/she charts the course for the firm. The major objective in this stage is to establish the legitimacy of the firm to act with or without the participation of the founder. This is done by recruiting individuals to fill key positions, delegating decision-making, developing procedural mechanisms, and establishing controls for monitoring and implementation.

Negotiating the difficult passage from stage 1 to stage 2 requires business skills. Some pragmatic considerations that help to successfully manage this transition are:

- Avoid having too many heirs;
- Avoid confusing the family and company roles.;
- Clearly state the basic principles of obligation to the community, customers, and employees;
- Train heirs rigorously before they assume responsibilities;
- Help family members move from rule to reign by uncoupling proprietary and managerial concerns.

Suggestions offered for successfully handling the departure of a founder include:

- The founder must retire when still in full command of his or her abilities and able to counsel senior managers when advice is sought;
- Retirement should be unequivocal;
- The founder should publicly commit to retirement;
- The founder should articulate and supervise the formulation of company principles regarding management accountability, policies, objectives, and strategies.

Key words: Organizational life-cycle stages, Succession planning.

BEROLZHEIMER, M.G. (1980). **The financial and emotional sides of selling your company.** *Harvard Business Review,* 58(1): 6-11.

An article based on the personal experience of the author.

Key points:

Growth of the family business, increasing age, career aspirations of family members or the founder, and marital situations may cause a company founder to sell the business. Many large corporations are constantly looking for fast-growing private companies. Before the actual sale process begins, the seller must find out where to go to find serious bidders and advisers, how many buyers to talk to at a time, when to let the employees know about the decision to sell, whether to continue as a consultant with the new company, how much to charge, and so on. Based on his own experience, the author makes the following suggestions:

- Before deciding to sell the owner should understand and weigh his/her personal objectives carefully;
- The owner sells a company rarely while buyers buy firms repeatedly; therefore, one must be thoroughly prepared before starting the selling process;
- Selling the company should not be delegated to a business broker;
- Be honest and candid about your business;
- Negotiate to keep the escrow amount as low as possible and sell for cash if you want liquidity and do not want to be tied up in someone else's company;
- Negotiate with two or more buyers at the same time and maintain a record of all prospective buyers;
- Do not tell your employees until the deal is finalized then involve them in the negotiating team to work out the final details;
- Carefully select those companies to whom your company will appeal the most;
- Develop a strategy for contacting potential buyers; a good way to approach potential buyers is through a close confidant;
- Plan for about 18 months to complete the deal;
- Do not be afraid to reject an offer;
- Once you negotiate the framework select the best possible lawyer to negotiate the details but draft your own letter of intent or memo of understanding to guide them through;
- Organize your company so that day-to-day operationa are ably handled without your interference, allowing you time to plan thoroughly about selling the company;
- Stay alert and healthy;
- Remember that a company is not sold until the money comes into your account;
- Be assertive regarding your own worth if you have to continue as a manager or consultant.

Key words: Termination of a family business.

BIRLEY, S. (1986). **Succession in family firm: The inheritors view.** *Journal of Small Business Management,* 24(3): 36-43.

Sample: 61 MBA and BBA students (potential inheritors)
Data collection: Questionnaires
Data analysis: Percentages, Means

Key points:

70 percent of inheritors indicate that the owner adopts an authoritarian style of management. 42 percent of respondents are certain about returning to the family business while 38 percent say they may return at an unspecified time. Females do not indicate certain return and sibling position is not correlated with the willingness to return. Most of the respondents believe that their parents give them an open option to decide their career paths.

Key words: Next generation.

BRADY, D. & C. STRAUCH (1990). **Who are the family foundations? Findings from the foundation management survey.** *Family Business Review,* 3(4): 337-346.

Sample: 285 family foundations
Data collection: Questionnaires
Data analysis: Percentages

Key points:

The study presents the findings of a 1990 survey conducted by the *Council on Foundations*. Family foundations have smaller boards, more female trustees, fewer limits on board services, and place higher work demands on staff and trustees than the general population of foundations.

Key words: Family foundations.

BROCKHAUS, Sr., R.H. (1994). **Entrepreneurship and family business: Comparisons, critique, and lessons.** *Entrepreneurship Theory and Practice,* 19(1): 25-38.

A conceptual article.

Key points:

Early research in both entrepreneurship and family business is primarily prescriptive, with practical suggestions offered to practitioners. In the early seventies, research began in entrepreneurship by academics more interested in teaching and providing consulting services than in developing and testing comprehensive theories.

Researchers that conduct research in these areas face special challenges that including: the unavailability of secondary data sources, an unwillingness of small business owners to participate in research, high discontinuance rates making follow-up difficult, a wide spectrum of small or family businesses, a paucity of theories for hypothesis testing, and no commonly accepted definitions. However, researchers in family business can learn from the development of entrepreneurship studies. Based on an examination of the two areas, the author suggests the following:

- Undertake comparative studies of family business and non-family business, as well as different types of family business based on factors such as size, number of family members involved in the business, mothers versus fathers as founders, daughters versus sons as second generation, etc.;
- Since many family businesses are more stable than the average small business, they may be better subjects for longitudinal studies;
- There is a need for sophisticated research designs and statistical techniques;
- Reaching a consensus on definitions has been a challenge in both areas;

Therefore, researchers should describe fully the subset of businesses in their studies.

Some areas suggested for future research include: the ethics and values of family firm managers; how they deal with conflicting goals of family and business; strategic management and international strategic planning; marketing strategies; financing needs, sources, and strategies; corporate venturing issues; characteristics of family firm owners; and educational needs of family firms.

Key words: Entrepreneurship and family business studies, Challenges for research in family firms, Research topics.

BROWN, F. H. (1993). **Loss and continuity in family firm.** *Family Business Review,* 6(2): 111-130.

A conceptual article based on a consulting experience.

Key points:

Helping a family deal with the loss or anticipated loss of a family member is a natural extension of succession planning. Losses such as death create three particular tasks for the family business: acknowledging and sharing the reality of death, reorganizing the family and family systems, and reinvesting in life and other relationships.

Factors affecting the family's reaction to loss are:

- Family context,
- Type of loss,
- Legacies of loss,
- Timing of the loss in the family's life cycle, and
- Position of the dying or deceased family member.

Guidelines to help business families deal with the loss of a family member:

1. Identify loss as an issue;
2. Educate the family and normalize the recovery process;
3. Keep lines of communication open;
4. Develop plans for loss of key players;
5. Know yourself and your belief system.

Key words: Founder's departure - coping mechanisms.

BUDGE, G.S. & R.W. JANOFF (1991). **Interpreting the discourses of family business.** *Family Business Review,* 4(4): 367-381.

A conceptual article.

Key points:

The authors stress the importance of listening to the narratives and stories told about both the family and the business, noting that differences arise when the voices of family and business compete for the final say on family business issues.

Three examples that serve to convey the differences in discourses of family and business are:

Time: In the business, time has a technico-rational basis - time is money - while in the family, calendar time is not as important as the development milestones of birth, death, marriage - time spent together is a valued reward;

Money: In the business, money is expressed in terms of profit while in the family, money is associated with blood and entitlement.

Career: For owner entrepreneurs, business signifies vocation while for inheritors, career entails a sale of one's labour in a competitive market.

Key words: Narratives, Stories, Consulting in family firms.

BURACK, E.H. & C.M. CALERO (1981). **Seven perils of family business.** *Nation's Business,* January: 62-64.

A conceptual article.

Key points:

The author identifies 7 perils and suggested remedies for the family business. They are:

- *One man show*: The owner should learn to delegate authority and responsibility;
- *The Immortality jag*: Name and train a successor;
- *Family only obsession.* Do not restrict key jobs to family;
- *Informality in operation*: Design procedures and policy manuals to formalize the operations;
- *Failure to separate roles of owner and manager*;
- *Tradition fever*;
- *Family fights*: Designate a person to mediate family feuds.

Key words: Challenges of family business.

BURKE, R.J., T. WEIR, & R.E. DUWORS, Jr. (1980). **Work demands on administrators and spouse well being.** *Human Relations,* 33(4): 253-278.

Sample: 85 male senior administrators of correctional institutions.
Data collection: Questionnaires completed independently by husbands and their wives.
Data analysis: Step wise multiple regression analysis

Key points:

Wives whose husbands have greater occupational demands report less marital and life satisfaction, decreased social participation, and increased psychosomatic symptoms and negative feeling states. In no case is the well-being of these wives enhanced by the husband's occupational demands.

Key words: Work and family conflicts.

CAMBRELENG, R.W. (1969). **The case of the nettlesome nepot.** *Harvard Business Review,* 47(2): p.14.

A case study of the Conlon-Fralley Company - a sales and service company.

Key points:

This article reiterates the importance of clear policies and open communication. The author suggests using a regular sales bulletin to provide a yardstick for performance. When this yardstick is used for promotions, objectivity in the evaluation process becomes obvious both to the nepot and other employees. If too many family members are concentrated in one location, ways should be found to spread them out. An interesting point brought out is that nepotism gives union organizers ammunition.

Key words: Nepotism.

CARSRUD, A.L. (1994). **Meanderings of a resurrected psychologist, or lessons learned in creating a family business program.** *Entrepreneurship Theory and Practice,* 19(1): 39-48.

A conceptual article

Key points:

This personal account of the author's life as the director of the UCLA's family business program discusses what universities and sponsors have to gain as stakeholders in family business programs and the process of creating such a program. The author stresses the importance of selecting sponsors who support the traditional roles of teaching and research. Other variables to be considered are: recognition of stakeholders' needs; size of the program; activities offered; program marketing, staffing and financing needs, and the development of an advisory council.

Key words: Family business program - setting up, Focus groups.

CATES, J.N. & M.B. SUSSMAN (1982). **Family systems and inheritance.** *Marriage and Family Review,* 5: 1-24.

A review article of inheritance practices.

Key points:

Inheritance laws and customs have changed over time in response to changing conditions. In France, following the revolution of 1789, the system used was equal partition among the children which left insufficient land for each member and generated conflicts and court disputes. In the U.S., land was abundant, the country was industrialized, and the need for labour was fulfilled by immigrants. Intestacy provided for the maintenance of surviving spouse (primary beneficiary), and for equal division of the remaining equities.

In contemporary U.S. society, the traditional family is becoming a minority. Families and individuals will be looking to non-family sources for adult care and may choose beneficiaries outside the family; the conjugal takes precedence over the family. New inheritance patterns that may evolve are:

- *Singlehood and child free marriages*: bequests to non-relatives and charities are likely in these cases;
- *Dual earner families*: in these families, the 'spouse takes all' pattern may be less prevalent because both spouses have retirement benefits; thus, the first spouse to die will likely include a bequest for the children and the surviving spouse will leave the estate to grandchildren. Tax laws in the U.S. (1982) allow an individual to leave everything to the spouse completely tax free; therefore, this may reinforce the pattern of leaving the entire estate to the spouse.
- *Cohabitation and remarriage*: estates may be willed to the spouse or divided among the marriages.

The social security system may not be able to support senior citizens in the coming years because of the sheer increase in number of claimants; consequently those with their own plans may be better off.

The authors believe that inheritance patterns will continue to reflect reciprocities, but these reciprocities will be oriented more toward those who provide services in the present and not necessarily follow the lines of kinship.

Key words: Culture in family businesses, Inheritance practices.

ÇHAGANTI, R. & J.Á. SCHNEER (1994). **A study of the impact of owner's mode of entry on venture performance and management patterns.** *Journal of Business Venturing,* 9: 243-260.

Sample: 345 firms (227 owner started firms, 61 family firms, 57 buy-outs)
Data collection: Mailed questionnaires
Data analyses: Chi-squared tests, ANOVA, ANCOVA, Factor analysis, Cronbach alpha

Key points:

This study examines whether firm performance and the associated patterns of management vary with the owner-manager's mode of entry into the firm. The three modes of entry examined are: (1) inheritance (FF), (2) start up (OS), and (3) buy-out (BO). The questions that guide this study and the corresponding findings are summarised below.

- *Are the performances of OSs, BOs, and FFs different?*
  Performance is dependent on the owner's mode of entry with OS firms having a higher average ROA but with FFs having a higher average annual sales.
- *What are the differences in the management patterns of OSs, BOs, and FFs?*

OS firms rated themselves significantly higher on business, competitive, and operational strengths.

- *Are variations in performance due to management patterns or mode of entry*?
  The higher sales of FFs is not linked to the management patterns adopted by these firms.
- *Is the management pattern-to-performance link the same across the three modes of entry*?
  In the OS firms, higher ROA is associated with operating in the service and retail sectors, developing a broad range of business strengths, offering competitive prices, higher quality goods, and using personalized management practices. Sales performance increases when trained staff are employed.
  High sales performance is found in FF firms where the owner-managers have extensive industry experience, are conservative in adding workers, emphasize product customization, rely on written reports, and avoid long-range operations planning. ROAs are enhanced by broad ranging operations strengths but are hurt by strategies based on cost efficiency and higher quality. FFs have the same selling and promotion expenses but higher purchasing and manufacturing costs and higher product prices.
  In the BOs, management patterns are not significantly linked to higher ROA, but sales are marginally higher when the owner-manager has extensive industry experience and employs a large work-force.

Key words: Family and non-family firms - performance, Management patterns, Success strategies.

CHAU, T.T. (1991). **Approaches to succession in East Asian business organizations.** *Family Business Review,* 4(2): 161-179.

A conceptual article.

Key points:

The Chinese and Japanese adopt different approaches to business succession with the Chinese practicing coparcenary and the Japanese practicing primogeniture. Coparcenary means equal division among all male descendants while primogeniture gives the bulk of the estate to the eldest son who also inherits the right to be head of the family. However, if the heir is considered incompetent to uphold or enhance the honour of the house, the eldest son may be replaced by another son, son-in-law, or even a non-kin member of the house. Primogeniture has greatly added to the longevity of Japanese family businesses, whereas coparcenary has negatively affected the survival rates of the Chinese ones.

Key words: Succession planning, Chinese family business, Japanese family business, Culture.

CHURCHILL, N.C. & K.J. HATTEN (1987). **Non-market based transfers of wealth and power: A research framework for family businesses.** *American Journal of Small Business*, 11(3):51-64.

A conceptual article providing a framework for research.

Key points:

The Family business provides an environment where change is inevitable, as one generation succeeds another transferring power and decision-making authority. By studying family business it may be possible to develop strategies for facilitating effective change.

Two critical differences between an owner-managed business and the family business are the involvement of family members in the business and the non-market based transfer of management control between family members.

The choice of a successor, his or her development and training, and the transfer of managerial power, is at the core of the family business and is the process that must be the prime focus of effective research. This article provides a framework for research in this area.

The inevitable path from birth to death, can be expressed in terms of the degree of influence that an individual can have on the direction and operation of a business. Four sequential stages in this path are:

1. The owner-manager,
2. Training and development of a new generation,
3. Partnership between generations, and
4. Actual transfer of power.

Key words: Succession, Research framework for family firms.

CORRELL, R.W. (1989). **Facing up to moving forward: A third-generation successor's reflections.** *Family Business Review*, 2(1): 17-29.

An article based on author's personal experience, as a third generation successor in a tannery.

Key points:

The struggle to achieve individuality is one of life's most basic and difficult tasks, especially for the successor of an established family business. This successor/individuality concept involves a person's awareness of two basic forces, emotionality and rationality. It entails both the balance of these two forces and an ability to make decisions and choices based on rationality rather than emotionality.

The author describes his struggle to achieve differentiation from his family and define his own individuality.

Key words: Next generation, Differentiation.

COVIN, T.J. (1994a). **Perceptions of family-owned firms: The impact of gender and educational level.** *Journal of Small Business Management,* 32(3): 29-39.

Sample: 115 undergraduate students and 108 graduate students
Data collection: Questionnaires
Data analysis: Descriptive statistics, t-tests, Factor analysis, MANOVA, ANOVA

Key points:

This study examines the general attitudes of university students toward family-owned firms. A family business is defined as 'a business owned and operated by a family that employs several family members'. The results indicate that:

- Participants strongly prefer working for their own family's business over any other type of employment opportunity;
- Few respondents express a preference for hiring family members;
- Participants are aware of the difficulties involved in managing the complex family-business relationship;
- Family-owned business are perceived to be as competitive as non-family owned business;
- The perceived general weaknesses of a family business include: informality in policies and procedures, preferential treatment for family members, and little opportunity for the advancement of non-family members;
- The perceived strengths of a family firm are higher organizational commitment to employee happiness and higher morale;
- Graduate students view family firms less favourably than undergraduates;
- Gender has no significant influence on the perceptions.

Based on these findings, the author suggests that family firms should: develop written policies for hiring, promoting, and compensating family members; require that family members work outside the family business for some time; and ensure that family members satisfy the same entrance requirements as non-family members. Management should treat non-family members with the same commitment and neutrality as family members. Also, educational institutions can help students make decisions about career opportunities by providing information about the potential benefits and challenges of working in family firms.

Key words: Family and non-family firms.

COVIN, T.J. (1994b). **Profiling preference for employment in family-owned firms.** *Family Business Review,* 7(3): 287-296.

Sample: 225 undergraduate and graduate students at a large state college in southeastern USA.
Data collection: Self administered questionnaire.
Data analysis: Discriminant analysis.

Key points:

This study aims to determine the perceptions of students about employment in family-owned businesses. Specifically, the two research questions are:

- What life history and job characteristics can distinguish between individuals who prefer working for a family-owned business and those do not?
- Do these factors differ for undergraduate and graduate students?

The family-owned firm is defined as "a business owned and operated by a family that employs several family members". The questionnaire contained several demographic background and job characteristic questions.

Almost 65 percent of the respondents indicate a strong preference for working in their family firms. Those who prefer a career in family firms are more likely to: have started their own business in the past, have worked for a family firm in the past, have worked for a greater number of companies, and be female. They have a stronger need for a job that provides for change and variety in duties and activities, permits working independently, encourages continued development of knowledge and skills, provides an opportunity to earn more income, and provides a feeling of accomplishment. They have a lower need for a job that is respected by other people, needs a specific educational background, and involves friendly associates.

Undergraduates and graduates who prefer working in family firms differ dramatically in terms of job characteristic profiles. Undergraduates who prefer family firms desire a job that provides a feeling of accomplishment and requires creativity, originality, and risk taking. They are less concerned about having a job that uses their educational backgrounds or is respected by others. Graduates, on the other hand, are more concerned about independence, continued development of skills, advancement, and working on problems of central importance to the organization.

Key words: Family and non-family firms - employment patterns.

CRANE, M. (1982). **How to keep families from feuding.** *Inc.*, Feb.: 73-79.

Sample: Case study of a Manhattan distributing company (a wholesale wine and spirits business)
Data collection: The author is a family member
Data analysis: Author's interpretations

Key points:

16 rules that should be followed by family firms are:

- Deal objectively with a son's or son-in-law's qualifications;
- The successor should acquire practical experience elsewhere;
- Clearly define responsibilities;
- Divide responsibilities;
- Establish working hours in advance;
- Find out who reports to whom;
- Plan office space and equipment carefully;
- Introduce the successor to key outside people;

- Discuss salary and perks in advance;
- Fight issues, not emotions;
- The successor should be free to do things;
- Define the roles of other family members;
- Work together on estate planning;
- The successor must begin to learn on his own;
- After a year or so, arrange a long vacation for the boss;
- Establish a family council.

Key words: Succession, Next generation.

CROUTER, A.C. (1984). **Spillover from family to work: The neglected side of work family interface.** *Human Relations,* 37(6): 425-442.

Sample: 55 employees in a large manufacturing plant
Data collection: Semi structured interviews at work and home (3-4 hours)
Data analysis: Frequencies, ANOVA, Pearson correlations to assess intercoder reliability

Key points:

Family life affects the morale, stability, and productivity of the work force. Women with young children at home are most likely to report high levels of family to work spill-over, when compared to mothers of older children or fathers.

Key words: Work and family relationships.

DAILY, C.M. & M.J. DOLLINGER (1992). **An empirical examination of ownership structure in family and professionally managed firms.** *Family Business Review,* 5(2): 117-136.

Sample: 104 small manufacturing firms, Response rate - 21 percent
Data collection: Mailed Questionnaires, Telephone interviews
Data analysis: K-statistic, t-test, Correlation analysis, Contingency analysis

Key points:

The five hypotheses tested in this study and the findings reported are:
1. *The professionally-managed firm will be larger than the family-owned and managed firm* (Supported);
2. *The professionally-managed firm will follow more aggressive growth-oriented strategies, than the family owned and managed firm* (Partially supported);

3. *The professionally managed firm will be older than the family owned and managed firm* (Supported);
4. *The professionally managed firm will rely more on internal control procedures than the family owned and managed firm* (Supported);
5. *The family owned and managed firm will achieve higher levels of performance than the professionally managed firm* (Not supported).

Key words: Family owned and managed firms, Professionalization.

DAILY, C.M. & S.S. THOMPSON (1994). **Ownership structure, strategic posture, and firm growth: An empirical examination.** *Family Business Review,* 7(3): 237-249.

Sample: 430 members of North American Heating and Air conditioning, Wholesalers Association (NHAW), Response rate: 22.5%
Data collection: Mailed questionnaire using a seven-point scale.
Data analysis: Factor analysis, MANOVA, Regression analysis

Key points:

This article examines the following research questions:
- Does ownership structure of the firm affect the strategic postures pursued?
- Does the ownership structure and strategic posture relationship affect firm growth?

Ownership structures are classified as: entrepreneurial, owner/managed, professionally-managed, or family firms. Strategic postures are characterized by: pattern and direction of scope, resource deployment, and competitive advantages, the direction in which these components are shifting over time, the way business tend to compete over time. Firm growth is measured by the percent increase in sales revenue between 1986 to 1989.

The results show no significant differences in the strategic postures pursued by firms run by founder, second generation founding family members, professional managers, or owner/managers, and neither ownership structure nor the strategic posture influences the level of growth. These results indicate that family firms behave no differently than entrepreneurial, owner/managed, or professionally managed firms when setting strategic postures or in terms of growth.

Key Words: Family and non-family firms - strategic posture, ownership structure.

DANCO, L.A. & J.L. WARD (1990). **Beyond success: The continuing contribution of the family foundations.** *Family Business Review,* 3(4): 347-355.

A conceptual article.

Key points:

Setting up a family foundation provides the aging business owner a new and challenging career, making transition toward the next generation easier. The owner (founder) is generally confused about the ways to pass on the family wealth. Although better than leaving the bulk of it to the government, passing too much passive wealth to the children may destroy positive values such as hard work, initiative, and self-reliance. Family foundations may be helpful in addressing this.

This paper describes the advantages of setting up a foundation, the psychological hurdles that family business owners may face, and the basic steps involved in setting up a foundation.

Key words: Family foundation - Steps to establish, Advantages, Psychological hurdles.

DAVIS, J.A. & R. TAGIURI (1989). **The Influence of life-stage on father-son work relationships in family companies.** *Family Business Review,* 2(1): 47-74.

Sample: 89 father-son pairs
Data collection: Questionnaires
Data analysis: Chi-square, F-statistics

Key points:

This study tests whether the quality of a father-son work relationship is affected by their respective life stages. Quality is measured along four dimensions: ease of interaction, enjoyment they derive from their relationship, level of accomplishment when working together, and how much they learn from working with each other.

The sons' results support the hypotheses that work relationships are affected by life stages; however, the fathers' do not because the latter reported low variation in their quality scores. Explanations for the low variation among fathers include denial, lack of sensitivity, and age.

The study suggests that swings in the quality of work relationships are natural. The son should not join the firm when both son and father are going through periods of identity formation. Father and son can co-exist within the family company, well into the father's 70s if the father relinquishes some authority in the company to his son; however, sons should also be given separate areas of responsibility to the extent that the operation of the company and their own competence allows. The father is emotionally attached to his company as to a child and this relationship competes with his attachment to his son. In the best of father-son relationships, fathers demonstrate a strong desire to see the son realize his potential.

Key words: Life stages, Father-son dyads, Quality of work relationship.

DAVIS, P. (1983). **Realizing the potential of the family business.** *Organizational Dynamics,* Summer: 47-56.

A conceptual article.

Key points:

Interactions between the family and the firm make the family business unique. Three types of families in business are identified:

- *Consensus seeking families*: In these families there is a constant tension to maintain close and uninterrupted agreement; individuals become enmeshed in the family system and members avoid conflict and addressing difficult issues. Major barriers to performance are a lack of differentiation, sibling rivalry that is not discussed, separation of key employees, boundary building, and triangulation. The owner should prevent consensus seeking from getting in the way of family businesses effectiveness.
- *Interpersonal distance seeking*: In these families each member has his or her own area of expertise and attends to that area only. Members tend to be more concerned about demonstrating their individual mastery than in joint efforts. This type of family is fragmented and cannot solve problems jointly.
- *Environment sensitive families*: In these families individual needs are balanced with family needs; thus forming an effective group.

In running the family business, owners should either:

1) Seek models of family business that are effective; or
2) Hire professional managers.

The author advocates the first option and uses intentionality and proficiency to analyze the family business. A family business with both high intentionality and high proficiency achieves corporate excellence; those with high proficiency and low intentionality survive skilfully with limited goals; those with low proficiency and high intentionality struggle uncomfortably; and those with low intentionality and proficiency fail in large numbers.

Key words: Family structure, Family systems.

DAVIS, P. & D. STERN (1988). **Adaptation, survival, and growth, of the family business: An integrated systems perspective.** *Family Business Review,* 1(1): 69-85.

A conceptual article

Key points:

In a family business, external factors (technology, environment, and contextual) and family (interpersonal) issues must be simultaneously accommodated to facilitate survival and growth. The ability to generate adaptive responses to a change in the market and technology is critical to the success of a family business. The author suggests that there are certain patterns in successful adaptation and that an awareness of these patterns can facilitate proactive approaches by which the firm shapes its own future and avoids being trapped in a debilitating reactive mode.

Four essential components of successful adaptation are:

1. Maintenance of an appropriate boundary between the emotional issues in the family and the tasks of the business;
2. Development of processes and mechanisms that enable the family to contain and resolve its own emotional issues;
3. Development of task structures and processes that are adapted to the requirements of the business environment and are not dependent on the resolution of family issues for successful performance;
4. Development of a valid legitimizing structure that maintains organizational cohesiveness.

Key words: Family business subsystems, External forces in family business, Adaptation process for growth and survival of family business.

DAVIS, S.M. (1968). **Entrepreneurial succession.** *Administrative Science Quarterly,* 13: 402-416.

Sample: 25 family firms in Mexico (5 case studies and 20 focused interviews).
Data collection: Interviews
Data analysis: Qualitative analysis

Key points:

This article identifies the three patterns of entrepreneurial succession observed among private enterprise in Mexico:

- *Strong father-weak son*: the father cannot let go of his command and son has no opportunity to exercise his initiative. In such situations, the firm is financially successful during the father's reign but ultimately fails because the father is incapable of preparing anyone to replace him;
- *Conservative father-progressive son*: differences in the personalities of the father and the son dominate the succession process. Although the son is given authority and responsibility, his mandate is to maintain the status quo. Chances are good that such as firm will make the necessary changes and succeed.
- *Branches of the family*: One offspring is in-charge of production and the other administration. The future of the firm depends on the extent of internal strife between the family factions. When internal strife is deep, the likely outcome is that one group will buy out the other. Firms generally benefit from this arrangement.

Key words: Succession - Mexico

DEAN, S.M. (1992). **Characteristics of African American family-owned businesses in Los Angeles.** *Family Business Review,* 5(4): 373-395.

Sample: 234 African American family-owned business owners (response rate -34%)
Data collection: Telephone interviews (2), Questionnaire
Data analysis: Content analysis, Descriptive analysis, Cronbach's alpha, Regression analysis

Key points:

The author classifies African-American families into four groups: (1) primary or nuclear families (37.2 percent), (2) extended families (15 percent), (3) augmented families (5.8 percent), and (4) modified-extended families (42%). The common assumptions about African-American businesses tested this study are:

- African-American family businesses do not incorporate standard business practices in their operations;
- Racism is the primary reason for most failures of African-American family businesses;
- Religion is the driving force behind the behaviour of the African-American owner manager;

In general, these assumptions are shown to be inaccurate. African-American business owners tend to be: preoccupied with business survival and management issues, primarily inward focused, and report little conflict and ambiguity about family dynamics. Succession is not a priority in these businesses as the business is generally viewed as a means to develop the children into professionals. Most owners do not seem bothered by racism, and do not attribute their success to the church or religion.

Key words: Strategic planning, African American family business, Racism, Religion, Succession planning.

DIETRICH, N.B. (1985). **Managing a successful transition.** *Small Business Report,* July: 61-64.

A case study of Oregon Worsted Company

Key points:

After attaining a business degree and establishing a career as a business professional outside the family business, the author joined the family firm. In her new position, she had to deal with the personnel problems, reorganization, establishing communication through regular meetings, and management training. In her opinion, being a woman adds to the challenges of managing the business.

Key words: Next generation, Women in family business.

DOERINGER, P.B., P.I. MOSS, & D.G. TERKLA (1992). **Capitalism and kinship: Do institutions matter in the labor market?** *Family Business Review*, 5(1): 85-101.

Sample: 2 New England ports of Gloucester and New Bedford
Data collection: Interviews with fishing crew and captains
Data analysis: Not mentioned

Key points:

Two systems, one based on kinship and the other on capitalism, are used in the New England fishing industry in regards to determine pay and employment. In the capitalist vessel, employment and pay respond to changing market conditions while in the kinship vessel, there are work guarantees and income-sharing rules. Kinship vessels have become dominant because the workers are willing to put in more effort and accept lower pay; they also tend to pool their savings, thereby providing easier and cheaper access to capital when it is necessary to reinvest in their boats. Furthermore, resources drawn into the business during good times are not released in bad times as they are in the capitalist vessel.

For labour intensive industries not subject to significant economies of scale, the kinship system may be highly competitive: it provides collective institutions in the labour and capital markets and, through income sharing, it can accommodate sales and profit fluctuations. When the industry is in decline, however, kinship system employees are more reluctant to seek alternative employment opportunities and often stress the community's welfare and other support resources.

Key words: Kinship, Capitalism, Fishing industry.

DONCKELS, R. & E. FROHLICK (1991). **Are family businesses really different? European experiences from STRATOS.** *Family Business Review,* 4(2): 149-160.

Sample: 1,132 Small and medium firms (less than 500 employees) in 8 European countries
Data collection: Structured interviews with pre-coded responses (90 minutes)
Data analysis: Chi-square test, Regression analysis, Cluster analysis

Key points:

This study finds that, compared to the non-family business, the family business is:

- A closely related system that is inwardly directed;
- Family business managers are less often pioneers but more often "all-rounders" and organizers, thus, most family businesses are risk averse. Creativity and innovation are considered less important in family businesses than in non-family businesses.

- Interdependencies with environment, culture, and macro-economic situations are less intense in family businesses;
- The family business is more inclined to pay above average wages and care significantly more about employee satisfaction while paying less attention to other progressive personnel issues such as employee participation in decision-making;
- The family business generally exhibits a conservative attitude toward business and is less prepared to start exporting and other internationalization strategies.

In the final analysis family businesses can be described as stable rather than progressive or dynamic, largely because their owner-managers are significantly less profit- and growth-oriented than managers in non-family firms.

Key words: Family business subsystems, Types of entrepreneurs.

DONNELLEY, R. (1964). **The family business.** *Harvard Business Review*, 42(2): 93-105.
Sample: 15 successful firms
Data collection: Interviews, Observations
Data analysis: Qualitative analysis

Key points:

The family business is viable, even in a complex business environment, if it can avoid common weaknesses, develop strengths, and heed the caveats. Weaknesses to be avoided are:

- Conflicts between the interests of family and the enterprise,
- Lack of discipline over profit,
- Failure to recognize market challenges and opportunities,
- Nepotism.

Strengths that should be developed in the family business are:

- Accumulation of resources through family sacrifices,
- Important community and business relationships stemming from respected name,
- A dedicated and loyal internal organization which helps to avoid expensive executive turnover,
- An interested, unified, management stockholder group which is less sensitive to short term performance,
- Sensitivity to social responsibility, and
- Continuity and integrity in management policies and corporate focus.

Caveats that family members should heed are:

- understand that their personal objectives can be realized only by the long-term success of the enterprise,
- establish policies to ensure that family participation contributes to the firm's long term strengths including impartial evaluation of both family and non-family members, and checks on favouritism.

Key words: Strengths of family business, Challenges of family business.

DREUX IV, D.R. (1990). **Financing family businesses: Alternatives to selling out or going public.** *Family Business Review,* 3(3): 225-243.

Financial advice for raising capital without going public or selling out.

Key points:

Family businesses are economic enterprises controlled by one or more families. Although they may be public companies, family businesses are generally privately held. Characteristics that differentiate the family business from other kinds of publicly-owned entities include the following:

- Family businesses are generally overcapitalized with little or no debt, maintain substantial liquidity, and have operating margins and return on investment that often exceed those of public companies.;
- Private family businesses possess two strategic advantages:
  - (1) They can invest in long-term value enhancement without worrying about short term results;
  - (2) Competitors generally have no access to information that is regularly disclosed by public companies;
- Family businesses generally operate without rigid bureaucracy and make decisions intuitively;
- Decision-making may not be completely rational as it is often influenced by estate, personal, or emotional considerations;
- Many family businesses are highly oriented toward "top-line" issues such as sales and production at the expense of "bottom-line" issues such as planning, finance, marketing;
- Family business owner managers generally operate with limited staff and are over-committed;
- In public companies succession is carefully monitored and anticipated but, in private companies, succession is generally not well-planned which may explain the high mortality rate of family businesses.

Family business shareholders and the business itself have different interests with respect to operational control, liquidity, and capital; the business needs capital while the family needs income and liquidity for the estate. Ideally, the company can meet both of these requirements through internally generated funds but, in most cases, the family business cannot do this without reassessing the fundamental issues of ownership, appropriate capitalization, and control of business.

Traditionally, selling the business or going public is used to resolve the business-capital and family-liquidity conflict. Investors, however, now increasingly appreciate the advantages of family businesses including: lower risks; strong management; loyal employees; supportive local constituencies; capital investments in partnership with the owner's capital; and management with long-term competitiveness and enhancement, rather than short term profits, in mind. Because of this recognition, family businesses now have non-public financing alternatives that can provide liquidity for shareholders and allow the family to maintain a high degree of control.

These alternatives include recapitalization, private equity, or equity-related securities, joint ventures with industry partners, employee stock ownership plans, subsidiary IPOs and spin-offs, and holding company reorganization.

Key words: Family business triangle, Financing alternatives, Recapitalization, Private equity, ESOPs.

DUMAS, C. (1989). **Understanding of father-daughter and father-son dyads in family-owned businesses.** *Family Business Review,* 2(1): 31-46.

Sample: 40 Family members in 18 family-owned businesses in Southern California (20 daughters, 15 fathers, 5 mothers)
Data collection: In-depth interviews (90 minutes - 4 hours), Group discussions
Data analysis: Inductive analysis, Percentages

Key points:

The father-daughter dyad in family-owned businesses is compared with the father-son dyad and a comprehensive review of the existing empirical studies on the relationship between fathers and sons. is presented. The findings of this study are categorized into four areas:

- *Carryover*: The role carry-over from home to work is found in both genders, although sons face less ambiguity in role definition because they are socialized to join the business and takeover as eventual successors;
- *Sense of identity*: Both sons and daughters face great difficulties in establishing their own identity in the organization: the son through conflicts with the father over control and power and the daughter, by accepting a submissive role. The key developmental issue is autonomy for sons and intimacy for daughters who are not considered potential successors, either by the fathers or by the daughters themselves, and need help with empowerment;
- *Triangulation*: The daughter's struggle for visibility, role management, and identity results in a triangulation between daughter, father, and a male manager or the mother;
- *Caretaker's role*: The male successor desires autonomy while the female successor attempts to establish her identity as a caretaker of both the business and the father.

The male and female inheritors face some similar difficulties and many different challenges; thus it is therefore dangerous to give daughters managerial advice based on studies of fathers and sons.

Key words: Next generation, Father-daughter dyad, Father-son dyad, Development stages, Review article, Triangulation.

DUNN, B. (1995). **Success themes in Scottish family enterprises: Philosophies and practices through the generations.** *Family Business Review,* 8(1): 17-28.

Sample: 15 interviews with family members of 10 firms in Glasgow, Scotland.
Data collection: Semi-structured interviews
Data analysis: Not specified

Key points:

The philosophies and practices of family businesses differ from the stereotypical rational model behaviour of firm with family firms demonstrating unique developmental characteristics and having different definitions of success.

While the definition of success for family enterprises may vary from one firm to another, it incorporates both objective and subjective criteria: for example, finding work for the owning family or for relatives of employees or sustaining the good name of the firm in the community may be included in a family firm's definition of success. All family firms subscribe to the idea that family members have a birthright to a job in the family business; however, a number of firms acknowledge sub-optimal performance as a result, but good family relationships are considered essential.

Family firms that view themselves as the family serving the business tend to use outside advisers, keep managerial control within the family, form family councils, display a healthy attitude to conflicts, have clearly defined roles and responsibilities, and monitor opportunities, threats, product and process improvements. On the other hand, family enterprises that view themselves as the business serving the family, on the other hand, do not use external advisers and spread ownership among the extended family but keep managerial control within the immediate family; roles and responsibilities are not clear and conflict resolution mechanisms are not well developed. Although product and process developments are pursued, family values are non-negotiable and at times hinder spending on developmental activities. In both cases, succession is neither planned nor discussed.

Key words: Scottish family firms, Goals and objectives, Philosophies and practices in family firms, Definition of success in family firms.

DYER Jr., W.G. (1988). **Culture and continuity in family firms.** *Family Business Review,* 1 (1): 37-50.

Sample: 40 Family firms
Data collection: Corporate histories, Annual reports, Leader's, memoirs, Interviews, Minutes of board meetings
Data analysis: Content analysis

Key points:

The culture of a family firm plays an important role in determining the success of the business. The study identifies four cultures in family businesses:

- *Paternalistic*: Relationships are arranged hierarchically in this culture, power and authority remains with family leaders, and outsiders are not trusted. This is the most common culture in family firms and works well when the leader has the necessary expertise to manage the business. Such firms rely too much on the leader and often neglect training and development of the next generation. As the business grows, the leader may not be able to manage ambiguity or complexity. Firms with this culture succeed when the business is small and the environment stable.
- *Laissez Faire*: This culture is similar to the paternalistic culture in that the relationship is hierarchial, family members are afforded preferential treatment, and employees are expected to achieve the family's goals; however, it differs in its assumptions regarding human nature and the nature of truth with employees being regarded as trustworthy and given decision-making responsibilities. Though the overall mission is set by family members, the means of achieving ends are left to the discretion of employees. This culture is more amenable to growth and individual creativity than the paternalistic culture; the major problem is that employees may not act consistently with the family's basic assumptions.
- *Participative*: This culture is relatively rare in family firms; relationships group oriented and the family's status is de-emphasized in favour of a community feeling. The advantages of this culture are high commitment and morale, ability to innovate and respond quickly to environment; while the major weakness of this culture is that decision-making takes longer. The challenge of working in this culture is to differentiate decisions that need to be taken rapidly from others that must receive more employee participation.
- *Professional*: This culture is generally found in firms where the owning family decides to turn management over to non-family professional managers; relationships within such firms are individualistic and employees focus on individual achievement and career advancement. Professionals can often improve the existing operational systems of the firm and bring in fresh perspectives; however, they may alienate the employees who used to work for the family leading to low morale and commitment.

The paternalistic culture is most common amongst the first generation family firms, but the culture changes as new leadership takes over because the paternalistic culture has not prepared the next generation for leadership responsibilities. For a successful transition family business owners must analyze their culture, plan a change in culture, and develop new leadership, an approach that helps to change the culture incrementally.

Key words: Culture - definition, Culture in family businesses, Paternalistic culture, Laissez Faire culture, Participative culture, Professional culture, Changing culture in family business, Succession planning.

DYER Jr., W.G. (1989). **Integrating professional management into a family owned business.** *Family Business Review,* 2(3): 221-235.

A conceptual article based on several case studies (number not mentioned) and the author's experience.

Key points:

The author discusses the meaning of professional management and the reasons why family businesses should professionalize. Business may move toward professionalization through evolution with incremental changes, by professionalising members of the family, by professionalising non-family employees, or through a revolution by bringing in outsiders.

The main problem in professionalising the family business is that family members are trained differently, have different values than those of professional managers. The author suggests that the options mentioned above are not mutually exclusive, and can be used in tandem.

Key words: Professionalization.

DYER, W.G. Jr. (1994). **Potential contributions of Organizational Behaviour to the study of family-owned businesses.** *Family Business Review*, 7(2): 109-131.

A conceptual article.

Key points:

Organization behaviour (OB) can be effectively used to study the. OB attempts to understand and influence behaviour at the individual, interpersonal, group, and organizational levels, all of which can be useful in the study of family firms. The areas of particular interest are listed below:

- *Individual level*: personal characteristics and leadership style, motivation, and career development;
- *Interpersonal level*: communication, role ambiguity and conflict, conflict management, and power and influence;
- *Group level*: group formation, group process, and inter-group conflict
  Models of group formation in the OB literature generally assumes that the individuals forming the group do not know each other before, an assumption that does not hold in family firms. However, the methods used to study groups can be applied to the family business;
- *Organizational level*: Strategic planning, structure and design, culture, and organizational systems

Various intervention techniques may be used to help the family business function more effectively. At an individual level, these include: t-groups, sensing meetings, feedback sessions, goal setting, career development and training, third-party role negotiations, training in communication and interpersonal skills. Team building, process consulting, intergroup conflicts, and confrontation meetings can help at the group level, while system planning, planning of change, and total quality management techniques can help at the organizational level. Existing theories need to be modified or new ones developed to account for the uniqueness of family firms; nevertheless, OB provides useful theories that can be put to test in family firms.

Key words: Organizational behaviour and family businesses.

DYER Jr., W.G. & W. HANDLER (1994). **Entrepreneurship and family business: Exploring the connections.** *Entrepreneurship Theory and Practice,* 19(1): 71-83.

A conceptual article.

Key points:

The two questions that have received the most attention in the entrepreneurship literature are: (1) who is an entrepreneur, and (2) what must an entrepreneur do to start a successful business? On the other hand, family business researchers have largely been interested in what happens to entrepreneurs near the end of their working lives. As a result, leadership and ownership transfers captivate most researchers in family business. This article attempts to tie the two streams of research to four "career nexuses" when the family's influence on entrepreneurial dynamics are strongest. The four nexuses are: early experiences in the entrepreneur's family, family involvement during the start-up, employment of family members, and ownership and management succession.

Key words: Entrepreneurship and family business literature, Research topics, Succession, Work family dynamics.

ERFURT, J.C., A. FOOTE, M.A. HEIRICH, & K. HOLTYN (1993). **Saving lives and dollars through comprehensive preventive health care.** *Family Business Review,* 6(2): 163-172.

Health care advise for small companies.

Key points:

The U.S. employee assistance and work-life welfare programs can help the small business gain access to preventive health care facilities although, in some cases the small firm may have to form a coalition to do this.

Key words: Preventive health care.

EWING, D.W. (1965). **Is nepotism so bad?** *Harvard Business Review,* 43(1): 22.

Sample: 2700 HBR executive subscribers
Data collection: Questionnaire
Data analysis: Percentages

Key points:

Nepotism is far less widespread than people believe with only 15 percent of respondents having directly observed it happen in companies. Generally, executives do not support nepotism, but they do not dismiss it blindly when presented with specific cases. It is less acceptable at the top levels although it may exist more there.

Some advantages of employing relatives are:

- They feel added responsibility toward the firm because of their family connections;
- When they are capable, the morale of the management team increases;
- Relatives have more than average commitment and interest in the long term growth of the company;
- They are more loyal and dependable;
- They are more outspoken because they do not have to fear termination;
- A salesman with the same surname as the boss has better chances of making a sale;
- Bankers and stockholders attach greater importance to their words and actions;
- Employing relatives assures continuity and effective carrying out of the policies.

Problems that firms may face as a result of nepotism are:

- Outsiders are discouraged from seeking employment in the firm;
- Nepots may stir up jealousy and resentment among employees;
- Nepots may be difficult to fire if incapable;
- Family interests may be put before corporate interest;
- Nepots may create doubt about the integrity and objectivity of top management.

Problems that nepots may face are:

- Others may suspect their authority;
- They may tend to take it easy if their job is protected;
- They may feel the pressure to live up to others' expectations;
- They may start doubting their ability and may never know their real worth;
- They may get unequal treatment, thus affecting their development.

What the firm should do:

- Have a group of the company's executives evaluate the qualifications of nepots;
- Let them work in another company for 2-3 years;
- Provide them with formal training and education;
- Provide them with extensive on-the-job training from superiors;
- Prepare them for undercurrents and backlash;
- Have written statement of management's policy on nepots;
- Evaluate their performance objectively.

What the firm should avoid:

- Employing a relative who is not qualified;
- Letting nepots work directly under a relative;
- Setting nepots' salaries above or below others in their position; and
- Going along with proposals limiting relatives in management to an ambiguous number or percentage of employment.

Key Word: Nepotism.

FIEGENER, M.K., B.M. BROWN, R.A. PRINCE, & K.M. FILE (1994). **A comparison of successor development in family and non-family businesses.** *Family Business Review,* 7(4): 313-329.

Sample: 357 firm (236 family firms and 121 non-family firms)
Data collection: Survey administered by telephone interviews
Data analyses: Regression analysis, Reliability coefficients, MANOVA, ANOVA

Key points:

This study compares successor development in family and non-family firms. A family firm is defined as a firm both owned and managed by members of the same family and where the next leader, who is currently employed by the firm, is related to the incumbent leader. Seven hypotheses are tested:

1. Family and non-family firms differ in the approach used to develop successors.
   1a. Family firms rely on task-centred development experiences to a lesser degree than will non-family firms.
   1b. Leaders of family firms are more directly (and informally) involved with their successors in relationship-centred development experiences than leaders of non-family firms.
2. Large and small firms differ with respect to their successor development practices.
   2a. Large family firms rely more on task-centred development experiences and less on relationship-centred experiences.
   2b. Size effects are more pronounced for non-family firms than for family firms.

The results support the first hypothesis. Family firms favour more personal, direct, relationship-centred approaches to successor development, while non-family firms rely more on formalized, detached, task-centred approaches. The family firm's approach is riskier because it is entirely dependent on the leader-successor interaction. The experience will be excellent if the relationship is healthy and affirming but dysfunctional otherwise.

Company size does not affect the approach used for successor development, perhaps because the largest firms in the sample have no more than 500 employees, a threshold size at which organizational scope begins to exert systematic pressure on successor development.

Key words: Family and non-family firms - successor development.

FILE, K.M. (1995). **Organizational buyer behavior of the family firm: A review of the literature and set of propositions.** *Family Business Review,* 8(1): 29-40.

A conceptual article.

Key points:

Family firms differ from non-family firms in three distinct ways: power is concentrated in the founder; non-family managers have less influence; and family members without formal authority can influence decision-making. This article suggests that the organizational buying behaviour of family and non-family firms should be different due to the specific characteristics of family firms. Seven propositions are espoused:

- Family firms can be meaningfully segmented into founder-active and founder-inactive firms with respect to buyer behaviour;
- Differences in power sources are more likely to affect purchasing processes in family firms than in non-family firms;
- Criteria and processes used in making the purchase decision in founder-led family businesses are likely to be different from those observed in professionally managed firms;
- Reliability in identifying members of the buying centre is low in family firms;
- As a procurement decision's impact on the family increases, non-employee family members' involvement in the buying centre increases;
- As the importance of the procurement decision increases, overall political activity increases as a result of conflicting social roles;
- Incumbents in managerial roles in family businesses have comparatively less influence over a decision than do holders of equivalent positions in non-family firms.

'Organizational climate' refers to the values, mores, customs, habits and traditions that influence the way organizational members act. The author has three propositions related to this:

- The more the family is valued within a culture, the more business decisions, including procurement, will be subordinated to family goals.
- Family businesses characterized by cultures other than professional cultures will engage in significantly different organizational buying processes.
- Family businesses will engage in different organizational buying behaviour processes during time of major family and business transitions.

'Organizational buying processes' are the decision-making processes by which formal organizations establish the need for products to be purchased and identify suppliers. It is suggested that:

- As the importance of procurement increases, and as family involvement in decisions increases, the organizational buying process will be longer than in non-family firms;

- Family firms will be slower to adopt product and service innovation than non-family firms;
- As the perceived impact of a purchase decision on the family as well as the business system increases, conflict between business and family goals increases;
- As the family influence on a procurement process increases, the ability of marketers to affect the outcome decreases;
- To the extent that family conflicts cannot be contained within the family but play out in the business, purchasing decisions in family firms will be affected by political factors.

As both rational and emotional motivations influence buying behaviour, family firms may differ from non-family firms in the following ways:

- Family security factors will be weighted more heavily in procurement decisions in family firms than in non-family firms;
- Factors linked to the personal set of family business CEOs will be weighted more heavily in family businesses than in non-family businesses;
- Family firms will weight confidentiality and discretion more heavily in procurement decisions than non-family firms;
- In procurement decisions, family firms weight the community responsibility orientation of their vendors more highly than non-family firms.

Two observations made about marketing strategies are:

- Marketers selling to family businesses will have less control over information flow;
- Adaptive selling approaches sensitive to discourses in both systems are more likely to be successful.

Key words: Family and non-family firms - buying behaviour.

FILE, K.M., R.A. PRINCE, & M.J. RANKIN (1994). **Organizational buying behaviour of the family firm.** *Family Business Review,* 7(3): 263-272.

Sample: 183 family investment management firms
Data collection: Questionnaires administered during personal interviews
Data analysis: Cluster analysis

Key points:

The data reveal four distinct categories of firms in terms of their objectives:

- *Firms uninvolved in issues of family dynamics*: 31.1 percent of the surveyed firms have objectives that are business rather than family oriented;

- *Balancing family and business goals*: 26.8 percent of the firms focus on incremental accumulation of capital shares and are sensitive to the issues of inheriting generations;
- *Family goals primary*: 22.4 percent concentrate on grooming the heirs and achieving inter-generational consensus, putting financial management secondary;
- *Adapting to changing conditions*: 19.4 percent are most concerned about being environmentally responsive and rapidly adapting to changing conditions; such firms are less concerned about family dynamics and the generation of incremental wealth.

This study also finds that family firms' priorities influence their decision-making, hiring policies, and buying behaviour.

Key words: Goals and objectives of family firms.

FIRNSTAHL, T.W. (1986). **Letting go.** *Harvard Business Review,* 64(5): 14-18.

A case study of Restaurant Services Inc.

Key points:

The author describes the emotionally difficult process of delegating authority, the problems faced in the delegation process, and suggests ways to effectively manage this process. Four problems faced by the owner-manager trying to delegate authority are:

- Learning to watch others make mistakes and learn,
- Shifting from a specialist to a generalist,
- Accepting that others can become experts too,
- Learning a whole new job of leadership that involves coaching and planning instead of doing.

A three part approach to make this process less painful includes:

- Recruiting the best people.
- Practicing what/why management.
- Thinking effectively.

Key words: Delegating, Succession.

FLEMONS, D.G. & P.M. COLE (1992). **Connecting and separating family and business: A relational approach to consultation.** *Family Business Review,* 5(3): 257-269.

A conceptual article with case examples.

Key points:

A family business is a unique combination of two sets of rules and expectations. Theorists may highlight the duality of this combination by focusing on inherent differences between family and business relationships or highlight the unity of this combination. A common suggestion given to family businesses is to separate the family and business systems. This is not only impossible to achieve, but the very effort expended to separation often brings them closer together. Instead, creative ways should be found to define new rules between the sibling-partners and incorporate the elements of both relationships.

Key words: Family business subsystem, Consulting.

FORBES, W.F. & A.C. PADDOCK (1982). **'Freeze' assets to lower estate taxes and keep control.** *Harvard Business Review,* 60 (6): 16-28.

Legal advice on estate planning.

Key points:

Asset freezing is a sophisticated technique that can be used to:

- Minimize estate taxes;
- Minimize gift taxes during the owner's life;
- Help current owner to maintain control;
- Provide continued income and control to the current owner and other beneficiaries not involved in business;
- Ensure that control passes to the owner's chosen successor.

Options that may be used for asset freezing include:

- Recapitalizing the existing company so that present owner receives the preferred stock and successors receive common stock;
- Forming a holding company;
- Forming a partnership in which the present owner receives a partnership interest with limits to its appreciation potential, while the successors receive general partnership interests, whose growth is unlimited.

Determining the correct value of each security or partnership interest is vital when freezing assets, otherwise the tax benefits can be negated. Some basic concepts important to this technique are:

- The fair market value of the preferred stock or the partnership interest exchanged for the common stock will not equal its par or stated value, unless its provisions are consistent with preferred stocks of similar quality trading at par in the marketplace;
- The valuation of a company's common stock is primarily based on the company's future earning capacity;
- The value of the company's stock after recapitalization cannot be computed by simply subtracting the par or market value of the new preferred stock from the total value of the shareholder's equity before the exchange; post-recapitalization common stock must instead be valued in light of the effect that the preferred stock will have on the earnings of the company;
- Book value, an accounting term that represents the accounts of the company stated primarily on a historical cost basis, cannot be used.

Key words: Asset freezing, Legal advice, Succession planning, Inter-generational asset transfer.

FORD, R.H., (1988). **Outside directors and the privately owned firm: Are they necessary?** *Entrepreneurship Theory and Practice,* 13(1): 49-57.

Sample: 325 CEOs (Response rate 56%, 91 Board members (Response rate 73%, Representing 35 companies

Data collection: Questionnaires, Interviews with owners and board members of 7 firms

Data analysis: t-tests, Regression analysis

Key points:

Two opinions exist in the literature about having outsiders on the board of directors of privately held companies. The proponents argue that these directors can help determine the objectives and strategies, provide specialized expertise, act as arbitrators for feuding family members and partners, bring an external perspective, provide independent assessments, are more representative of stockholders and society, and provide checks, balances, advice and support. Others claim that outside directors are rarely in a position to start challenging the owner's judgement, since their livelihood depends on his funds, goodwill, and continued blessings. Some suggest that insider dominated boards perform better than those with outside members, because the outsiders are quite powerless and cannot make changes effectively.

This study tests these conflicting opinions focusing on the perceptions of CEOs and board members about the relative value of inside versus outside board members. The results indicate that outside board members do not have a positive influence on firm performance. Two reasons for the ineffectiveness of outside board members cited are:

- Their lack of knowledge about the firm and its environment,
- Their lack of availability to the firm.

Key words: Board of directors, Outsider directors, Inside directors, Performance.

FOX, H.W. (1984). **Managing the transition to professional direction.** *Management Review,* December: 42-45.

A conceptual article.

Key points:

As a business grows, structure tends to replace simplicity as expansion requires a larger scale of operation, diversification, specialization, etc.. Options available to owner include:

- Retaining full control and keep the business small;
- Adopting bureaucratic procedures to change from a small entrepreneurial business to a big business;
- Withdrawing partially or completely by seeking a partner with complementary skills, merging with another small firm, selling to a large company, joining a large company through franchising, or retaining ownership and delegating management to executives.

Professional management does not guarantee a productive future for the company and many large corporations are discovering that superior performance can come from restructuring into small units, each using informal, personalized approaches. Smaller firms should try to find ways to combine the benefits of large and small size.

Key words: Professionalization.

FRANCIS, A. (1991). **Families, firms, and finance capital: The development of U.K. industrial firms with particular reference to their ownership and control.** *Family Business Review,* 4(2): 231-261.

Sample: 250 large U.K. firms - 17 studied in depth
Data collection: Not mentioned
Date analysis: Not mentioned

Key points:

Most of the growth of large-scale corporations in the U.K. has taken place outside elite English society, under the direction of men from marginal social groups, and without large amounts of capital. A theoretical model describing the three stages of control through which firms are likely to pass is presented. The stages described are:

1. *The beginning* - the industrial enterprise is set up by minority members of society with capital from themselves, relatives, and friends. Minorities are prevalent because their mobility in other pursuits is blocked.
2. *The transition* - control passes into the hands of other industrial owners or the financial institutions, only rarely to professional managers as is frequently believed.
3. *The emergent exercise of control by finance capital* - Financial institutions begin to move into the industrial areas and their influence in the management of industrial firms increases.

Key words: Organizational life cycle stages, Control.

FRIEDMAN, S.D. (1991). **Sibling relationships and inter-generational succession in family firms.** *Family Business Review,* 4(1): 3-20.

An article based on clinical experience and theoretical research, using a grounded theory building technique.

Key points:

Sibling rivalry is caused by competition for parental love; inevitable in families. Parental responses to this contest determine whether siblings become rivalrous or develop a healthy relationship. Areas in which parental response can have significant effect are:

- *Inter-sibling comparisons*: Parents should appreciate each child's individual qualities; explicit comparisons are constructive only if they are based on characteristics that can be influenced by a child's efforts.

- *Mode of justice - equity versus equality*: Siblings' individual needs are not equal. The allocation of parental love will create a sense of fairness when it is done on the basis of needs. Allocations on the basis of equality often causes siblings to compete continually for their share of parental love and attention.
- *Conflict resolution*: Parental interference in sibling conflicts can exacerbate rivalry and create a dependency on parents to resolve conflicts.

The author suggests intervention strategies to help turn specific dysfunctional sibling relationships into healthy ones. These include:

- *Stereotypes to individuation*: Collaborative relationships can be developed among siblings by helping them view themselves and their siblings as unique individuals, with unique needs and abilities; discussion among siblings about the roots of their rivalries are helpful in achieving this understanding.
- *Resentfulness to fairness*: Establishing empathy through role reversals and open communications amongst siblings may lead to better understanding of each other's position.
- *Dependency to autonomy*: By airing and bringing to attention historical differences, siblings can be encouraged to redefine current relationships and formulate collaborative problem solving abilities.

Key words: Sibling conflicts, Succession, Equity in succession planning, Equality in succession planning, Consulting.

FRUIN, W.M. (1980). **The family as a firm and the firm as a family in Japan: The case of Kikkoman Shoyo Co. Ltd.** *Journal of Family History,* Winter: 432-449.

A case study of a Japanese family firm

Key points:

Changes in the relationship between the family and the firm in Japan since pre-industrial days can be divided into four stages:

1. *Late 17th century to 1887*: The complete separation of management and ownership.
2. *1887-1917*: Owners formed cartels to reduce risk, management was still separate from ownership, and family competition continued.
3. *1918*: Joint Stock companies were formed through the merger of cartel members, families that merged were related by descent or marriage, owners became managers, and employees had life time jobs. After the 1927-28 strike, owners started to promote family spirit.
4. *After WWII*: Democracy arrived and the family-firm analogy lost ground, the emperor was demythologized, and employees demanded rights. The 'family' concept continued though in a modified form.

Japanese owners have carefully planned for succession since the earliest of times and adoption has been widely practised in order to provide competent male heirs if such heirs did not exist or if the existing male heirs do not measure up to the job. Families groom their eldest son as the heir and help him with his education. A second mechanism commonly adopted has been to find daughters husbands who can fill the position of a competent male heir.

Two highly advocated principles for family business success are careful planning of succession and separation of ownership and management, both of which have been practised in Japan since the 17th century.

Key words: Japanese family business, culture, succession planning, strategic planning.

GALLO, M.A. & J. SVEEN (1991). **Internationalizing the family business: Facilitating and restraining factors**. *Family Business Review,* 4(2): 181-190.

An article based on the consulting experience of the authors, previous studies, and a series of interviews (number not specified).

Key points:

Five factors that affect a company's ability to change are discussed along with their effects on the internationalization of family businesses. These factors are:

- *Strategy and general objectives*: Family businesses generally focus narrowly on customer needs and have a hierarchical organization structure while internationalization involves dedicating resources to develop new markets or establishing structures in new countries. If family business owners focus on the short term and distribute the profits as dividends instead of reinvesting them in the new internationalization process, then they are bound to be unsuccessful. Achieving internationalization is more easily achieved if the owners are committed to long term growth.
- *Organizational structures and systems*: Top positions in family businesses are often held by family members who have no management abilities. Internationalization requires organizational changes that may not be supported by family members. It also requires a strong management in order to motivate the organization and pull it through when the company meets with difficulties. Many family businesses, especially those in the first generation, have the strong leaders who can motivate and lead the company through difficulties. Moreover, a new company can be created for internationalization, with minimal impact on the parent company and new family members in charge.
- *Company culture*: Family businesses are usually deeply integrated in the local culture. Old timers may fear the negative effects of internationalization on the

culture of the company; however, families that already place an emphasis toward internationalization may have already prepared its members for the changes.

- *Developmental stage of the company*: The locally-oriented generation may not be in favour of internationalization; thus the stage in which the company finds itself may be an important restraining or facilitating factor for internationalization.
- *The family's international characteristics*: Exposure of various family members to international business can be a great facilitator in the internationalization of the company.

Family businesses in the first and second generations generally move slowly toward internationalization. In order to enter the global markets, companies do not have to give up their family orientation, rather they need to broaden their local orientation and attitudes.

Key words: Strategic planning, Internationalization, Culture.

GEERAERTS, G. (1984). **The effect of ownership on the organization structure in small firms.** *Administrative Science Quarterly,* 29: 232-237.

Sample: 142 small and medium Dutch businesses
Data collection: The data was collected through 84 consultants employed by 15 consulting firms. A questionnaire was administered and an interview that lasted for 3 hours was conducted for each case.
Data analysis: Regression analysis

Key points:

An organization's structure is dependent on both its size and the ownership status of its management. This dependency may explain why studies on the relationship between an organization's size and its structure have produced erratic results since these studies have typically ignored ownership status of management. Firms controlled by professional managers are more horizontally differentiated, more formalized, and have higher internal specialization, than those controlled by owners. Owner-managers are clearly reluctant to share power and do so only if forced by a situation. Consequently, size produces decentralization only in owner-managed firms.

Key words: Strategic planning, Differentiation.

GERSICK, K.E., I. LANSBERG, & J.A. DAVIS (1990). **The impact of family dynamics on structure and process in family foundations.** *Family Business Review,* 3(4): 357-374.

Sample: 6 case studies of family foundations, 31 interviews
Data collection: Semi-structured interviews, Questionnaires
Data analysis: Inductive approach

Key points:

How family dynamics affect the family foundation changes from one generation to the next. Founders see the foundation as a personal enterprise and makes all the decisions; but as the foundation's control moves through the second and third generations, the structure and procedures increase in formality, the geographical focus weakens, and the priorities become more oriented toward social action.

In families where a family business has not survived, the foundation may remain the only avenue in which enduring family dynamics can continue. In these cases, it is hypothesized that the intensity of family dynamics on the foundation board will be greater.

Sibling rivalry, not inter-generational conflict, is often the source of stress. Related conflicts can develop into "branch competition", with each sibling heading a branch of the family. Over time, the branch that has the strongest interpersonal ties will dominate the foundation.

Many of the rewards available to the first and second generation family members from foundation related activities are reduced for third and later generations and as family identification and status rewards diminish, recruiting board members becomes more difficult. To maintain continuity, new incentives for later generations must be built into the succession plan; the transition from second to third generation is usually a good time to rethink purpose, structure, and procedures. If self-analysis does not lead to an adequate redesign, many family foundations will dissolve or become publicly controlled.

Key words: Family foundations, Organizational life cycle, Family dynamics, Sibling conflicts.

GILBERT, N. (1989). **Can a family business survive mergermania and divorce?** *Management Review,* January: 38-42.

A conceptual article.

Key points:

Mergers and divorces often end the family firm legacy. As the number of buyers increase, higher purchase prices may entice family business owners to sell. Divorce, on the other hand, often leads to legal, financial, and emotional problems that can devastate a family business or force the owner to sell. Crisis situation is a bad time to make strategic long range plans; therefore, owners should give early consideration to protect their companies from the ravages of divorce.

Key words: Succession planning, Mergers, Divorces, Challenges to family business, Strategic planning.

GILLIS-DANOVAN, J. & C. MOYNIHAN-BRADT (1990). **The power of invisible women in the family business.** *Family Business Review,* 3(2): 153-167.

A conceptual article.

Key points:

Women with varying degrees of visibility in the family business may nonetheless hold considerable power and influence; ascertaining the extent of their actual influence is difficult, however, because the power is often executed through other people.

Men and women distribute their tasks and responsibilities differently; women organize their lives around the needs of their families while men organize their lives around the demands of their work. In the family business, there is a broad range of responsibilities and work for women including less visible roles such as confidante and personnel adviser, informal nurturer of employees, and public relations representative. Women may also be involved in more visible roles and actively participate in business decisions. Family respectability and life cycle changes, etc. influence how a woman will function in a business.

Key words: Women in family business.

GOFFEE, R. & R. SCASSE (1985). **Proprietorial control in family firms - Some functions of 'quasi-organic' management systems.** *Journal of Management Studies,* 22(1): 53-68.

Sample: 12 firms in general building and personal services
Data collection: Interviews with proprietors and senior managers
Data analysis: Content analysis

Key points:

Business proprietors may be reluctant to delegate control because: they lack formal management training, knowledge, and skills; they believe that separation of ownership and management leads to poor decision-making and higher overhead; and they believe that managers often take up unproductive tasks. As a result, proprietors often resort to quasi-organic structures in which non-family executives are given a large extent of control and informal, adaptive, and flexible work practices are emphasized. Control is the maintained by regulatory mechanisms such as: autonomy with proprietorial prerogatives, management by objectives, divisionalization, control on the nature and amount of information available to managers, and recruitment, training and appraisal.

Key words: Professionalization, Quasi-organic management, Strategic planning.

GOLDBERG, S.D. & B. WOOLRIDGE (1993). **Self confidence and managerial autonomy: Successor characteristics critical to succession in family firms.** *Family Business Review,* 6(1): 55-73.

Sample: 254 CEOs of small firms (less than $10 million in gross revenue and 500 employees). The sample included 2nd, 3rd, 4th generation successors, 34 women CEOs and a diverse sibling order.
Data collection: Questionnaires (Response rate - 34%)
Data analysis: Factor analysis, MANOVA

Key points:

The two hypotheses tested in this study are:

1. The attitudes concerning the predecessor, the business, the family, and self differ among the successors of effective and ineffective successor groups.
2. Successor attitudes concerning the predecessor, the family, the business, and self differ because of the successor's birth order.

The findings indicate that effective successors score significantly higher on self-confidence and managerial autonomy and that success in succession is not affected by the birth order of the successor.

Key words: Next generation, Succession planning.

GREENHAUS, J.H. & N.J. BEUTELL (1985). **Sources of conflict between work and family roles.** *Academy of Management Review,* 10(1): 76-88.

A literature review on conflict between work and family.

Key points:

This study finds that there are three sources of conflict between work and family roles:

- Time devoted to meet the requirements of one role makes it difficult to fulfil requirements of the other role;
- Strain from participation in one role makes it difficult to fulfil the requirements of other role;
- Specific behaviour required by one role makes it difficult to fulfil requirements of other role.

Work-family conflict is related to a person's career success and role demands, and depends on the support of the spouse. Men are exposed to stronger sanctions for non-compliance with work demands, whereas women are exposed to stronger sanctions for non-compliance with family related demands.

Key words: Family business subsytems, Work-family conflicts.

GRISANTI, D.A. (1982). **The agony of selling out to relatives.** *Harvard Business Review,* 60(6): 6-14.

Sample: A case study of a restaurant business in Louisville
Data collection: Anecdotal
Data analysis: Author's interpretations of the business

Key points :

The author's tips for selling a business or an interest in a business to a relative are listed below:

- Hold all negotiations away from the business;
- Give the buyers control and confidence during the negotiating process;
- Expect that selling out to a relative will be a long drawn out process;
- Seek valuation of the company from independent sources;
- Entertain other potential suitors;
- Make all arrangements formal and legal;
- Do not expect business concessions to improve family relationships.

Key words: Termination of family business.

GUMPERT, D.E. & D.P. BOYD (1984). **The loneliness of the small business owner.** *Harvard Business Review,* 62(6): 18-24.

Sample: 2 surveys of 700 owners (Response rate - 83%)
Data collection: Questionnaire using Likert scales and open ended questions, Semi structured interviews (2 to 3 hours).
Data analysis: Regression analysis

Key points:

Small business ownership is closely associated with loneliness, which may lead to stress, other health problems, and ineffective decision-making. Based on the findings of two surveys, the authors suggest ways to deal with the problem of loneliness. These include:

- Rearrange the work environment;
- Participate in peer group activities;
- Be attentive to family and friends;
- Modify attitudes that reinforce job-related isolation.

Key words: Loneliness.

GUNDRY, L.K. & H.P. WELSCH (1994). **Differences in familial influence among women-owned businesses.** *Family Business Review,* 7(3): 273-286.

Sample: 832 women-owned businesses
Data collection: Mailed questionnaire
Data analyses: ANOVA, Factor analysis, Regression analysis

Key points:

The authors develop a theoretical concept of 'family intensity' and use it to understand the influence of family on different decisions made by female-owned firms. Family intensity is defined 'by the number of family investors and family members employed in the business'. Firms in the sample are divided into four categories according to the degree of family intensity.

Respondents from high family intensity firms are more likely to:

1. Perceive that finding competent leaders/managers and technical people, and locating sources of financing are important contributors to entrepreneurial growth;
2. Engage in activities involving technological change;
3. Report high levels of projected sales performance and ideal sales performance, despite similar current sales;
4. Report stronger affiliations with their families than with their business;
5. Pursue a career path outside the business.

This study suggests that the degree of family involvement in women-owned businesses exerts significant influence on various dimensions of their businesses as well as the long-term career plans of such women.

Key words: Family intensity, Women-owned family firms, Ownership and management issues.

GUZZO, R.A. & S. ABBOTT (1990). **Family firms as utopian organizations.** *Family Business Review, 3*(1): 23-33.

A conceptual article.

Key points:

Utopias are voluntary, value-based communal societies rooted in religious, social, or politico-economic beliefs. Utopias and family firms share the following similarities in regard to organizational ideals, mechanisms of commitment, and the exercise of authority:

- *Ideals*: positive social identity, perfectibility, harmony, and order.
- *Mechanisms of commitment*: sacrifice and investment of members, transcendence, communion including practices such as meetings of members.
- *Exercise of authority*: authority is exercised by a leader or founder who is well respected by other members.

Key words: Utopias.

HALL, P.D. (1988). **A historical overview of family firms in the United States.** *Family Business Review,* 1(1): 51-68.

An article tracing the historical development of family firms in US.

Key points:

In 1835, Tocqueville saw inheritance law as the single most important factor shaping American life and character. As responsible citizens, virtually all Americans agreed that accumulation of vast fortunes was inimical to democracy; thus, they supported the passage of laws favouring the division of estates. However, as individuals, they continuously sought ways of passing their farms, firms, and fortunes on to the next generation, devising a variety of adaptive strategies to counter-act the erosion of family resources.

Over time, different strategies have been adopted to keep the family property intact. In the 18th century, kin marriage, sibling exchange, marriage of widows to the husband's brother, and preventing the marriage of daughters were used while in the post revolutionary era, children (usually older ones) were sent out to seek their fortunes, legal mechanisms such as equity jurisprudence were adopted, and family trusts were formed. By the 19th century, charitable endowments, formation of partnership firms, and encouraging vocational diversity amongst descendants were common and in the late 1930s, family charitable foundations were created.

As the nineteenth century industrial system grew more complex, three forces persistently worked against family firms: diversification, changing scales of market activity, and opposition to dynasticism. Furthermore, dynastic families in America were not protected by 'Special Legal Status' as in Europe where the lands and titles must pass undivided to the eldest son. The survival of the "great" families in the United States depended on their ability to participate effectively in the capitalist economy and to defend their place in the democratic polity. The establishment of elite boarding schools and universities was one way of legitimizing the wealthy as a class.

Key words: Historical development of family firms, Dynastic families, Adaptive strategies to retain property, Factors against the family firms.

HAMILTON, S. (1992). **A second family business: Patterns in wealth management.** *Family Business Review,* 5(2): 181-188.

Sample: 100 families with net worth of more than 100 million
Data collection: Telephone surveys (45 minutes)
Data analysis: Percentages

Key points:

Taking capital out of their business may seem risky to many owners who are accustomed to being in direct control of their assets; but as firms grow in size, the diversification of assets provides many advantages. In this study the asset management behaviour of four types of investors: those with operating businesses, recent sellers of businesses, sellers who sold their businesses more than five years previous to the study, and families who sell their services as registered investment advisers or private trust companies, are studied.

Another topic discussed is respondent selection of investment managers. It appears that business managers go through a process of referrals and checks basing their decisions on the performance record, investment philosophy, personality fit, consistency in investment strategy, risk orientation, integrity, and credibility of the investment managers.

Key words: Diversification, Strategic planning.

HANDLER, W.C. (1989). **Methodological issues and considerations in studying family businesses.** *Family Business Review,* 2(3) 257-276.

A review article.

Key points:

In this article, five methodological issues and their potential contributions to both theory and practice of the family business are discussed. The issues examined are:

- *Defining the family firm*: Various definitions have been proposed for family firms but there is no consensus. Different theorists focus on different aspects of family business and base their definitions on family ownership, family management, degree of family involvement, inter-generational transfer, or multiple conditions; these aspects of family businesses vary according to the size and type of firms. Any definition of family business needs to take into account this range of configurations as well as the features that distinguish family firms from other forms of organizations. The author defines the family business as "an organization whose major operating decisions and plans for leadership succession are influenced by family members serving in management or the board".

2. *Using process reporting*: Most studies of family business provide only limited discussion of the research methodology. The author argues that the value and utility of any study is based, in part, on the way it is conducted, and therefore must be described in detail.

3. *Using self-analysis*: The researchers must be explicit and honest about their own personal backgrounds, roles, and assumptions guiding the research, to enable the reader to better understand the context of the research and personal influence of the researcher.
4. *Alternatives to research based on individual consulting efforts*: The suggested alternatives are to use action science or teams of individuals as consultants and researchers.
5. *Broadening the range of research methods*: The field of family business has overused case studies. Other methods such as surveys, interviews, participant observations, archival data, and quasi-experiments need to be combined and used, to improve the quality of analysis and enhance the validity and reliability of the results.

Key words: Review article, Definitions of family business, Methodological issues.

HANDLER, W.C. (1992). **The succession experience of the next generation.** *Family Business Review,* 5(3): 283-307.

Sample: 32 next generation family members
Data collection: Interviews, Questionnaire
Data analysis: Content analysis

Key points:

The next generation's experience and views about succession are very important as they may be different from those of the existing generation; yet these have not been documented. This study tries to identify the influences affecting the quality of the next generation's experience. These influences include:

- Individual factors such as personal need fulfilment and personal influence, both of which positively affect the quality of the experience of the next generation.
- Relational factors such as mutual respect and understanding, sibling accommodation, and commitment to family business perpetuation.

Key words: Next generation, Succession, Research framework.

HANDLER, W.C. (1994). **Succession in family businesses: A review of the research.** *Family Business Review,* 7(2): 133-157.

A review article.

Key points:

This literature review of family business succession identifies five streams of research:

- *Succession as a process*: Succession involves distinct stages, each with characteristic problems. To progress through these distinct stages, different personal skills are needed and the family and organizational must go through certain processes.
- *Role of the founder*: The founder's sense of immortality and indispensability contributes to problematic succession. Changing the founder's attitudes about retirement prior to the event is important to effective and harmonious succession.
- *The next generation's perspective*: Accession planning is as important for the successor as succession planning is for the incumbent. The successor's satisfaction from working in the family firm depends on the fulfilment of career needs, psycho-social needs, life-stage needs, and relational factors such as exposure to the business and personal relationships with parents and siblings.
- *Multiple levels of analysis*: This stream of research tries to identify the causes of resistance to succession planning and find ways to help families overcome such resistance.
- *Characteristics of an effective succession*: The determinants of effective successions include appropriate selection and grooming of heir, degree of harmony in family relationships, and the presence or absence of outsiders in an advisory capacity. Four areas requiring future research are: succession planning in different ethnic groups, the impact of family dynamics on the issue of succession, comparative studies of effective and ineffective successions, and the role of gender in succession planning.

Key word: Succession, Streams of research.

HANDLER, W.C. & K.E. KRAM (1988). **Succession in family firms: The problem of resistance.** *Family Business Review,* 1(4): 361-381.

A conceptual article that summarizes the literature on succession issues.

Key points:

The existing literature on succession has focused on narrowly defined issues and has not dealt with the multi-level forces that increase or decrease resistance to succession. Four different levels of influences contribute to the problem of resistance to succession in family firms. A brief discussion of each level follows:

- *Individual*: Succession problems are tied to psychological elements that originally motivated the founder to start the business. Over time, the business becomes an extension of the owner who is reluctant to let go.
- *Group*: Interpersonal and group dynamics, including family system perspectives and family business system perspectives influence succession resistance. The family system perspective may be described by interaction typologies, structural typologies, and family paradigms. The family business system perspective recognizes family and business as two distinct but overlapping groups or systems of organization and attributes succession difficulty to diverging values.
- *Organizational*: Two perspectives are addressed here. The cultural perspective addresses the various values and assumptions held by the founder, the family, and the firm. As the firm approaches succession, the transition mechanisms must address these values and assumptions. The organizational development perspective adds time as a factor, suggesting that the functional hierarchy developed during the start up of a firm can be dysfunctional to the firm's future.
- *Environmental*: Most studies of family business succession have looked at factors internal to the firm. Contingency theory and population ecology can help explain the external factors influencing succession in a family firm.

Based on the four levels of influence discussed above, the authors present a model of resistance to succession.

Key words: Succession planning, Culture, Psychological factors, Interaction typology, Structural typology, Family paradigm, Family business system, Family system, Problems of transition, Contingency theory, Population ecology.

HANSEN, R.W., A.C. HALLETT, S. FREDRICKS, J.K. HEALEY, & R.L. PAYTON (1990). **Continuing in the family foundation.** *Family Business Review,* 3(4): 405-420.

Opinions of 5 authors on the problem of continuity in family foundations.

Key points:

The authors discuss ways to find, attract, select, train, and integrate new members into family foundations.

- Using the case of Prentice Hall Publishing Co., the author describes how the creation and use of an adjunct board proved helpful to maintain continuity of the organization. Experience on the adjunct board provides in-depth experience of the issues involved in the foundation and the values of giving while developing an ability to understand different people's positions. Adjuncts join the senior board when nominated by the existing members of the senior board. (R.W. Hansen)
- Bringing diversity to a board in terms of ethnicity, gender, and adding professionals, can have a positive impact on a foundation. (A.C. Hallett)
- There are additional advantages of using an adjunct board. (S. Fredricks)
- Methods to solve the problem of lazy or incompetent board members include: rotation of board members, long range planning, and a special sensitivity towards individual family members and branches of a family. (J.K. Healey)
- A summary of the above accounts and brings up some interesting points regarding continuity in family business. (R.L. Payton)

Each stage of transition may raise its own continuity issues and require a different training and recruitment strategy. As families grow in size, the costs of formal boards may become too heavy and unjustifiable for the business; thus, there should be a regular assessment of the foundation's usefulness. Just as succession is a process, not an event, the foundation's self-assessment should be a process too and issues such as board diversification, merger considerations, or transfer of assets to other organizations must be regularly evaluated.

Key words: Family foundations, Adjunct boards, Diversity, Ethnicity, Board of directors.

HARRIS, D., J.L. MARTINEZ, & J.L. WARD (1994). **Is strategy different for the family-owned businesses.** *Family Business Review,* 7(2): 159-176.

A conceptual article.

Key points:

The process of formulating strategies and the means of implementing strategies are similar in both non-family and family businesses; however, special elements of family businesses affect strategy formulation and implementation. First, strategy formulation includes the development of a mission statement, industry analysis, company strength and weakness analysis, and strategic choice. For family businesses there are some special issues to consider in each of these areas. Second, implementation of strategies deals with the structure, systems, or processes that help a company implement the chosen strategy effectively. The authors suggest several research areas related to strategy implementation in family business. For example, do certain traits of family businesses affect implementation? Do family firms have inherent advantages in some implementation activities? Do boards of directors play a different role in family-owned businesses?

The authors suggest that case histories provide a good first step for research in this area as they can highlight the effects of family ownership on strategic decisions. The next step will be to develop data bases for empirical research.

Key words: Strategy formulation, Strategy implementation, Family and non-family firms.

HARVEY, M. & R.E. EVANS (1994a). **The impact of timing and mode of entry on successor development and successful succession.** *Family Business Review,* 7(3): 221-236.

A conceptual article.

Key points:

The timing and mode of a potential successor's entry into the business can have a significant influence on his/her development. Assuming that family business owners wish to perpetuate their organizations, owners must prevent qualified family members becoming disinterested in joining the family firm and unqualified members laying claim to leadership. These situations can be avoided by managing the timing of entry and the involvement of family members in the business.

The most appropriate mode and timing of entry for next generation family members can be optimized by an analysis of their life cycles, i.e., career life cycle, family life cycle, and business life cycle. Less predictable events such as death in a family, involuntary termination of a key employee, divorce, and so on, can also affect a successor's mode and timing of entry. Preparation for such events can be made by assessing a potential successors' aptitude and personality using standardized tests. With this analysis, potential successors can plan to build skills and knowledge they do not have possess but are needed by the family firm.

The succession process can be more effectively managed by following five steps: assess business and family life cycle, assess critical timing junctures in career and family life cycles, evaluate timing options, establish time table for each sibling, and assess the potential impact of sibling entry on existing employees.

Key words: Succession planning, Strategic windows, Life cycle stages, Career stages of successors.

HARVEY, M. & R.E. EVANS (1994b). **Family business and multiple levels of conflict.** *Family Business Review,* 7(4): 331-348.

A conceptual article.

Key points:

The close interaction of family members with both internal and external stakeholders causes multiple levels of potential conflicts in the family firm.

- Reasons for high level of conflict in family firms include:
  - No participative management,
  - Overlap of family and business concerns,
  - No organizational mechanisms,
  - Unclear roles and obligations,
  - Perception of unequal opportunity among siblings and employees.
  - Founding individual's reluctance to let go and to recognize talents of other individuals in the organization.
- Three levels of conflict that may be found in family firms and the suggested conflict resolution mechanisms.

A conflict that occurs within one group of family stakeholders (the business, the family, the external stakeholders) and does not interact with the other two is a level 1 conflict. This type of conflict can be resolved with interpersonal skills of family members and modification of interactions. The entrepreneur can generally play an important leadership role in resolving such a conflict. There are little or no post-conflict resolution monitoring necessary.

A level 2 conflict occurs when any two of the three stakeholders are involved. Resolving this type of conflict may require addressing some core issues and alter both organizational units involved. Generally, this requires a team of individuals and will need some post conflict resolution monitoring.

A level 3 conflict involves all three stakeholders and may need system-wide changes, and in most instances, correction requires the participation of external consultants or experts. Longitudinal monitoring of change is necessary in these conflicts.

Key words: Conflict - forecasting, levels, resolution; Life-cycle stages.

HARVEY, M. & R.E. EVANS (1995). **Life after succession in the family business: Is it really the end of problems?** *Family Business Review,* 8(1): 3-16.

A conceptual article.

Key points:

To attain complete success, an installed successor must identify and manage the problems and conflicts created by the transfer of leadership. It is naive to assume that conflict among family members and managers will subside just because the power has been transferred; rather, the centrality of succession in the family business and the involvement of a number of stakeholders can lead to resentment and negatively influence business and personal relationships.

The authors present a simple three stage model of succession: pre-succession, succession mechanism, and post-succession. The pre-succession stage focuses on siblings before they enter the business and involves the diagnostic analysis of potential successors and managing their entry into the business. The second stage covers the training of potential successors within the organization in various positions and determination of the future leader. The final stage includes the following six components:

- An objective assessment of the conflicts generated by the succession process aimed at identifying discontentment among family members and employees;
- Clarification of new roles and redefinition of responsibilities;
- Agreement on past incumbent's role in the business;
- An audit of the business in order to benchmark the business at the point of power transfer and enable an evaluation of the progress and changes made in the future;
- Identification of changes that need to be made;
- Monitoring of the change process.

Key words: Succession process, Post-succession conflicts, Predecessor-successor relationships.

HAYES, J.L. (1981). **All in the family.** *Management Review,* July: 4.

Sample: 350 family and non-family businesses
Data collection: Questionnaires (mail and telephone)
Data analysis: Percentages

Key points:

The advantages of working in a family business are: a warmer, more family-like atmosphere, a high degree of decision-making authority once accepted as an insider, executive longevity in the company, and a greater latitude for entrepreneurial decision-making. The disadvantages or the difficulties include: lower level of professionalism, unclear lines of authority, and a lack of stock options for non-family members. An employee can achieve the status of "insider" in a family-owned company by being flexible.

Key words: Strengths of family business, Challenges of family business.

HAYES, J.T. & R.M. ADAMS (1990). **Taxation and statutory considerations in the formation of family foundations.** *Family Business Review,* 3(4): 383-394.

Taxation advice regarding family foundations.

Key points:

A family foundation is a charitable foundation that derives, at most, one-third of its financial support from the general public and the rest from a family. Individuals may claim income, estate, and gift tax deductions for contributions made to a family foundation while the income realized by the foundation is almost entirely tax-exempt. However, family foundations are regulated by the Internal Revenue Service using an elaborate regulatory system and non-compliance entails severe penalties. These laws are so strict, arbitrary, and complex that competent legal and accounting advise are necessary. Examples of how to reduce the cost of charitable giving include: pre-funding, appreciated property, and private operating foundation status.

Key words: Family foundations, Taxation advice.

HECK, R.K.Z. and R. WALKER (1993). **Family-owned home-businesses: Their employees and unpaid helpers.** *Family Business Review,* 6(4): 397-415.

Sample: 508 sole proprietors
Data collection: Telephone interviews (30 minutes)
Data analysis: Descriptive statistics, Regression analysis

Key points:

Family-owned home-businesses employ paid workers, contract workers, and unpaid helpers who may be family, related, or unrelated. This study finds that family workers, family helpers, and unrelated workers (paid or contract) contribute positively to business output. While unpaid related helpers tend to decrease net income, related contract workers tend to increase the owner's working hours, and unrelated unpaid helpers are associated with lower business outputs. Thus, using extended family or other relatives as employees may actually decrease business output. Such individuals are often less employable in the regular labour market and depend on family ties for employment; yet they frequently receive wages that are above their market value and/or their willingness to contribute effectively to the company. However, the aforementioned employees may provide long-term benefits such as continuity, loyalty to the family during times of succession. In order to achieve the highest level of output the owner may fare better by utilizing paid and contract family workers or unrelated workers.

Key words: Home based business, Work force contributions.

HEIDRICK, G.W. (1988). **Selecting outside directors.** *Family Business Review,* Fall, 1(3): 271-285.

A conceptual article.

Key points:

This article discusses the advantages of outside board members, the characteristics of a good outside director, the functioning of boards, the compensation for outside directors, and advisory boards.

Independent outside directors, not reliant on the family for their incomes, are valuable to the family business as a sounding board for the owner, by increasing the owner's self discipline, by contributing sound input to the decision-making process, and by providing interim leadership when the CEO dies or is disabled and a successor has not been chosen. Outside directors are an unequivocal bargain to management.

Suitable candidates should be: friendly, compatible, independent thinkers who provide advice or counsel; well informed, intelligent, analytical team players with management experience and familiarity with the business; have personal integrity and a good standing in the community. They may be found among the second and third level executives of large companies, as well as professionals, management consultants, academics, ex-government employees, and so-called professional directors.

For companies with $100 million plus in sales, the total compensation for the board of directors should range from a few thousand to $20,000 annually plus travel expenses. This total must be broken down into retainer, board and committee meeting fees and perquisites, an allocation that should encourage attendance. It is easy to augment payment but very difficult to reduce it.

The critical steps in developing a board of directors are: review the firm's present situation and objectives; define the ideal board; prepare the board manual; develop the list of candidates; check a candidate's references thoroughly; determine personal chemistry; extend an invitation to the acceptable candidate; and lay out policies of periodic reviews to reaffirm mutual satisfaction.

Role definition is also important; directors govern but advisers merely recommend. Advisers are easier to change, face a lower threat of liability, and make a smaller time commitment; advisers cannot vote and agreements in advisory boards are achieved by consensus.

Key words: Advantages of outside board members, Finding outside directors, Compensation of board members, Steps in developing a board, Advisory boards.

HINSZ, V.B. (1990). **Family farmers' reactions to their work: A job diagnostic survey.** *Family Business Review,* 3(1): 35-44.

Sample: 54 family farmers in Upper Mid-West region (Response rate 57%)
Data collection: Survey (Job diagnostic survey instrument used)
Data analysis: Means, t-tests

Key points:

Family farming is an example of a well-designed job that requires only greater pay and job security to improve it. Family farmers appear to derive a sense of fulfilment from their work; they are highly motivated and continue in their work despite adverse factors such as low financial returns, bad weather, and job insecurity. Family farmers appear to derive a sense of fulfilment from their work.

Key words: Farm families.

HIRSCHHORN, L. & T. GILMORE (1980). **The application of family therapy concepts to influencing organization behavior.** *Administrative Science Quarterly, 25:* 18-37.

Sample: A social welfare agency
Data collection: Interviews, Historical analysis
Data analysis: Content analysis

Key points:

The author reports on a consulting assignment for a social welfare agency that grew from 45 professional staff to 90 in 5 years and then stagnated. The agency needed a new developmental mission and changes in its administrative structure. Some innovative diversionary tactics were used to improve relationships.

Key words: Strategic planning, Consulting.

HISRICH, R.D. & D.J. CAHILL, (1995). **Buried at the crossroads at midnight with an oak stake through its heart: An entrepreneurial replication of Ross and Staw's extended temporal escalation model.** *Family Business Review,* 8(1): 41-54.

Sample: A case study of InfoVision, a project started by DECOY corporation
Data collection: Ethnographic record by participant observation. One of the authors was a project manager for InfoVision.
Data analysis: Not stated

Key points:

This case study replicates Ross and Staw's research on extended temporal escalation. It starts by presenting the case of InfoVision which is an integrated system of personal computer, super-high resolution monitor, and printer. DECOY Corporation suffered considerable losses and finally abandoned the project four years after its inception. After comparing this case with the one reported by Ross and Staw, the authors suggest six propositions related to a losing project in an small or mid-sized entrepreneurial or family-owned firm:

- When internal stakeholders are strong enough to continue a losing project or service, it will create a permanently failing operation, especially in entrepreneurial enterprises or where the developer of the project is very senior in an organization;
- Efforts to de-institutionalize a project in an entrepreneurial company when the projects initiated by those other than the entrepreneur or shareholders will

probably cause the entrepreneur to proceed more forcefully with the losing project;

- Changing the reality of a project's economics in an entrepreneurial firm will mean little without changing the psychology of the project for the entrepreneur;
- Innovation causes escalation problems only when the project does not come in on time and on budget; thus, the more experience a firm or an entrepreneur has with successful innovation, even innovation unrelated to the current project, the more likely it will be that escalation/exit difficulties will occur when a project is delayed or has cost overruns;
- When termination of a project will prevent an entrepreneur from increasing the asset value of the firm, project termination will be difficult;
- Once hard costs have been spent, it is easier to hide soft costs (even from oneself) and the organization has less incentive to terminate a project. Conversely, if hard costs continue to run, the organization will be forced on a regular basis to confront the "terminate or continue" issue.

Key words: Termination of projects.

HOLLAND, P.G. & W.R. BOULTON (1984). **Balancing the family and the business in a family business.** *Business Horizons,* 27(2) 16-21.

Sample: Number is not mentioned in the article, although all the firms were in food processing industry
Data collection: Interviews
Data analysis: Content analysis

Key points:

The four structures of family business relationships presented are: *pre-family* (founding stage - power is concentrated); *family* (entry of relative into management and/or ownership - power is dispersed); *adaptive family* (stock is sold to non-family members - power is based on stock ownership and management position); and *post family* (family stock liquidated - power is based on ability to function in a new organization).

The decision process in a family business depends on the power of an individual in the family (based on age, gender, etc.) and power in the business (based on expertise and experience). Persons with high power both in the business and family can take actions effectively and achieve what they want while those with high power in the family but low power in the business need to rely on their political skills to achieve their goals. Because of their family clout, the latter can afford an occasional confrontation. Family members with high power in the business but low power in the family should make use of negotiations and family members with low power both in the family and the business should make use of mediations. Both need considerable interpersonal skills and communication abilities.

Key words: Organizational life cycle stages, Family business sub-systems.

HOLLAND, P.G. & J.E. OLIVER (1992). **An empirical examination of the stages of development of family businesses.** *Journal of Business and Entrepreneurship,* 4(3): 27-38.

Sample: 41 family businesses (17 family members, 24 outside employees)
Data collection: Questionnaire administered during family business seminar at a university
Data analysis: ANOVA, Duncan Multiple range tests

Key points:

The literature proposes a four-stage development model for the family business:

1. The owner manager is in complete control, makes all business related decisions, and the successor has not yet been selected;
2. Family members share control of the business, resolve conflicts through discussions, and a successor is being trained.
3. In this transitional stage, work is shared between family and non-family members, the founder's retirement is imminent, strife and conflict are rampant, and information is shared with some family members and not with others;
4. The family firm becomes publicly owned and professionally managed and a successor is selected from outside of the family.

The empirical results do not support the existence of stage 3.

The delegation of responsibility and power to non-family members is significantly different in each stage; however, family harmony and perceived organizational effectiveness are not systematically different from stage to stage, suggesting that the adjustment from family to professional management may not be as conflict ridden in all firms as is generally believed to be the case.

Key words: Organizational life cycle stages, Professionalization.

HOLLANDER, B.S. & N.S. ELMAN (1988). **Family-owned businesses: An emerging field of inquiry.** *Family Business Review,* 1(2): 145-164.

A review article.

Key points:

Four approaches are used to study the family business: the rational approach, focus on the founder, phases and stages of growth, and the systems approach. All four approaches recognize that because of the family/business linkage, events that directly affect one side can influence the other side. What follows is a brief description of the assumptions associated with each approach:

- *The rational approach*: Family firms are not operated in a highly business-like manner. The firm's interests should be placed before those of the family, thus, excising the family concerns from the business. If the family is unable to do this, the business should be managed by outside managers.
- *Focus on the founder*: Considerable attention has been given to the founder's personality, psychological traits, roles, and management techniques inspite of the fact that the founder is only a part of the family business system. Notably, most of the literature is based on male founders and may not be applicable to female founders or mixed groups, such as co-preneurs.
- *Phases and stages approach*: The family business has a predictable pattern of growth and change occur over time, with alternating periods of stability and transition. Researchers using this approach can be differentiated by the part that each chooses to emphasize, such as family generational progression, stage of life of individuals crucial to the firm, or the interaction of the life cycles of firm, family, and key individuals.
- *Systems approach*: This approach emphasizes the whole as a unit of focus and focuses on the interrelatedness of its parts.

Key words: Phases and stages models, Rational approach, Systems approach, Founder characteristics.

HOLLANDER, B.S. & W.R. BUKOWITZ (1990). **Women, family culture, and family business.** *Family Business Review,* 3(2): 139-151.

A conceptual article.

Key points:

Automatic and unquestioned rules, roles, structure, and triangles are the four components of family culture and all evolve from patterns developed around major emotional issues. A family's culture establishes perceptions about who should be doing what in the family and in the family business. It is important for family members to explore how they have internalized and played out these automatic processes since problematic cultures can lead to sub-optimal family and business decisions. By understanding these processes and their effects, family businesses can lead the way toward building a business community that supports family and economic activities for both male and female participants.

Key words: Women in family business, Culture.

HORTON, T.P. (1982). **The baton of succession.** *Management Review,* July: 2-3.

A conceptual article.

Key points:

For the baton of succession to be passed effectively, the successor should:

- become a student of the organization and gently explore its many dimensions, history, culture, people, and its external and internal relationships before ascending to the leadership role;
- develop trust through open communication and easy exchange of ideas;
- demonstrate objectivity and strive to maintain balance;
- help others settle uncertainties, calm fears, and ensure that his/her words and actions are consistent;
- look to the long-term future and view the transition time as a ripe time to make changes and mobilize the people toward shared values and mutual goals.

Key words: Succession planning, Next generation.

HORTON, T.P. (1986). **Managing in a family way.** *Management Review,* Feb.: 3.

A conceptual article.

Key points:

This article lists the advantages of a family business as being:

- The convergence of values held dear by the family members,
- The ability to pool resources when needed,
- Cohesiveness afforded by working long hours,
- The ability to survive periods of uncertainty,
- Living through failure and success.

The problems associated with family businesses include:

- Conflicts between family members,

- Lack of confidence of the founder in other members.

In order to run a family business successfully, two key types of relationships need to be properly handled: the fist among family members and the second between family members and professional managers.

Key words: Strengths of family business, Challenges of family business, Family business subsystems

---

HOY, F. & T.G. VERSER (1994). **Emerging business, emerging field: Entrepreneurship and the family firm.** *Entrepreneurship Theory and Practice*, 19(1): 9-23.

A conceptual article.

Key points:

The fields of entrepreneurship and family business have both separate and distinct themes and overlapping ones including interest in the entrepreneur, innovation, organization creation, value creation, profit status, uniqueness, and the owner-manager. For example, while both stress the importance of the entrepreneur, the entrepreneurship literature focuses on risk taking, creator, and founder roles and the family business literature emphasizes the entrepreneur's role as a manager, relative, and employer. Some topics for future research in this area are: mechanisms to transfer the founder's vision to other family members, the timing and implication of a new venture becoming a family business, and strategies to oust a founder when that is necessary for the growth and survival of business.

Key words: Entrepreneurship and family business literature, Research topics.

JAIN, S.K. (1980). **Look to outsiders to strengthen business boards.** *Harvard Business Review*, 58(4): 162-170.

Sample: 120 small and medium mid-western companies
Data collection: Questionnaires administered through mail and telephone
Data analysis: Percentages

Key points:

The author argues for the extensive employment of non-family members as board members suggesting that outsiders can help small companies in public relations, the mediation of a wide range of internal issues, and provide valuable expertise, including:

- Help to form and guide company policies and confront management;
- Determining long range objectives of the organization;
- Allocation of major resources;
- Help in dealing with merger, acquisition, and divestment bids;
- Assisting in top management performance appraisal, succession, and compensation;
- Providing links to the public;
- Providing a buffer zone and mediate conflicts and prevent emotional outbursts;
- Helping the company to realize the importance of R&D and presenting an objective view of the technical growth of the company.

Key words: Outside directors, Finding outside directors, Role of directors.

JONES, W.D. (1982). **Characteristics of planning in small firms.** *Journal of Small Business Management,* 20(3): 15-19.

Sample: 69 firms in 7 seven different S.I.C codes in the state of Virginia (Response rate - 34.5%)
Data collection: Questionnaires with questions using 7 point Likert scales
Data analysis: Canonical correlation

Key points:

The study compares firms that plan with those that do not. Non-planners react to changes they had not anticipated and use the knowledge and intuition of only a single planner or limited group. Planners scan the environment for opportunities, identify the future through research, involve organizational members in the planning process, and are more successful.

Key words: Strategic planning.

JONOVIC, D.L. (1989). **Outside review in a wider context: An alternative to the classic board.** *Family Business Review*, 2(2): 125-140.

A conceptual article.

Key points:

The classic board with outside directors may not be suitable for the family business; rather, a review council with broader membership and mandate may be better. A review council is an advisory board formed of professional advisors, other business owners, other family members, other stakeholders, successors from other companies, non-family managers, and minority shareholders.

Council members have a mandate to review family business decisions and directions with a mission to broaden the width and depth of ideas available to the family business. The council should meet periodically and various committees may be formed within the council. Members serve for a limited period of time and may be expected to provide replacement for themselves. Professionals should be paid their normal fee for the time involved and should serve principally as devil's advocates and provide peer review to colleagues on broad ideas, rather than providing specific directions. Non-professional members should receive a council fee for their services that should be high enough to make shareholders want to listen to the council and respect its advice. Finally, professional council members should be precluded from acting as fee-paid advisers of the company during their tenure on the council and a reasonable period thereafter.

As the company grows, professionalises, and adjusts to the committed reviews of outsiders, the council can be replaced by an advisory board with all the features of a classic board, but without formal appointment or authority of directors. Eventually, presuming success and continuing professionalization of management and business, a classic board can be created.

Key words: Review council, Classic board, Professionalization.

KAHN, J.A. & D.A. HENDERSON (1992). **Location preferences of family firms: Strategic decision-making or "Home Sweet Home"?** *Family Business Review*, 5(3): 271-282.

Sample: 990 firms in South-East Michigan, consisting of 435 family firms and 555 non- family firms (Response rate - 44%)
Data collection: Questionnaires
Data analysis: Factor analysis, t-tests

Key points:

This article attempts to understand the reasons that underlie the location decisions of family and non-family firms. The hypotheses and whether they are supported by the findings follow:

1. Relative to non-family firms, family firms prefer locations that provide a better quality of life for family members. (Not Supported);
   - 1a. Relative to non-family firms, family firms prefer locations that provide secure locations with access to cultural and entertainment attractions, quality health care, and recreational opportunities. (Not Supported);
   - 1b. Relative to non-family firms, family firms prefer locations that provide closer proximity to owner's residence. (Strongly Supported);
   - 1c. Relative to non-family firms, family firms prefer locations that provide better access to quality housing. (Marginally Supported);
2. Relative to family firms, non-family firms prefer locations that minimize their costs. (Strongly Supported);
   - 2a. Relative to family firms, non-family firms prefer locations that offer lower labour costs. (Strongly Supported);
   - 2b. Relative to family firms, non-family firms prefer locations that minimize their facilities costs. (Marginally Supported);
   - 2c. Relative to family firms, non-family firms prefer locations that offer an available pool of skilled labour. (Strongly Supported);
   - 2d. Relative to family firms, non-family firms prefer locations that offer a superior technical infrastructure. (Strongly Supported).

The data provide mixed support for the notion that family firms seek locations that improve the family's quality of life and strong support for the notion that non-family firms seek locations providing the lowest cost of operation. Both family and non-family firms rank proximity to markets and customers as their highest preference, suggesting that business success is a primary concern regardless of the ownership form.

Key words: Family and non-family firms - location of business.

KANTER, R. (1989). **Work and family in US: A critical review and agenda for research and policy.** *Family Business Review,* Spring, 2(1): 77-114.

A review of the work and family subsystems and their interrelationships.

Key points:

Contemporary social scientists agree that there is a strong link between economic variables and family life; however, it is a myth that in a modern industrial society work life and family life exist in two separate and non-overlapping worlds, with their own functions, territories, and behavioral rules. This myth suggests that each world operates by its own laws and can be studied independent of the other.

This myth exists because organizations require loyalty and commitment from employees and attempt to neutralize ties that compete with these needs. The family is an especially insidious source of particularistic loyalties. Family members may band together as a political force, may favour one another in decisions on grounds far removed from the organization's purposes or interests, and may exclude fellow workers from organizationally relevant deliberations because of a family's right to withdraw privately to it's own quarters. Organizations need either to incorporate the family into serving organizational needs or keep it outside the corporate boundaries.

The history of family relationship to the evolving capitalist-industrial system indicates that the family was first incorporated into the organization's life (first few decades of the 19th century) and then pushed outside. Industrialization was unpleasant and employees wanted to shield the family from it; this separation of occupational and family sectors in the society was considered essential to the smooth functioning of each institution and to the society as a whole. Occupational life was perceived to be organized around impersonal objective standards of competence, whereas the family rested on emotional criteria.

Work operates as a dominant constraint on family life, as well a source of economic and personal sustenance; aspects of the structure and organization of work life influence family life and vice versa. These are described in depth by the author.

Key words: Family business subsystems, Work and family relationships, Review article.

KAYE, K. (1991). **Penetrating the cycle of sustained conflict.** *Family Business Review,* 4(1): 21-44.

Based on a consulting experience.

Key points:

Family conflicts are fundamentally different from conflicts between separate parties with issues running deeper than those over which they claim to be incensed. Often, the reasons for sustaining their conflicts may not be clear even to the parties concerned. and may be stronger than the desires to resolve such conflicts. By charting the chronic, often repeated dynamics of escalating and retreating conflicts, consultants can encourage communication between members and help resolve conflicts.

Key words: Sustained conflicts in family firms, Consulting.

KAYE, K. (1992). **The kid brother.** *Family Business Review,* 5(3): 237-256.

Sample: 10 case studies
Data collection: Not mentioned
Data analysis: Not mentioned

Key points:

Structural family dynamics that place one sibling, usually the youngest son, in an outsider role can have powerful repercussions for a family business. The author refers to this as the 'kid brother syndrome' and suggests ways for dealing with it. Four specific features of this syndrome are:

- The family member affected is usually much younger than other siblings and has been raised in a more affluent family with a value system that differs from that of the older siblings.
- The "kid brother" displays a tendency toward defensiveness and making excuses.
- The family feels an obligation to carry him along.
- The kid brother feels trapped in the business.

Some ways of preventing this syndrome from developing include:

- Establishing constructive expectations for every employee in the business, including the owner's children;
- Raising responsible children by building values and expectations into children from infancy;
- Cultivating a team of differentiated siblings; fostering respect, independence and loyalty among children for each other;
- Establishing mechanisms to transfer wealth among siblings.

The recommended treatment of the "kid brother" syndrome is to confront the situation realistically and explore and expand options for the affected sibling both within and out of business.

Key words: Kid brother syndrome, Sibling relationships.

KEPNER, E. (1983). **The family and the firm: A co-evolutionary perspective.** *Organizational Dynamics,* Summer: 57-70.

A conceptual article.

Key points:

Both the family and the firm are subsystems of a larger metasystem, in which the boundary conditions are overly diffused and permeable. The family's purpose is to provide affection, intimacy, a sense of identity and a healthy environment for the social and emotional development of family members. The firm, on the other hand, provides for economic needs of its stakeholders. The conflict between the family and firm may lead to serious problems.

The demands of business can seriously intrude on a family's energy and time. Because of the economic interdependence of family and business and pressures to maintain an image of cohesiveness, conflicts may be suppressed resulting in the family's failing to learn healthy negotiating skills and/or healing mechanisms. Family members may feel the pressure to behave in certain expected ways; however, the business may be in a different stage and may require different behaviours. Family members' perceptions of the external environment may be tainted as they have always been associated with the firm and they often develop a bloated sense of self importance. Family and firm culture may be different, even though a parent is the head of both and new members often go through a period of culture shock when they join the firm. It is natural for children to compete for parent's attention and love; however, when they grow older and go their own ways, they usually learn to relate to each other better more effectively. This distancing of siblings does not take place when the family members continue to be associated with a family business; thus, childhood rivalries may persist. Usually sons want to emulate fathers but they also compete with the fathers for the mothers' attention. Family businesses usually operate on the principle of primogeniture and the disappointed daughters often attempt to exert their influence vicariously by promoting their husband's career in family firms.

Family business founders can prevent tensions by communicating their thoughts or decisions regarding: who will be considered for roles in the firm, what criteria of competence will be required, how performance will be evaluated, and how the inherited assets will be distributed. These considerations should be made clear as early as possible. The owner-manager may consult family members to make these decision, or persuade them to accept his decisions by using formal or informal means.

Key words: Challenges in family business, Family subsystem, Women in family business, Communication in family firms.

KIRCHHOFF, B.A. & J.J. KIRCHHOFF (1987). **Family contributions to productivity and profitability in small businesses.** *Journal of Small Business Management,* 25(4): 25-31.

Sample: 647 firms
Data collection: University of Minnesota data base
Data analysis: Regression analysis

Key points:

Family members are more productive than other employees in family businesses; a productivity, however, that does not increase profitability, because wage and salary expenses are higher. The family firm goes through a cycle of family members being underpaid or unpaid when the business starts and then paid generously as it becomes profitable. Being overworked and underpaid does not appear to affect the productivity of family members.

Key words: Productivity and profitability in family businesses.

KLEINSORGE, I.K. (1994). **Financial and efficiency differences in family-owned and non-family-owned nursing homes: An Oregon study.** *Family Business Review,* 7(1): 73-86.

Sample: 34 administrators of nursing homes (10 family-owned, 24 non-family owned)
Data collection: Public data set (Oregon senior services division, Financial audit unit)
Data analysis: Data envelopment analysis

Key points:

The findings of this study indicate that, compared to non-family-owned nursing homes, family-owned nursing homes in Oregon are less efficient in providing care, have lower occupancy rates, spend more on room and board salaries, and less on patient care salaries. Furthermore, family-owned nursing homes have significantly fewer assets and higher liabilities than non-family owned homes.

The greatest weakness of the study is that it assumes the same objectives for both family and non-family firms.

Key words: Family and non-family owned nursing homes, Profitability, Efficiency.

KRENTZMAN, H.C. & J.N. SAMARAS (1960). **Can small businesses use consultants?** *Harvard Business Review,* 38(3): 126-136.

Sample: 200 managers of small businesses (Response rate - 30%)
Data collection: Questionnaires
Data analysis: Percentages

Key points:

Although small businesses encounter a host of problems, only 32 percent of the responding firms have ever used consultants. Two reasons for this are that:

- other sources of help are available to small business owners (literature, friends, bankers, lawyers, accountants, boards of directors, advisory boards, and the small business administrator);
- attitudes and fears of small businessmen (fear of fees, failure, hiring the wrong consultant, information being passed to competitors, and loss of time) prevent them from hiring consultants.

Recommendations to small businesses consultants include:

- The person who solicits the assignment should be the one who works with them;
- Establish a relationship of trust with the manager and other employees;
- Spend time with employees and explain the function of the program;
- Be well prepared for all appointments and do not discuss other clients;
- High pressure sales methods only scare the small business owner away;
- Flexibility in fees arrangements and time spent is necessary;
- Keep operations small and flexible to keep overhead costs to a minimum;
- Be prepared to get out on the firing line, rather than being an advisor;
- Be willing to maintain a continuous relationship with the company, and be available to give advice.

Key Word: Consulting.

KURATKO, D.F., H.B. FOSS, & L.L. VANALST (1994). **IRS Estate freeze rules: Implications for family business succession planning.** *Family Business Review,* 7(1): 61-71.

Legal advice.

Key points:

This article examines the estate freeze rules of the United States Internal Revenue Service with respect to their implications for family business succession planning. The authors review the tax impacts of the valuation rules for transfers of certain interests, transfers in trust, buy-sell agreements, and lapsing rights. Although they suggest that there is no single best answer to the challenge of ownership transfer in a family business, some possible alternatives include:

- Gift of personal use property,
- Establish a grantor retained annuity trust or grantor retained unit trust,
- Buy-sell agreements,
- Sale in exchange for private annuity,
- Reverse freeze,
- Special trusts (credit shelter trust, estate freeze at will, and life insurance trusts).

Key words: Legal advice, Trusts, Estate freeze.

LANDES, D.S. (1993). **Bleichoders and Rothschilds: The problem of continuity in the family firm.** *Family Business Review,* 6(1): 85-101.

A case study, from Rosenberg, C.E. (ed.) (1975). *The family in history.* University of Pennsylvania Press.

Key points

This article is a case study of two historical merchant banking families of Germany: the Bleichoders and the Rothschilds. The former lost their identity while the latter were able to preserve both their family's and the firm's identity. The author asserts that the behaviour of businessmen is partly determined by their tacit or expressed ideology (self image, self esteem, and force of personality) and partly by the place accorded to them by the world around them; thus. societies get the businessmen or business families they deserve.

Key words: Continuity in family firms, Cultural influences.

LANE, S.H. (1989). **An organizational development / team-building approach to consultation with family businesses.** *Family Business Review,* 2(1): 5-16.

Consulting advice.

Key points:

The author espouses a consulting approach that uses a planned, guided change to enhance the family members' problem solving capacity by developing their adaptiveness and self-renewal skills, thus, fostering the client's independence. The approach consists of a number of distinct but overlapping stages:

1. *Entry*: Problems are related to the succession issues and the call for help generally comes from the owner-manager or other family members, with the consent of the owner-manager. If his/her consent is absent, the consultant's ability to work effectively is hampered.
2. *Assessment and diagnosis*: Family interactions should be conceptualized as a system. Data are collected via non-structured interviews with family members, and non-family managers.
3. *Feedback*: Feedback is presented in the form of a written report describing the overall transition that needs to take place both in the family and the business. Specific steps to solve current problems are suggested.
4. *The planning process*: Establishing a game plan of action steps.
5. *Implementation*: Developing change mechanisms and monitor progress with process consultation.
6. *Termination*: The consultant becomes an adviser and is called in when needed.

Consulting for family businesses requires a broad knowledge base, although there is also a need for specialists such as lawyers to develop an estate plan, accountants to develop improved reporting systems, financial planners to establish financial plans, or therapists to resolve specific and deep process issues.

Key words: Consulting, Board of directors.

LANSBERG, I. (1983a). **Conversation with Richard Beckhard.** *Organizational Dynamics,* Summer: 29-38.

An interview.

Key points:

Succession is both central and critical to family firms. Business founders need to think about and plan for their families, themselves, and their business. Succession is an economic and emotional one for everybody involved and company founders do not easily give up their leadership role. Family involvement in planning the future is desirable but not always possible. Advisors need to be aware of the whole system and the underlying dynamics and male-female advisory teams are particularly effective in consulting with family firms.

Key words: Succession, Consulting.

LANSBERG, I. (1983). **Managing human resources in family firms: The problem of institutional overlap.** *Organizational Dynamics,* Summer: 39-46.

A conceptual article.

Key points:

Families and businesses exist for different, often contradictory purposes, leading to many difficulties for family firms. These contradictions include:

- *Reason for existence*: Families exist to take care of and nurture its members while a business exists to produce goods and services.
- *Selection*: The family should provide opportunities for children, regardless of competencies but the business should hire only the competent.
- *Appraisal*: Parents should not differentiate between siblings but the CEO should differentiate between employees on the basis of performance.
- *Allowances*: Parents should allocate allowances in accordance with the developmental needs of family members but CEOs should allocate salaries based on the performance history and market worth of employees.
- *Training*: Parents should provide learning opportunities designed to satisfy individual needs of children but CEOs should provide training opportunities to satisfy organizational needs.

Two commonly adopted coping strategies of family firms and potential hazards are outlined:

- *Compromise between family and business principles*: Compromises may lead to sub-optimal decisions from the point of view of the firm.
- *Oscillate between family and business principles*: Relatives and employees become discontented as they perceive the founder to be inconsistent and unpredictable.

The separation of management and ownership can be the key to effectively managing the inherent family/firm contradictions. From an ownership perspective, relatives are subject to norms and principles regulating family relations; but from the management perspective, they are affected by the firm's principles. The following principles should be adopted from the point of view of the accompanying family/firm perspectives:

- Only relatives with necessary skills should be taken into the business (management perspective);
- Relatives keen on joining the firm should be given opportunity to acquire the necessary skills (family perspective);

- The salary of relatives should be based on their market worth (management perspective);
- Any extra income should be distributed through stocks and dividends. (family perspective);
- Relatives should be subject to objective evaluation by peers, subordinates, and superiors (management perspective);
- If found incompetent or unsuitable for organizational responsibilities, family members should explore alternative career paths (family perspective);
- Employment of relatives whose interests or needs fail to mesh with the organizational goals should be reconsidered (management perspective);
- Such relatives should maintain a share of the family's assets (family perspective).

Key words: Sociological differences between family and business, Nepotism.

LANSBERG, I. (1988). **The succession conspiracy.** *Family Business Review, 1*(2): 119-143.

An article based on author's experience as son of a family business entrepreneur.

Key points:

Leadership succession is seldom planned for family businesses although its importance is clearly recognized. The reason for this inconsistency is that most stakeholders in family business are ambivalent towards succession planning:

- Company founders experience strong psychological deterrents to succession planning because it entails a letting go of power and influence and a fear of losing their central role or identity within the family, since the business has become an integral part of their sense of self. These influences may cause powerful feelings of rivalry and jealousy toward potential successors.
- Family members avoid succession planning for fear of loss of identity, loss of family harmony, and loss of privacy. Parents may also differ significantly in their preferences for the successor while the younger generation may want to avoid succession planning as it arouses fears of parental death, separation, and abandonment.
- Senior managers who have worked with founders for a long time are reluctant to shift from a personal relationship with the founder to a more formal one with the successor. Discussions regarding the founder's retirement and death also makes it necessary for managers to confront their own aging and retirement.
- When ownership is separate from management, the owners may be reluctant to see a change in leadership.

- External agents such as clients and suppliers may regard the founder as their primary business contact and may be reluctant to see changes in a firm.

The author suggests some strategies for different stakeholders to assist in addressing the issue of succession planning. Some salient points are stated below:
Mobilizing the founder:

- Help the founder to develop a supportive network of persons who can emphasize and share learning;
- Heighten the sensitivity of family to the needs of the founder;
- Help the founder to design a role for his/her self in the future.

Mobilizing the family:

- Help the founder and his/her spouse to develop a shared vision of their future;
- Develop a family council that facilitates meetings of the family in which members discuss their values and expectations for the business and for one another.

Mobilizing the managers:

- Create a succession task force and build incentives that reward serious involvement in developing the succession plan;
- Encourage succession planning for senior managers as well as for the founder.

Mobilizing the owner:

Create a board of directors appropriately staffed to provide an independent perspective that can safeguard the interests of owners.

Key words: Succession planning, Family business system, Restraining factors, Intervention strategies.

LANSBERG, I. & J.H. ASTRACHAN (1994). **Influence of family relationships on succession planning and training: The importance of mediating factors.** *Family Business Review,* 7(1): 39-59.

Sample: 130 participants from 109 family businesses (Response rate - 36%)
Data collection: Questionnaires from owner-managers as well as successors, Telephone follow-up interviews
Data analysis: Cronbach alpha, Descriptive statistics, Regression analysis

Key points:

This article addresses the degree to which family adaptability and cohesion affect management succession planning and training are mediated by the family's commitment to the business and the quality of the relationship between the owner-manager and the successor. The hypotheses tested and their respective findings are:

1. Family cohesion is positively associated with the quality of the relationship between the owner-manager and the successor. (Not supported);

2. Family adaptability is positively associated with the quality of the relationship between the owner-manager and the successor. (Supported);
3. Family cohesion is positively associated with the family's commitment to the firm. (Supported);
4. Family adaptability is positively associated with the family's commitment to the firm. (Supported);
5. The family's commitment to the business is positively associated with the extent of succession planning. (Supported);
6. The family's commitment to the business is positively associated with the degree of successor training. (Supported);
7. The quality of the relationship between the owner-manager and the successor is positively associated with the extent of successor training. (Supported).

The results indicate that family commitment to a business serves as a mediator to the influence of family cohesion on both succession planning and successor training. The study also reveals that the quality of the owner-manager and successor relationship mediates the influence of both family cohesion and adaptability on successor training; however, family cohesion and adaptability variables do not directly affect the dependent variables succession planning and successor training.

Key words: Succession planning, Successor training, Family influences.

LANSBERG, I. & E. PERROW (1991). **Understanding and working with leading family businesses in Latin America.** *Family Business Review*, 4(2): 127-147.

Sample: 25 family businesses in 9 Latin American countries
Data collection: Not mentioned
Data analysis: Not mentioned

Key points:

Most Latin American economies are dominated by large cosmopolitan family businesses called grupos. The unique economic, political, and socio-cultural characteristics of Latin America affect the ownership, management, and family dynamics of these organizations.

The unique strengths and factors that contribute towards the survival and proliferation of these organizations are:

- Comparatively low domestic competition and protection from foreign competition;
- The social structure of Latin American societies which creates a climate for members of upper circles support each other's activities;
- Grupos are favoured by government and given exclusive rights to lucrative entrepreneurial endeavors;

- Most leading families value their children's education leading to highly skilled family managers;
- The spirit of entrepreneurship is instilled in children from an early age by encouraging them to turn their ideas into business proposals that may be funded by the family;
- Most grupos adopt socially responsible policies and make tangible contribution to the community helping to mitigate envy and resentment.

Specific stressors associated with this system and interventions that may alleviate them are:

- *Stressor*: The grupos lack the governance mechanisms to handle complex family business issues.
  Suggested intervention: The formation of a family council can provide a forum in which family members can articulate their values, needs, and expectations regarding the company and develop policies.
- *Stressor*: Rapid expansion of families from one generation to the next and the effects of rigid patriarchal authority on the younger generations.
  Suggested intervention: The functional integration within the clan is enhanced by stimulating differentiation among the backers. Regular family meetings with members of all generations and gender can be helpful; a three step format suggested by the authors is to have all members meet together, break up into subgroups to discuss their concerns, and then present their ideas in a plenary session to all the members.

Key words: Latin-American family businesses, Ethnicity.

LANSBERG, I., E. PERROW, & S. ROGOLSKY (1988). **Family business as an emerging field.** *Family Business Review,* 1(1): 1-8.

Editors notes.

Key points:

As an introduction to the first issue of the *Family Business Review,* the editors comment on the existing state of the discipline. Their observations are outlined below:

- *There is no consensus on the definition of a family business*:
  Agreement about the definition is important for any discipline so that researchers can build on each other's work and develop a usable knowledge base; moreover, knowing the type of organization studied in a given project helps managers and consultants to decide whether the findings are applicable to their situations.

- *There is a prevalence of the family business*:
  If the commonly used definition of family business is adopted; "a business in which the members of a family have legal control over ownership, 90 percent of all businesses in US are family businesses".
- *Demographic trends suggest that succession and retirement will accelerate*:
  The increasing number of women in the labour force will have important implications for succession issues.
- *Family firms have been neglected by scholars*:
  Social scientists seem to believe that control of the business sector no longer rests in the hands of families. Researchers are trained to study either the business or the family and they find it difficult to study both simultaneously, a factor compounded by the belief that firms and families exist as two separate and self-contained systems.

Key words: Definition of family business, Scholarly neglect, Prevalence of family businesses, Demographic changes.

LEVINSON, H. (1971). **Conflicts that plague family businesses.** *Harvard Business Review,* 49(2): 90-98.

A conceptual article.

Key points:

Father-son conflicts and sibling rivalries are common in family businesses. If more than one sibling sits on the company board, only one should be an operational executive. Family businesses should try to move toward professional management where ownership and management are separated, alleviating problematic situations where siblings are senior-subordinate in the organization but equals on the board.

Establishing a new venture or separating the areas of operation (either under the same corporate umbrella or out of it) can help provide necessary autonomy to all of the family members in a business.

Key words: Sibling conflicts, Inter-generational conflicts, Professionalization.

LEVINSON, H. (1974). **Don't choose your own successor.** *Harvard Business Review,* 52(6): 53-62.

A conceptual article.

Key points:

If the leadership successor of a family business is chosen by the incumbent, chances of failure are higher than when other members select the successor. Most people tend to seek immortality and omnipotence in an unconscious way by having their achievements stand as enduring monuments. Sometimes that can be achieved by showing that an organization cannot do without them. This pressure is particularly strong for entrepreneurs and those who have held their positions for a long time and may result in executives unconsciously selecting inadequate successors. A committee-based selection of successors to important managerial positions may lead to more effective choices.

Key words: Succession, Successor - choosing strategies.

LEVINSON, H. (1983). **Consulting with family businesses: What to look for, what to look out for.** *Organizational Dynamics,* Summer: 71-80.

A conceptual article.

Key points:

The three categories of family businesses and the degree to which they are open to the use of consulting services are:

- *Traditional*: These have been established over generations and the issues of succession have been clearly determined. Growth is slow and steady and difficulties are handled with refined self-control. Consultants are called in to address specific well-defined problems.
- *Conflictful*: Members of these family firms differ in their opinions about power and/or the strategic direction of the business. Consultation usually fails because the rift is already wide by the time the consultant is called.
- *Entrepreneurial*: This form of family business is ripe for consultation. A typical scenario is that of a business started by the father and inherited by the sons but where the father does not let go and allow the sons to make any decisions, a situation ripe for family feuds. Consultants are usually called in by those with little or no power within the business and need to establish individual trust and ties before bringing the family together. If family members wish to stay

together, then the differences can be worked out, but when commitments are weak, it may be better to let them go their own ways.

In most cases family members have 3 options:

- Each family member is assigned his/her own operation/department;
- Each family member manages his/her own operation but buys together to create synergies;
- Some family members leave or the firm is sold.

Key words: Consulting, Types of family businesses, Inter-generational conflicts.

LEVINSON, R.E. (1974). **How to make your family business more profitable.** *Journal of Small Business Management,* 12(4): 35-41.

A conceptual article.

Key points:

This article outlines eight guidelines to make family business more profitable:

- Cash in on flexibility;
- Keep emotions outside the business;
- Seek outside viewpoints;
- Depersonalize key business decisions by using built-in controls;
- Make employment attractive to non-family members;
- Apply business-like financial techniques;
- Personalize your approach to important matters;
- Make hereafter business plans; if no one wants to step in after the incumbent leaves, plan on selling the company.

Key words: Profitability in family businesses.

LICHTENSTEIN, J.H. (1993). **Factors affecting the provision and cost of health insurance in small family businesses.** *Family Business Review,* 4(2): 173-178.

Health care advise for small businesses.

Key points:

Health care premiums are 10 to 40 percent higher for small firms because of the costs associated with medical underwriting and administration. Small firms may control costs by increasing deductibles, changing carriers, and requiring second opinions before surgery.

Key words: Health care in family firms.

LIEBTAG, B. (1984). **Problems tracked in transition from owner to professional management.** *Journal of Accountancy,* October: 38-40.

Sample: 20 major family controlled businesses in U.S., Europe, Latin America
Data collection: Not specified

Key points:

The timely withdrawal of a company founder from active management and the corresponding transfer of leadership to professionals is the most critical factor in transforming a family firm into a professional company. Although a traumatic experience, familial disengagement is vital to the success and growth of the business.

Effective disengagements are marked by actions on four fronts:

- The owner relinquishes control when still in full command and can lend support and counsel;
- Withdrawal from active management is final and clearly communicated;
- The owners publicly commits to an orderly plan of succession;
- The owner articulates and supervises a formal statement of the company's mission, objectives, policies, strategies, and accountability.

Once owners relinquish control, they may still focus their attention on specific aspects of the business that they enjoy or are good at, and may even retain positions on the board.

The authors also believe that large numbers of heirs have the potential to dilute management and may ultimately paralyse the ability to manage. Heirs should be chosen for leadership roles only after objective consideration of their merit and effective support systems should be provided to deal with family members who are not equipped to carry out the responsibilities of the firm.

Key words: Succession planning.

LITZ, R.A. (1995). **The family business: Toward definitional clarity.** *Proceedings of The Academy of Management*: 100-104.

A conceptual article.

Key points:

This article outlines two approaches that are used to provide definitional clarity to the term 'family business':

Structure-based approach: The ownership and management of an organization can be controlled by an individual or a family or may be widely held; a three-by-three matrix is provided to understand the different possible combinations of management and ownership in a firm. It is suggested that 'a business may be considered a family business to the extent that its ownership and management are concentrated within a family unit'.

Intention-based approach: This approach is based on the intentions of one or more organizational members to increase or decrease family ownership and/or management control. Using this approach 'a business firm may be considered a family business to the extent that its members strive to achieve and/or maintain intra-organizational family-based relatedness'.

An integration of the above two approaches provides the following definition for family businesses:

'A business firm may be considered a family business to the extent that its ownership and management are concentrated within a family unit, and to the extent its members strive to achieve and/or maintain intra-organizational family-based relatedness'.

Key words: Definitions of family businesses.

LONGNECKER, J.G. & J.E. SCHOEN (1978). **Management succession in the family firm.** *Journal of Small Business Management*, 16(3): 1-6.

A conceptual article.

Key points:

Succession is a process, not an event. Family successors are gradually prepared for leadership roles through a lifetime of learning from experience gained by filling successive preparatory positions or roles. The different stages of a father-son succession and their characteristics are:

1. *Pre-business*: The passive unplanned orientation of the potential successor by the family.

2. *Introductory*: The part time employment of the potential successor in the firm.
3. *Introductory functional*: The education and full time work of potential successor in another organization.
4. *Functional*: The potential successor joins organization as a full time employee with a non-managerial job.
5. *Advanced functional*: The potential successor assumes managerial position.
6. *Early succession*: The successor assumes presidency.
7. *Mature succession*: The successor becomes leader of organization.

Key words: Socialization of successor, Stages in succession process.

LOSSBERG, J.T. & R.M. ADAMS (1990). **The role of the non-family administrator in family foundations.** *Family Business Review*, 3(4): 375-382.

Based on authors experiences and interviews with 5 other non-family administrators.

Key points:

Managing a family foundation poses a special challenge to non-family administrators because the task combines family and corporate non-profit board dynamics. As a foundation's asset base increases, so does the need for non-family administrators (NFAs). NFAs bring new levels of professionalism to family-run foundations, lessen the burden placed on family board members, are more accessible to the public than family members, and bring fresh perspectives to discussions. In return for this expertise and objectivity, family members must share family confidences and some degree of control with NFAs.

Generally, the NFAs of family foundations have a low turnover rate, especially in families that work well together. But in families that are caught in conflict, NFAs are trapped in the political web and impaired in their ability to perform even routine tasks.

Key words: Family foundations, Non-family administrators.

LUNDBERG, C.C. (1994). **Unravelling communications among family members.** *Family Business Review*, 7(1): 29-37.

A conceptual article.

Key points:

The field of organization communications has not yet provided models that can assist in unravelling the complex communications among family members in family firms. Family members relate and communicate both as business colleagues and as family members, finding themselves in at least four different roles: the family member role, the role associated with their position in the firm, a role describing their ownership or equity, and a more personal role outside the other three. The role that is prominent at any given moment will be a function of whichever of the four general roles is cued by the situation. The author distinguishes between the complementary-role and cross-role communications. Effective communications are more likely when complementary roles are being performed.

Two common sources of miscommunication occur when a person adopts an inappropriate role or when the cues in a situation reflect role conflict and ambiguity. In order to enhance communications among family members in the business, there should be clearly articulated purposes or agenda for meetings. When a shift in agenda is inconsistent with the setting, it should be communicated clearly to the members. Moreover, members should remain vigilant of role-inappropriate behaviours.

Key words: Communications in family firms, Family influences.

LYMAN, A.R. (1988). **Life in the family circle.** *Family Business Review,* 1(4): 383-398.

Sample: 73 business women (39 family business women, 34 non-family business) women
Data collection: Interviews (face-to-face and telephone)
Data analysis: Wilcoxon two-sample test

Key points:

Interpersonal networks are defined as a combination of immediate and extended family, friends, and associates with whom significant interaction occurs. Such networks act as boundary guides, by establishing and reinforcing norms for appropriate behaviour.

The interpersonal networks of family business and non-family business women are examined in this article. The family business woman's interactions with family members dominate her personal and professional lives. These women describe their contacts with family at work as being necessary but they seldom mention non-family interactions. Non-family-business women indicate that they consciously work to separate family interactions, believing that their personal sanity and professional progress would be enhanced by such separation. The limited homogenous networks of family business women may limit their ability to pursue and test new ideas, by imposing limitations on the expression of individuality. Though the stability of these networks can be very helpful in turbulent times, the effects of their limitations may outweigh the benefits.

Key words: Women in family business, Interpersonal networks.

LYMAN, A.R. (1991). **Customer service: Does family ownership make a difference?** *Family Business Review,* 4(3): 303-324.

Sample: 78 business managers and 48 family members in family owned businesses in Davis, California.
Data analysis: Interviews, telephone surveys
Data analysis: Percentages

Key points:

Five areas describe the different orientations of family and non-family business managers toward customer service:

- Family business managers have a more personal orientation to customer service transactions. They do not adhere to standard rules;
- Family business managers talk about the impact of a policy in terms of its ability to help employees and customers be happy. Non-family business managers talk about their policy in terms of its ability to get employees and customers to exhibit appropriate behaviour or responses;
- Family business firms are more likely to have unwritten policies whereas non-family business firms are more likely to have written policies;
- Family business managers are more likely to trust their employees than non-family business managers;
- Non-family business managers focus on the behaviour to be elicited from the customers, whereas family firm managers focus more evenly on the sentiment and behaviour that results from the implementation of a policy.

Key words: Family and non-family firms - customer service.

LYMAN, A.R., M. SALGANICOFF, & B. HOLLANDER (1985). **Women in family business: An untapped resource.** *SAM Advanced Management Journal,* Winter: 46-49.

A conceptual article.

Key points:

The authors discuss the importance of considering women for family business jobs. As caretakers of family concerns, women are in a perfect position to hear about the family business and may know it inside out. They may, therefore, be in a position to manage the business effectively. To enable women to participate in family business management, businesses need to address family development issues. The women should acquire skills needed for taking over and develop networks with other working women. This may provide continuity in family business, ensure its longevity, and give an opportunity for male heirs to pursue other interests or careers.

Key words: Women in family businesses.

MALONE, S.C. (1989). **Selected correlates of business continuity planning in the family business.** *Family Business Review,* 2(4): 341-353.

Sample: 58 CEOs of wholesale lumber dealerships (Response rate - 19.5 percent)
Data collection: Questionnaire, telephone interviews
Data analysis: Cronbach's alpha

Key points:

Propositions regarding the factors likely to influence continuity planning in the family business, and the findings with respect to the propositions are listed below:
Organizational characteristics:
1. There is a positive relationship between the size of the business and the level of business continuity planning. (Not supported);
2. There is a positive relationship between the level of strategic planning and the extent of business continuity planning. (Supported);
3. There is a positive relationship between the level of perceived family harmony and the extent of business continuity planning. (Supported);
4. There is a positive relationship between the percentage of outsiders on the board and the extent of business continuity planning. (Supported).

Personal characteristics:

5. There is a positive relationship between the age of the owner and extent of business continuity planning. (Not supported);
6. The more internal the owner-manager's locus of control, the higher the level of business continuity planning. (Supported).

Although continuing the family business is generally considered desirable, 26 percent of the respondents in this study rated family business continuity as undesirable or highly undesirable.

Key words: Succession planning, Strategic planning, Outside directors.

MALONE, S.C. & P.V. JENSTER (1992). **The problem of plateaued owner manager.** *Family Business Review,* 5(1): 25-41.

A conceptual article.

Key points:

Management succession is an important event that occurs only once every 20 to 30 years. On the other hand, revitalizing the firm, perhaps several times within a single generation, may be necessary to help survive to the next succession.

An owner-manager may become plateaued because of:

- boredom with the business (but cannot quit easily);
- lack of pressure to perform better;
- having worked in the same job for 3 to 4 decades; and/or
- other career interests that resurface.

The plateaued individual does not derive satisfaction from the business and seeks fulfilment through increased involvement with family, hobbies, and civic or church groups. Less time is devoted to the business, lower performance is expected from the employees, and the business ceases to grow.

The symptoms of a plateaued owner-manager are:

- Same product, same customers over a decade. Few industries are so stable that requirements do not change over a decade;
- Same key employees;
- Too much cash. One possible reason for the excess cash may be a lack of new ideas; debt in such companies may be non-existent or small.

Some methods to deal with plateauing are:

- Take a break from the business and use the time to visit similar companies in different areas of the country or to attend executive seminars;
- Establish a board of advisors to serve as committed listeners, friendly co-pilots, supporters, and moderators;

- Hire a new employee to provide new ideas. This also provides the owner with a mentoring opportunity which may bring back the lost excitement;
- A percentage of current earnings can be allocated to development of new businesses.

The concept of a plateaued owner-manager is antithetical to the image of an energetic entrepreneur. This behaviour is difficult to detect because the affluent firm is able to tolerate the behaviour for extended periods. This is a personal phenomenon; advisers need to develop close relationships with the individuals before addressing the problem because the individual may be offended at the suggestion of its presence.

Key words: Plateauing of owner-managers, Revitalization of family business, Advisory boards, Sabbatical for owner-managers.

MANDELBAUM, L. (1994). **Small business succession: The educational potential.** *Family Business Review,* 7(4): 369-376.

Sample: 57 small business owners (Response rate - 20%)
Data collection: Mailed questionnaires, a focus group discussion with professionals
Data analyses: Frequencies, percentages

Key points:

The barriers to succession planning, and educational programs that could prove helpful in such planning, are examined by sending separate questionnaires to business owners with a succession plan (40 percent) and those without (60 percent).

The barrier to planning most frequently cited by both groups is a lack of time. 41 percent of the respondents without a plan cite business barriers only, 21 percent cite emotional barriers only, and 13 percent cite both business and emotional barriers.

Informational seminars are the most desired form of assistance cited by the respondents; assistance manuals and reasonably-priced professional assistance are other important tools. An effective education plan should explain the benefits of, and options for, succession planning, identify barriers to such planning, indicate sources of assistance, and estimate the cost of the options.

Key words: Succession planning - barriers, Modes of assistance.

MARCUS, G.E. (1991). **Law in development of dynastic families among American business elites: The domestication of capital and the capitalization of family.** *Family Business Review,* 4(1): 75-111.

Sample: 2 dynastic families of Galveston, Texas.
Data collection: Not mentioned.
Data analysis: Not mentioned

Key points:

Legal rules and instruments that are being used to adapt the family capital become an integral dimension of family relationships. This is because the legal arrangements define relationships, and specify rights and obligations, more authoritatively than the other sources of family authority. Therefore, the legal arrangements shape the tone and substance of extended family relationships. Moreover, wealth in the form of business capital is fundamentally an abstract, metaphysical phenomenon. Laws provide an objectified form of property as a set of relationships in a complex society.

Key words: Dynastic families - legal arrangements.

MARSHACK, K.J. (1993). **Coentrepreneurial couples: A literature review on boundaries and transitions among copreneurs.** *Family Business Review,* 6(4): 355-369.

A literature review on co-preneurs.

Key points:

Co-preneurs are defined as couples who share ownership of, commitment to, and responsibility for, a business. These couples represent a dynamic interaction of systems of love and work. Research suggests that:

- Equity rather than equality contributes to marital and personal satisfaction of dual career couples;
- These couples adhere to the traditional sex role orientations in the division of household labour and child care;
- The wife generally does more household chores and sacrifices her career ambitions to promote the husband's career, but there are high levels of satisfaction with this life style for wives;
- The husband also reports a high level of satisfaction, although he experiences high stress due to the challenge that comes with the traditional sex role encouraged by their life style;

- Some couples report that working together enhances their relationship.
  Some suggestions for future research are:
- Replicating dual career studies to determine if there are differences between dual career couples and co-preneurs in areas such as household labour, child care, power, and decision-making;
- Replicating studies of entrepreneurs to determine if there is a 'copreneurial personality';
- Designing the studies of co-preneurs to follow the principles of integrated systems;
- Comparing co-preneurs in home-based businesses with co-preneurs who work outside the home in how they manage the boundaries and transitions between personal relationship and business partnership.

Key words: Co-entrepreneurship, Equity and equality in family businesses, Boundary zone.

MARSHACK, K.J. (1994). **Copreneurs and Dual-Career Couples: Are they different?** *Entrepreneurship Theory and Practice,* 19(1): 49-69.

Sample: 60 couples: 30 co-preneur and 30 dual-career
Data collection: 3 mailed 24-item personal attribute questionnaires
Data analysis: Chi-squares, t-tests, percentages

Key points:

This is a comparison of co-preneur couples with dual-career couples in terms of sex-role orientation, self-concept at work and home, and marital and business partnership equity. Co-preneurs are married couples who are 'full-time partners in their own business or professional practice. They share ownership, commitment, and responsibility for their enterprise'. Dual-career couples are 'currently engaged in full-time work in their respective careers'. The findings are as follows:

- Co-preneurs are quite traditional in their sex-role orientations, while dual-career couples are more androgynous. Husbands are the leaders both at work and at home, while wives are the support persons in co-preneurial families. Dual-career couples are leaders at work. They are 'more focused, formal, task-oriented, active, extroverted, and serious. At home they move from their unilateral leader role to a more bilateral sharing of power with their spouses';
- Regardless of their division of labour, both co-preneurs and dual-career couples are satisfied as married and business partners. The author interprets this as an indication that they consider the distribution of work equitable.

Co-preneurial couples can make use of their strong family values and follow the pattern of relationship adopted by dual-career couples. This adaptation enables them to divide work assignments according to talent rather than to gender, and will lead to healthier succession planning and opportunities for all family members willing to work in the family firms.

Key words: Dual-career couples, Copreneurs, Work-family boundaries, Women in family firms.

MASTROMARCO, D.R. (1992). **The family owned business in tax policy debates.** *Family Business Review,* 5(2): 191-200.

An article discussing 3 of the most significant federal initiatives from 1989-1992 affecting the family businesses.

Key points:

In this article three U.S. federal initiatives are discussed in great detail.

- Section 2036(c) eliminates estate freezes as a technique to reduce tax liability and transfer future appreciation of business to a successor.
- Section 1361 sets a single-class-of-stock requirement for subchapter S corporations.
- Chapter 14 focuses on the method for valuing intra-family transfers.

A look at these initiatives confirms that policy-makers do not recognize the attributes of family owned businesses, their mode of operation, and their unique contributions. Laws and regulations developed in a vacuum have a negative effect on the family businesses.

Key words: Estate freeze, Inter-generational asset transfer, Legal advise.

MATHILE, C.L. (1988). **A business owner's perspective on outside boards.** Family Business Review, 1(3): 231-237.

A conceptual article.

Key points:

The author discusses the advantages of outsiders on a board of directors, the reason why outsiders should serve on a family firm board, and characteristics that family firm owners should look for in an outside board member. An outside board of directors can be very useful for a closely held company for a variety of reasons:

- It can act as the inside sparring partner who tests the owners' perceived strengths and weaknesses before they get to the main arena, i.e., the marketplace;
- They have nothing to win or lose by telling the owners the truth about business plans/strategies, key employees, and excessive salaries that are draining the company;
- The owner manager of a closely held company can be very lonely and unsure of the decisions he/she makes. The board can help reduce the loneliness and increase objectivity.

Helping others is the prime reason for outside directors to serve. Characteristics to look for in outside directors are:

- Risk taking peers, i.e., those engaged in a similar position as owner-manager;
- High degree of honesty and integrity proven in past business dealings;
- Functional strengths needed by the firm;
- Compatibility with the owner manager, i.e., there should be mutual trust and respect;
- Compassion. This quality can be assessed during personal visits, e.g., how he/she treats his/her secretary, etc..

Key words: Outside board of directors - CEOs views, Advantages, Characteristics of board members, Compensation of outside directors, Selecting board members, Working with board members.

MATTHEWS, G.H. (1984). **Run your business or build an organization?** *Harvard Business Review,* 62(2): 34-44.

An article based on the author's experience as the founder and President of College Marketing group - a Massachussets-based supplier of mailing lists.

Key points:

By not delegating authority, the owner is tied to the job, an obligation that can be frustrating and create stress, job dissatisfaction, and burnout. The employees are not sufficiently challenged and do not learn to think or act for themselves. The result is that no successor is trained to take over the organization and, thus, the business has difficulty growing.

Effective delegation of authority is an art that requires practice, patience, experimentation, study, and trust. In order to start this process, one should resist the temptation to solve all problems. Instead, one should ask the employees to provide alternate solutions for problems at once; this helps to test the abilities of individuals. For the employees who do not prove capable of providing alternative solutions, the organization should be reorganized so that the incapable employees report to those who can provide specific guidance.

While delegating, a few points to be kept in mind are:

- Define goals succinctly;
- Select an individual for the task;
- Ask the delegate to suggest options regarding how the job could be done;
- Agree on the approach to be followed;
- Schedule and implement progress checkpoints, discussing the work in progress at these previously agreed upon checkpoints;
- Encourage delegates to summarize in writing the approach used, and provide recommendations for improvement.

Based on the capabilities of individual employees and the trust that the owner has in them, various levels of responsibility/authority can be laid out in an organization. For example:

- No responsibility except to do the job right; explain even the simplest jobs clearly, and check that they are understood correctly;
- Work out alternative solutions through discussions with the employee, but make the final decisions;
- Give pre-packaged decisions to the employee;
- Clearly define the responsibilities of the employee and ensure that he/she is informed of these responsibilities. Let him/her make the decisions, but ask to be kept informed;
- The responsibility and authority should rest with the employee; the owner should remove him/herself from the particular decision-making role of the employee. This is generally not recommended for small businesses, except when the owner is unwell or travelling. In those situations, encourage team work among decision-makers, but one individual should be left in-charge.

Key words: Delegating, Levels of responsibility.

MATTHEWS, G.H., D.P. VASUDEVAN, S.L. BARTON, & R. APANA (1994). **Capital structure decision-making in privately held firms: Beyond the finance paradigm.** *Family Business Review,* 7(4): 349-367.

A conceptual article.

Key points

This article brings together three different streams of literature to provide a model for understanding the capital structure decision in privately held firms. Specifically, research from strategic management (strategic choice), decision sciences (decision-making models), and social psychology (theory of reasoned action) are brought together to highlight the behavioral factors involved in capital structure decision-making for privately held firms.

The capital structure decisions are influenced by the firm owner's attitude toward debt. This attitude-capital structure decision-making is moderated by the decision maker's knowledge of the market, financial constraints, and organizational form. Attitude toward debt is a function of one's belief about debt, which in turn, is influenced by the individual's need for control, risk propensity, past experiences, social norms, and personal net worth. Based on this theory eight propositions are suggested that provide a foundation for future research.

Key words: Capital decision-making, Theory of reasoned action.

McCOLLOM, M. (1988). **Integration in the family firm: When the family system replaces controls and culture.** *Family Business Review,* 1(4): 399-417.

Sample: Case study (3 department stores owned by one family)
Data collection: Structured and unstructured observation and interviews
Data analysis: Qualitative analysis

Key points:

Using the open-systems model, wherein an organization is seen as sub-units with interdependent relationships, the family system can be the key integrating mechanism of a family firm, which in turn meets the needs of the family. The activities among system subunits must be coordinated and regulated to ensure the system's stability. In a family firm, the two subsystems of family and firm seek stability through reciprocal adjustments. The type of family, enmeshed or disengaged, influences the structure and processes of the business.

There may be a variety of combinations in which the two systems can achieve stability. For example, the combination of an enmeshed family and a differentiated work environment can achieve stability. As the business grows, different relationships may evolve between the two systems.

Key words: Family business system, Integrating mechanisms, System stability.

McCOLLOM, M. (1990). **Problems and prospects in clinical research on family firms.** *Family Business Review,* 3(3): 245-262.

Sample: Case study of a retail company (3 stores)
Data collection: Structured and unstructured observations and interviews
Data analysis: Qualitative and quantitative methods (details not mentioned)

Key points:

The author argues that clinical methods (qualitative research techniques) offer a distinct advantage for research in family firms. Family-owned businesses are different in fundamental ways from other businesses in terms of structure (complex), tasks (multiple), culture (emotionally competing), and roles (obscure). This is because the family and business systems overlap. Principles used in clinical methods are:

- The researchers' immersion in the system,
- Trust in relationships between researchers and system members,
- Participation of client system members in the research, and
- Self-scrutiny by researcher.

Because of these characteristics, clinical methods can provide intensive relationship research in family firms. Some problems with this research method are:

- Lack of control by the researcher,
- Over-involvement in the system,
- Role confusion, and
- Emotional involvement.

Three ways suggested to address these problems are:

- Develop an explicit and clear contract,
- Conduct research in teams,
- Be carefully trained in clinical methods and have access to family therapy expertise.

Key words: Methodological issues, Clinical methods.

McCOLLOM, M. (1992a). **Organizational stories in a family-owned business.** *Family Business Review,* 5(1): 3-24.

Sample: 565 organizational stories in 1 organization narrated by 48 individuals
Data collection: Structured and unstructured observations, informal conversations, formal interviews
Data analysis: Content analysis, intercoder reliability tests

Key points:

The author uses a specific form of narrative - stories (brief accounts of specific events) - to reveal how family and non-family employees experience membership in a family business system, i.e., how they perceive membership in the system, and illuminate the power relations. The purpose is to describe how the relations between the two systems of family and business are determined and maintained in daily interactions.

Stories told by employees focus on closeness to colleagues at work, frustration with management dysfunctions, difficulties in dealing with customers, and unworthy co-workers. They reflect both positive and negative feelings for family members, and a clear dominance and power of these members. In contrast, the stories of family members focus on security issues and frustration with incompetent employees.

Key words: Methodological issues, Family business sub-system, Narratives, Stories.

McCOLLOM, M. (1992b). **The ownership trust and succession paralysis in the family business.** *Family Business Review,* Summer, 5(2): 145-160.

A case study of a 25 million dollar construction company in New Hampshire (based on a consulting assignment)

Key points:

A trust is a legal entity created by an individual to hold property for the current or future benefit of others, thus separating ownership of the property from its use. In the family business, a trust helps reduce taxes, supports family members with business revenues, and runs the business on a temporary basis until family successors are able to take over. However, a badly designed trust agreement can limit the family business system from functioning productively. By illustrating the ill effects of trust formation in a construction company, the author stresses the importance of two elements in a trust:

- Flexibility - The more flexibility written into a trust, the better it is. If not carefully designed, trust and business can be fundamentally at odds on the key dimension of risk-taking. If the trust agreement constrains management from making decisions that will help business grow, it is not meeting its intended use;
- The emotional consequences that may be caused by the elegantly designed technical solutions to the legal, tax, and financial problems of a family business should be given considerable importance.

Key words: Trust in family businesses, Succession paralysis, Legal advice.

McGIVERN, C. (1989). **The dynamics of management succession: A model of chief executive succession in the small family firm.** *Family Business Review,* 2(4): 401-411.

2 case studies (a merchant co. & furniture manufacturing business)

Key points:

In 1971 Merrett-Cytrax Associates revealed that, in the UK, management succession and financial failure are the top two equal causes of firms ceasing to exist as independent organizations. Dun & Bradstreet (1972) calculated that, in the USA, 45 percent of all business failures are caused by appointing incompetent managers to the chief executive position. Management thinkers have not identified the complete set of variables that exist in all succession situations and that have predictable effects. Any serious attempt to deal with succession must apply contingency theory, which suggests that when designing a strategy to cope with particular succession problems, the main variables affecting the situation must be identified, and the ways by which they influence the process worked out.

Succession issues can occur at different stages of development in different companies.

1. *Dormant stage*: Succession is not a live issue;
2. *Stage 1*: The need to replace the CEO some time in the foreseeable future is recognized and a debate over whether to continue the business or sell it begins.
3. *Stage 2*: A decision has been taken to appoint someone some time (perhaps unspecified) in the future. The problems that must be solved within this period are the training of the successor, his/her designation, preparation of employees and other family members, and the retirement process of the outgoing chief executive;
4. *Stage 3*: The formal succession has happened. The successor must actually take control, introduce changes, and handle the outgoing executive's influence.

5 important groups of variables that influence the succession are:

- The five stages reached in the firm's development:
    1. Initiation - Exploiting ideas,
    2. Development - Maintaining and developing the business,
    3. Growth - Growing, stable organizational structure whose activities need coordinating,
    4. Maturity - Effective maintenance of status quo, or
    5. Decline - Need to find successor/organizer.
- Motivation of owner-manager;
- Extent of family domination;
- Organizational climate within the firm; and
- Business environment.

A model of succession in the small family firm is used to illustrate these groups of variables.

Key words: Succession planning.

McGOLDRICK, M. & J.G. TROAST (1993). **Ethnicity, families, and family businesses: Implications for practitioners.** *Family Business Review,* 6(2): 283-300.

An article based on consulting experiences.

Key points:

This article provides some insights into the:

- interaction patterns (communication patterns, handling of conflicts and differences, organizational structure, and influence of outsiders);
- involvement (loyalty, independence, and gender roles);
- management succession;
- ownership.

Understanding these issues can be important for all those involved in a family business.

Irish: In this community, relationships are not discussed openly. Conflicts and resentments are allowed to linger. This can cause serious problems for succession. Family members are silently cut off from each other. During transition, the roles and responsibilities are divided according to the capabilities of each child, although the parents' favourite may be given more. For outsiders, it is best to approach each individual of the family, build some trust and understanding of the family dynamics, and then bring the family together.

African-Americans: In this community, there is a highly developed ability to understand non-verbal messages and contexts of speech, but there is also a strong mistrust of outsiders. Thrift, loyalty, and shared responsibility are at the core of their relationships; a large number of family members are brought in. Succession is a low priority issue in these businesses, as the purpose of the business is to promote upward mobility of family members.

Jews: Jews have open, democratic relationships with a high value placed on reasoning and verbal explanations. When resolving conflicts, they are direct and believe in talking things out. They value loyalty, success, intellectual ability, and achievement. Women are encouraged to participate in business.

Italian-Americans: Communication in this community is ritualistic and there are no problems dealing with and understanding emotions. There are clear values of right and wrong and the family is given priority over all else. Women's roles are clearly defined and centred around family. It is common to name the eldest son as the successor but to leave equal shares for other children. Quite often daughters are given other assets but no share in the business.

Anglo-Americans: In this community, the children are brought up to be independent. Convention and fairness reign supreme. Business is usually passed on to the eldest son and shares are divided among the others.

Key words: Ethnicity, Italians in family business, Jews in family business, Anglo-Saxons in family business, African American in family business, Irish in family business.

MILLER, E.J. & A.K. RICE (1988). **The family business in contemporary society.** *Family Business Review,* 1(2): 193-210.

A conceptual article.

Key points:

The primary task of the family is different from that of the business. This creates conflicts and dilemmas generic to the family business. The unconscious basic assumptions of the family frequently produces behaviour that interferes with the adaptability of a business. The family business makes demands that may be difficult to fulfil in modern conditions. These difficulties are:

- A distinguished name can be a handicap to a family successor. Many will assume that he got his job because of his name, and not because of his qualifications;
- Some enlightened families make a conscious attempt not to put pressure on members to take roles in the family business and applaud their success in other fields. The parents' feeling of disappointment, however, is often detectable if the children do not join the family firm. Success in other fields is frequently taken to imply that, if those who succeed outside are less selfish, they could have made a valuable contribution to what is essential to the family - the business. This causes grief and guilt;
- Members who join the family firm have no external criteria to judge themselves;
- A family business that requires male members as top level executives in business creates pressure for the family to produce male babies;
- In a family business, the internal non-competitive culture of the family, and the external reality of competition, are frequently incompatible;
- The business requires more capital and skill than a family can provide. Family businesses often face the conflict about allocation of profits, i.e., reinvest or pay dividends to family members;
- Family business is a climate in which established relationships are more important than performance. Employees who stay in a family business may be

those who expect to be looked after, not only when they are at the height of their powers; but also when they grow older and no longer hold significant roles or powers.

Mechanisms for dealing with the difficulties of family businesses include:

- Introduction of sons-in-law;
- Examine the tasks carried out by the family sentient group and devise an appropriate organization for each, e.g., separation of ownership and management roles.

The authors conclude that a modern industrial enterprise can survive as a family business only with the most exceptional families.

Key words: Family business sub-system, Problems of family business, Mechanisms to deal with problems, Future of family business.

MINTZBERG, H. & J.A. WATERS (1990). **Tracking strategy in an entrepreneurial firm.** *Family Business Review,* 3(3): 285-315.

Sample: Case study of Steinberg Inc. in Montreal (1917-1974)
Data collection: Interviews, organizational records, personal records
Data analysis: Content analysis, inferring the patterns, graphs and bar charts

Key points:

Strategy is 'a pattern in a stream of decisions'; it is consistency in the behaviour of an organization. These consistencies render the concept of strategy operational for the researchers. The search for strategy-making becomes a search for consistencies in decision-making behaviour, the investigation of their appearance and disappearance, and the analysis of intended and realized strategies.

By collecting information on the major events (turning points) of a company that grew from a tiny fruit and vegetable store in Montreal's ethnic area in 1917 to sales of over $1 billion in 1974 with 191 supermarkets, 32 department stores, 33 catalog stores, 119 small restaurants, 15 pharmacies, and other establishments, the authors chart out the different strategies used by the company.

The company went through the entrepreneurial and planning mode, although it stayed in the entrepreneurial mode for a longer time. The study found the existence of entrepreneurial ownership and management in the firm. The entrepreneurial mode was effective as long as the owner-manager knew the firm's operations intimately. Decisions could be based on his vision and intuition. In this mode the structure followed strategy. Strategy-making was an interplay between a leader and the environment. The leader reacted pro-actively to the environment and kept the structure lean and flexible to adapt to any changes in the environment.

Once the operations spread beyond the comprehension of one man, a decentralized, more analytic, but less flexible, less integrated, less visionary, and less deliberate mode of strategy arose. Eventually strategy, to some extent at least, had to follow structure, as well as environment.

The authors feel that the literature on strategy formation is in great need of an operational definition of planning. Is planning 'future thinking' (which this company was always doing) or an exercise carried out by the planners (in the case described, planning had nothing to do with strategy formation)? At Steinberg's planning was never really strategy-formation, it was programming. It involved justifying, elaborating, and making public a strategy it already had - the one based on the leader's vision. The plan articulated, quantified, and elaborated the vision.

They tentatively conclude that when a company's intended strategy is based on the owner's vision, the company plans in order to give form to the vision, for the sake of formalized structure and environmental expectations. Planning operationalizes strategy. However, by keeping his vision personal, the entrepreneur can adapt it at will to the changing environment. When he/she is forced to articulate and program the vision, flexibility is lost. Thus, planning forces out the entrepreneurial mode, procedure replaces vision, and strategy making becomes more an extrapolation than an intervention. When the vision is absent, planning extrapolates the status quo, leading to marginal changes in practice. Two points brought out in this discussion are:

- In the entrepreneurial mode, planning is programming a given strategy rather than formulating a new one;
- The planning mode is an inevitable result of the organization's growth and development of a more formalized structure.

In this company, which achieved unprecedented growth in its earlier years, the owner-manager retained absolute control of the company till his death. After his death, legal battles for control of the company embroiled the family members. The company was eventually sold to an outside investor.

Key words: Entrepreneurial mode, Planning mode, Succession planning.

MUELLER, R.K. (1988). **Differential directorship: Special sensitivities and roles for serving the family business board.** *Family Business Review,* 1(3): 239-247.

A conceptual article.

Key points:

Outside directors bring distinct advantages for the family business but they must deal with special sensitivities. The benefits they yield are:

- Objectivity to provide preventive maintenance and keep the business on course;

- Help in prioritizing issues and providing escape from insider thinking;
- Arbitration in case of family conflicts and disagreements;
- Expertise to fill gaps in the owner's experience or qualifications;
- Individuals with whom the owner can share concerns, hopes, desires, and talk confidentially;
- Credibility to the firm by their association with it;
- Provocation for the firm to make significant changes;
- Enlargement of the firm's corporate network;
- Objectivity to deal with emotional issues such as estate planning; and
- Perspectives to watch out for the interests of all stakeholders, including employees, government bodies, environmentalists, community members, etc.

Despite the pressures, exposure, and emotional climate that can prevail on the boards of family firms, outsiders serve on family firm boards for the following reasons.

- Psychological rewards:
  - tackling strategic issues provides exhilaration;
  - ethics of service can be rewarding;
  - serving on an effective board can provide self-confidence, sense of identity, and power to one's psyche.
- Material rewards:
  The pay and perquisites received for giving advice can be significant.

Key words: Advantages of outside directors, Compensation of outside directors.

MURDOCK, M. & C.W. MURDOCK (1991). **A legal perspective on shareholder relationships in family businesses: The scope of fiduciary duties.** *Family Business Review,* 4(3): 287-301.

A legal perspective on shareholders' relationships in family businesses, especially the position of minority shareholders.

Key points:

The situations that generally lead to legal problems in the family business are:

- Two players with equal share-holding and a dead-lock; and
- Two or more players with a minority player claiming unfair treatment.

When disputes arise, the response of the courts follows the following principles:

- *Duty-of-care and the business judgement rule*: Those in control can argue that their actions are in the best interest of the corporation. The business judgement rule protects their actions as long as no duty-of-care toward the plaintiff has been breached. The plaintiff has the burden of proof, which is very difficult to establish;

- *Duty-of-loyalty and self-dealing*: This implies that corporate directors will not use the property under their control for personal benefits. For a disgruntled shareholder this is a more fertile approach. The main benefit for the minority shareholder is that this may stop the majority shareholders from benefiting themselves to the detriment of the corporation. It may also give the minority shareholder some leverage to negotiate a buy-out at a reasonable price.
- *Fiduciary duties for controlling shareholders*: Since the mid 70s, the courts have alluded to the existence of a fiduciary duty of fairness owed by the majority or controlling shareholders toward minority shareholders. In this case, when a minority shareholder alleges a breach of fiduciary duty by the majority, the majority shareholder is entitled to demonstrate that it had a legitimate business purpose for its actions. Even then, the minority shareholder can demonstrate that the majority's business purpose could have been achieved by an alternative less harmful to the minority shareholder. While this has greatly improved the position of the minority, he/she is still exposed to further wrongful conduct in the future.
- *Dissolution or exit strategy*: The statutes in most states permit a court to dissolve a corporation when actions of those in control are illegal, oppressive, or fraudulent. When a corporation is dissolved, its assets are sold, creditors are paid off, and the equity is distributed to the shareholders. However, the minority shareholder must be able to convince the court that:
    - the conduct of the majority is oppressive,
    - the dissolution is a necessary 'drastic remedy', and
    - he/she will realize value upon dissolution equivalent to the value of the live corporation as a going concern.
- *Development of alternative remedies and the recognition of 'reasonable expectations'*: In the 70s, the courts began dealing with the concern that dissolution was a drastic remedy and looked for alternatives. An alternative used is for the court to order a corporation or controlling shareholders to buy out the complaining minority shareholder.

The reasonable expectations test focuses not on the wrongdoing of the party, but on the basis of the bargain between the parties (explicit or implicit), and on its fulfilment. The courts have to determine what the expectations of the parties were at the time they associated themselves with each other. In most cases in family businesses, these understandings are not worked out properly and are not in writing. The authors suggest that family business consultants should insist on written agreements covering the firm's mission and issues related to management, succession, compensation, ownership, and family member employment and responsibilities. The real product of designing these statements is the process that leads to clarification and forestalls litigation. It is better for family business professionals to work at the front end, than for the legal professionals to work at the back end.

Key words: Legal advice.

NASH, J.M. (1988). **Boards of privately held companies: Their responsibility and structure.** *Family Business Review,* 1(3): 263-369.

A conceptual article.

Key points:

The author was the president of the National Association of Corporate Directors. In the article he describes the advantages of boards and the duties and responsibilities of board members.

Advantages of a board:

- For a small fee, directors are available for consultation virtually 24 hours a day, which is not true of consultants;
- Experienced outside directors can save the owners considerable time and energy by helping them to avoid pitfalls;
- They can review the important decisions, without being immersed in day-to-day operations;
- A good board enhances a firm's credibility with its customers, suppliers, bankers, etc.;
- A good board can act as an arbitrator in family conflicts or in dealing with hostile interests;
- Outside board members can provide advice and expertise that are not available in-house;
- In case of an owner's death, a board helps to provide continuity and preservation of firm with minimal turmoil.

A few points discussed regarding the working of boards are:

- The composition of a board depends on the particular needs and circumstances of each firm. However, NACD's experience suggests that 5-9 directors in a board form an effective group for most firms. In a seven member board, four outsiders and three insiders is a good mix;
- Boards can be assisted by committees, the type and number depending on the firm's needs;
- The chairman is responsible for setting agendas for board meetings and seeing that all members receive information and feedback. Though in smaller companies the CEO or the president generally acts as chairman, it is helpful to have an outside board member to act as chairman;
- Individual members have no authority in any board; authority rests with the full board;
- In order to be effective, members must receive adequate communication.

Although an advisory board has been recommended in the literature, this author suggests the need for a legally constituted board. He argues that because the advisory board has no power or authority, the CEO may not heed its advice.

Key words: Advantages of a board, Functioning of board, Advisory boards, Characteristics of board members, Legal requirements of board members.

NAVIN, T.R. (1971). **Passing on the mantle.** *Business Horizons*, 14(5): 83-93.

Sample: 105 companies
Data collection: Historical analysis
Data analysis: Qualitative analysis

Key points:

The study examines the process by which top management evolved in 105 companies. Most companies follow five stages of development, although the duration of time spent in each stage varies. These stages are:

1. *Initiator* - The entrepreneur starts the business;
2. *Founder* - The enterprise takes a viable form under an individual who is not necessarily the initiator, but is often a member of the original team;
3. *Founder's heirs* - The company becomes highly successful and the founder appoints a second-in-command who may be the heir or the surrogate heir;
4. *Technicians* - After existence for 40 to 50 years, the company comes to the end of the "founder's heirs" experience. At this stage the organization becomes institutionalized. The president appears to be making the decisions, but he/she is strongly influenced by the executive group. Usually the person chosen has been the head of the most prestigious department for some time, is not a young man, and generally has no overall management experience. The tenure is likely short and not very successful.
5. *Professional managers* - Very few firms reach this stage. A professional manager has a business degree, broad experience in another industry, has spent a decade in the present organization, has headed a profit centre or an independent unit in the present company, and has some experience with government relations.

Key words: Organizational life-cycle stages.

OWEN, A.J., M.L. CARSKY, & E.M. DOLAN (1993). **Home-based employment: Historical and current considerations.** *Family Business Review,* 6(4): 437-451.

A conceptual article.

Key points:

The authors present a conceptual model for family work activities. They suggest that any study of home-based work should begin with recognition of the differences in work styles, family goals and opportunities, the nature of the work, and the work environment. Important variables are:

- *Nature-of-work variables.* These include variables such as the form of employment, skill level, location, and absorptiveness (level of concentration required, level of family commitment required, etc.).
- *Work environment variables.* These variables include those components of work associated with quantitative aspects of resource allocations and of projected outcomes, such as time, space, remuneration, rewards, family paradigms (family's image of itself).

Key words: Home-based businesses, Women in family business, Review article, Research framework on home-based businesses.

OWEN, A.J. & M. WINTER (1991). **Research note: The impact of home-based business on family life.** *Family Business Review,* 4(4): 425-432.

Sample: 899 households
Data collection: Telephone interviews (2)
Data analysis: Factor analysis, regression analysis

Key points:

The hypotheses about how the functionings of the family and the business are intertwined in the home-based business are:

1. Women are less disrupted by home-based business than men. Households with fewer or older children are less disrupted than those with either more or younger children. (Supported).
2. Higher-income businesses generate less perceived disruption because family members understand that the business contributes to their economic welfare and, therefore, view it more positively. (Not supported).
3. The longer a family business has operated, the less perceived disruption because the family has increased opportunity to get used to it and incorporates business obligations into everyday life. (Not supported).

4. Family businesses that require more family members' time are more disruptive. (Supported).
5. Those that use established managerial techniques for home life and for the business perceive less disruption, as such techniques assist in anticipating and avoiding difficulties and in solving problems as they arise. (Supported).
6. Marketing and agricultural workers perceive the most disruption because of the seasonality of their work. (Supported).

The results indicate that the age of the business, revenues from the business, and the hours worked are positively related to the perception of family disruption. Success in financial terms may be more disruptive to a family.

Key words: Home-based businesses, Family business sub-system, Women in family business.

PEISER, R.B. & L.M. WOOTEN (1983). **Life cycle changes in small family businesses.** *Business Horizons,* 26(3): 58-65.

A conceptual article.

Key points:

There are three stages in a small business' life cycle: survival, success, and take-off. Life cycle crisis precipitates when goals of two generations collide. Symptoms of this are increased interpersonal conflicts, attention to short term profits rather than long term growth, no defined process to integrate new family members, and difficulty in valuing diverse contributions of family members.

When a firm goes through a life cycle change, the family goes through a change too; an outsider may help in disseminating the information kept in the entrepreneur's head. The clean-up process should start with carefully delineating responsibility and accountability, and designing mechanisms to reduce the first generation's authority. Procedures need to be explicitly defined when more family members join the business or when the business grows. Mechanisms for solving management problems and defining the responsibility of each family member in clear, realistic, and time bound terms becomes important.

Key words: Inter-generational conflicts, Organizational life-cycle stages, Project oriented industries, Consulting.

PERRIGO, A.E.B. (1975). **Delegation and succession in the small firms.** *Personnel Management,* May: 35-37.

A conceptual article.

Key points:

Delegation of authority is by far the most difficult problem for owner-managers of small firms, and succession is an important step in the process of delegation. With growth, an owner-manager preoccupied with the firm's day-to-day affairs will ignore long term planning. As new managers join the firm, the owner-manager must adopt a relationship-oriented style of leadership by delegating responsibilities. Many owners confess that they are afraid subordinates will not do the jobs as well as they do, an opinion that arises from an inflated view of their performance relative to others. Moreover, they need to keep in mind that delegation is required to let them do more important things for the firm, not for the purpose of finding someone who does the delegated job better than they.

Key words: Delegation, Succession.

PETTKER, J.D. & A.D. CROSS (1989). **The new anti-freeze law: A meltdown for the family firm?** *Family Business Review,* 2(2): 153-172.

Legal advice regarding transfer of ownership to the next generation.

Key points:

A new section 2036(c), the anti-freeze law, has been added to the Internal Revenue Code. This changes the tax consequences of many transactions intended to pass all, or a portion of, a family business to the next generation. This new law expands the circumstances under which an estate or gift tax will be retroactively imposed on portions of a business that have already been transferred away.

The new anti-freeze law has four components (tests) all of which need to be satisfied for the law to be applied.

- *Substantial interest test*: A transferor must hold a substantial (10 percent or more) interest in the enterprise;
- The transferor must make a transfer of a property interest in the enterprise either to a family member, in which event this test is satisfied even if the recipient pays full value for the property transferred, or to a non-family member, if the transferee does not pay full value for the property transferred.
- The property transferred must have a disproportionately large share of the potential appreciation in the transferor's interest in the enterprise.

- *The retained interest test*: The transferor, after the transfer, must retain an interest in the income of, or rights in, the enterprise other than in an interest protected as a safe harbour exception.

When all these tests are satisfied, and if at the transferor's death the transferee still owns the original property transferred, the transferred property is taxed in the transferor's estate. This law, its intricacies, and possible strategies for passing along the family business are discussed in great detail.

Key words: Anti-freeze law, Tax advice, Transfer of ownership, New anti-freeze law, Legal advice.

PONTHIEU, L.D. & H.L. CAUDILL (1993). **Who's the boss? Responsibility and decision-making in copreneurial ventures.** *Family Business Review,* 6(1): 3-17.

Sample: 184 respondents (80 male and 104 female, Response rate - 28%)
Data collection: Questionnaires
Data analysis: Factor analysis, MANOVA, t-tests, regression analysis

Key points:

While the husbands tend to be the primary decision-makers, wives are equal partners since these relationships are based on a clear division of responsibility, mutual trust, and confidence. Financial decisions, however, are made jointly by the couple. Though the husbands report confidence in their wives' decision-making ability, the wives do not believe that their spouses trust them. The males tend to be dominant at work but neither claims dominance at home.

Key words: Co-preneurship.

POST, J.E. (1993). **The greening of the Boston Park Plaza hotel.** *Family Business Review,* 6(2): 131-148.

A case study describing the greening of Boston Park Plaza Hotel (Saunders family).

Key points:

The case study demonstrates the harmony that can be created between economic success, family success, and social responsibility. The owners were looking to find a way to be environmentally friendly and save money too. A green team consisting of the owners and 25 employees from various departments of the hotel was formed to discuss various implementable ideas of greening. Customers were involved and educated as part of the program.

The business lessons learned from this case are:

- Environmental responsibility need not mean less service or lower quality;
- A long term perspective is essential when integrating environmental initiatives into business practices;
- Top management commitment is required, but words alone are not sufficient;
- Communication and creative thinking are vital to any major change program;
- Recognition of and reward for employees' efforts are essential;
- The environmental program must become a core element in the management approach if it is to take root in a business.

The case study shows how the values, the interests, and the needs of a family can be integrated into the strategies, missions, and operations of a hotel business.

Key words: Environmental friendliness, Strategic planning.

POST, J.M. & R.S. ROBINS (1993). **The captive king and his captive court: The psychopolitical dynamics of the disabled leader and his inner circle.** *Family Business Review,* 6(2): 203-221.

Sample: 40 case studies of political leaders ailing while in seat of power.
Data collection: Documented records, diaries of physicians and advisors, medical records, public media
Data analysis: Qualitative factor analysis

Key points:

When a leader is ill, there are contradictions between the requirements for patient comfort and those of leader competence. Four major factors associated with the effect of disability upon the relationship between the leader and his inner circle are listed below:

- *Factors associated with the disease*:
    - suddenness of the disease,
    - course of the disease,
    - degree of disability, and
    - type of psychiatric illness.
- *Factors involving the leader and his reactions to his illness*:
    - the leader's political power,
    - the leader's personality and acceptance of mortality;

  - the leader's awareness or denial of his illness, and
  - interaction between the partially disabled leader and his inner circle.
- *Factors in the social and political environment that affect the political functioning of the ailing leader*:
  - existence of well established procedures for transfer of power,
  - availability of alternative leaders,
  - scrutiny from public media,
  - environmental demands on the leader.
- *Medical management of the ailing leader.*

Key words: Ailing leader.

POZA, E.J. (1988). **Managerial practices that support interpreneurship and continued growth.** *Family Business Review,* 1(4): 339-359.

A conceptual article based on author's observations and consulting assignments.

Key points:

A business is interpreneuring when it organizes to revitalize the business just prior to, or during the tenure of, the next generation. Measures to help set the stage for interpreneurial activity include:

- *Strategic explorations*: Strategic analysis and planning force the next generation to envision the future and to sometimes increase the entrepreneurial propensity of the founder. It is important for the second generation to frame interpreneurial efforts as a natural progression that builds on the founder's legacy and acknowledges the contribution that the founder has made.
- *Organizational change and development*: Changes in strategy are often accompanied by changes in structure, and vice versa. Innovative changes in structure can be made to help institutionalize the process of growth. Steering committees, asset boards, outside boards, in-house management education for family members, hiring of non-family professionals, and venture review boards can all be used to promote continued growth.
- *Financial restructuring*: Options available for financial restructuring include: real estate trusts, preferred stock, stock swaps, buy-sell agreements, private annuities, instalment sales, limited partnerships, family capital corporations, and employee stock option plans.
- *Family system change*: Reaching a consensus among family members, the board, and the firm on what is a desirable future for the firm, and how to get there, is important for any interpreneurial activity.

  Obstacles to interpreneurship include:

- Absence of growth vision on the part of both the preceding and the following generation;
- Distance from customers, employees, operations, and competition;
- Short term focus;
- High overhead;
- Perception of high social image risk;
- Obsession with data and logic; and
- Inappropriate boundaries between management, owners, and interpreneurs.

Intervention strategies include:

- Diversification or specialization;
- Formation of a venture capital firm or a new venture division within the existing business;
- Task and business teams;
- Reward systems changes;
- Information system changes;
- Ownership structure changes; and
- Human relations policies.

The choice of intervention strategies will have to be guided by the business and family cultures as well as the firm's technical and marketing expertise.

Key words: Interpreneurship, Strategic planning, Diversification, Innovation, Organizational change, Growth barriers, Intervention strategies to increase growth.

PRINCE, R.A. (1990). **Family business mediation: A conflict resolution model.** *Family Business Review,* 3(3): 209-223.

Sample: 18 law firms
Data collection: Not mentioned
Data analysis: Not mentioned

Key points:

Family firm disputes can cripple the firm. Methods for resolving interpersonal conflict include:

- *Litigation*: This sets family members against each other and severely damages the business. Moreover, litigation is often a time consuming and costly process.
- *Binding arbitration*: This method has two drawbacks in the family business situation. Not all parties may agree to binding arbitration. Arbitration imposes a solution and an imposed solution generally generates animosity.

- *Mediation*: This is less destructive and often strengthens both the business and family relationships.
  What makes mediation different are the following:
- The mediator is impartial.
- The mediation process is voluntary.
- Confidentiality is maintained when appropriate.
- The mediator has considerable procedural flexibility.

Moreover, in mediation the past only provides background material. The process is oriented toward present and future. The objective of mediation is not to alleviate deep-seated psychological conflicts, but to resolve specific substantive issues under dispute. The mediator functions primarily as a facilitator and a catalyst to enable concessions without loss of face to either party.

The stages of mediation process are:

1. *Issue identification*: In this stage the mediator adopts a passive stance and solicits information, attempts to sift facts from rhetoric. Next, the issues are identified and the parties made to agree to an agenda. Compliance with an initial small request can dramatically increase the likelihood of compliance with a more demanding request in future.
2. *Negotiations*: In this stage, the mediator becomes more assertive as the exchange of proposals and counter proposals take place.
3. *Formalization of agreement*: The concerned family members must fully understand and agree with the decisions made. Conditions of agreement must be explicit and unambiguous.

Key words: Litigation, Arbitration, Mediation, Family conflicts.

RAPPAPORT, A. (1995). **Farm women as full-time partners: Some evidence of sharing traditional gender-based tasks.** *Family Business Review,* 8(1): 55-63.

Sample: 632 married male respondents of farm families, 592 respondents' wives' work off the farm, 40 respondents' wives work full-time on the farms

Data collection: Survey conducted by *Farm Futures* magazine, Circulation 205,000 (0.3% response rate)

Data analyses: Percentages, chi-square version of the Kolomogorov-Smirnov two-sample test

Key points:

Full-time partner wives do not assume dominant responsibility for any decision or task area on the farm, but they have a greater role in some operating decisions as compared to wives who work off the farms. In terms of household tasks, husbands who consider their wives as full-time partners share a higher number of home tasks, although the primary responsibility for these tasks rest with the wives.

Key words: Farm families, Women in family firms.

ROGAL, K.H. (1989). **Obligation or opportunity: How can could-be heirs assess their position?** *Family Business Review,* 2(3): 237-255.

An article based on author's experiences as a potential heir.

Key points:

Owners need training to evaluate and plan their succession and heirs need training to evaluate and plan their accession. The characteristic overlapping boundaries of management, ownership, and family can cause heirs to confuse family obligation with business opportunity or, conversely, spurn potential emotional or investment gain because of familial discord.

Could-be heirs should engage in a pre-decision period of systematic soul-searching, perform a rigorous and disciplined self-analysis, analyze career alternatives, and hold discussions with family members and other experts before making the decision to join the family firm.

Key words: Next generation, Accession.

ROSENBLATT, P.C. (1991). **The interplay of family system and business system in family farms during economic recession.** *Family Business Review,* 4 (1): 45-57.

Sample: 42 adults from 24 Minnessota farm families
Data collection: Face-to-face and telephone interviews
Data analysis: Not mentioned

Key points:

In pursuance of family goals, family farms pay inadequate attention to the economies of inter-generational transfers. As a result, farms are expanded to make room for offspring and risky investments are made in farm land. This may have led to the increased vulnerability of family farms to economic recession in the mid-80s. Unpaid family help during the start up of family farms may have helped but, in general, meeting family goals has increased the vulnerability of farm families. Careful long range planning is required and expert advice can help.

Key words: Farm families, Inter-generational asset transfer, Strategic planning.

ROTHSTEIN, J. (1992). **Don't judge a book by it's cover: A reconstruction of eight assumptions about Jewish family businesses.** *Family Business Review,* 5(4): 397-411.

Sample: 45 Jewish sons in family businesses in Montreal, Canada
Data collection: Telephone conversations, structured interviews (2 hours)
Data analysis: Content analysis, percentages

Key points:

Eight assumptions regarding the Jewish family based on the experience of the author and others in Jewish families are tested in this study.

Assumption 1:

Jewish families have divorce and marital disruption rates similar to those of other groups in the general population. (98 percent of the sample are from intact families while 52 percent of marriages in the U.S. and Canada end in divorce).

Assumption 2:

Jewish men attain a college education before entering the family-owned business, probably majoring in business. (Over 75 percent of the respondents have some post-high school education. Most report that education is a vehicle to pay off a loyalty debt to their parents. However, only about 30 percent have business related degrees).

Assumption 3:

In choosing to continue their education, Jewish men have the opportunity to leave home and experience some independence. (87 percent of the respondents stay with their parents. Family togetherness is so strong in Jewish families that Jewish children rarely leave home to attend university).

Assumption 4:

Conversations about higher education is an important part of family discussions and parents advise their children on the academic path. (100 percent of the respondents say that going to college is a given in their families but the details are rarely discussed. Respondents express a yearning for more real contact with their parents).

Assumption 5:

Sons who work with their fathers in family businesses have warm earliest memories of their fathers and report strong emotional support from their mothers during childhood. (The respondents' earliest memories are of a distant father and an overburdened mother).

Assumption 6:

Jewish children grow up with a strong value system in relation to school, family, loyalty, money, and work. (Despite the father's absence, his value system resonates throughout the home. This value system passes from one generation to another through family dinners, rituals, vacations, and storytelling).

Assumption 7:

All adolescents "act out", even Jewish sons who end up in their family businesses. (Only 25 percent of the respondents reported any serious "acting out").

Assumption 8:

Jewish sons who join the family business lack creativity and focus entirely on the business. (90 percent of the respondents are highly creative in their spare time. Those who see themselves as creative in their spare time do not perceive their work as a creative outlet).

Key words: Ethnicity, Jews in family businesses.

ROWE, B.R., G.W. HAYNES, & M.T. BENTLEY (1993). **Economic outcomes in family-owned home-based businesses.** *Family Business Review,* 6(4): 383-396.

Sample: 620 family-owned home-based business units.
Data collection: 2 telephone interviews (5mts and 30 mts)
Data analysis: Regression analysis, factor analysis, Cronbach Alpha

Key points:

Reasons for the increase in home-based businesses are:

- A shift in the national economy from an industrial base to an information and service base;
- Advanced telecommunication equipment makes possible the transfer of service-related work away from a centralized work site;
- Changes in family structure and allocation of work and family roles between men and women;
- That it now takes two workers in a family to maintain a decent standard of living;
- That it is a way to balance work demands and family responsibility particularly for women;
- The elimination of legal restrictions on work at home.

The census bureau reports 5.6 million home-based businesses in the U.S. in 1993. These businesses are generally proprietorships, with less start-up capital, fewer employees, lower cost of doing business, and less business income. Factors affecting profitability in home-based business are the characteristics of the owner and the features of the business. The results show that personal and family characteristics of owners are more important variables than features of the business.

Key words: Home-based businesses, Profitability.

RUSSELL, C.S., C.L. GRIFFIN, C.S. FLINCHBOUGH, M.J. MARTIN, & R.B. ATILANO (1985). **Coping strategies associated with inter-generational transfer of the family farm.** *Rural Sociology,* 50(3): 361-376.

Sample: 92 inter-generational farm families in Kansas state, (89 fathers, 91 mothers, 89 sons and 73 daughter in laws)
Data collection: Questionnaires
Data analysis: Factor analysis

Key points:

Coping strategies in inter-generational conflicts include individual coping, discussion, expression of anger, use of professionals, and farm management.
Individual coping and discussion are most often used by all family members. Daughters-in-law report using expression of anger most frequently. Mothers and fathers report using professionals. This reflects the basic values of rural America: self reliance (individual coping), family (discussion), and then community (professionals).

Mothers usually act as a bridge between father and son, while daughters-in-law report high stress due to their limited access to coping strategies or social support. Discussion is significantly associated with the well-being of the father, but negatively associated with the perceived ease of making transfer decisions. In general, the receiving generation appears to be more stressed than the parent generation.

Key words: Farm families, Inter-generational asset transfer, Inter-generational conflict, Coping mechanisms, Women in family businesses.

RUTIGLIANO, A.J. (1986). **Family businesses need help from outside.** *Management Review,* February: 26-27.

A conceptual article.

Key points:

Succession is more problematic when there is more than one heir. Rapidly growing firms have the ability to generate a new strategy with every generation coming into business. Outside board members should be appointed, three to four meetings should be held per year, and these members should be paid between 5 and 10 thousand dollars annually.

Key words: Strategic planning, Outside directors.

SALGANICOFF, M. (1990). **Women in family business: Challenges and opportunities.** *Family Business Review,* 3(3): 125-137.

Sample: 91 women in family businesses
Data collection: Questionnaires, Discussions during the course of a workshop
Data analysis: Percentages

Key points:

Women have particular qualities, such as sensitivity, compassion and caring, that can be of vital importance to the survival and success of family businesses. Family businesses provide a ripe ground for women to pursue their careers, as these businesses can provide them with flexible schedules, job security, and a chance to work in male-dominated industries. It is, therefore, to the mutual advantage of family businesses and women for the latter to join the former.

Family businesses should expose female as well as male family members in each generation to the business, and encourage early know-how and positive feelings for the business. Women and men who have an aptitude and interest in business should receive appropriate formal education and training. Women who think they want a career in the family firm should understand the possible conflicts, interpersonal dynamics, and power. It may be beneficial for them to work in other organizations before joining the family firm.

Key words: Women in family businesses, Succession planning.

SALOMON, R. (1977). **Second thoughts on going public.** *Harvard Business Review,* 55(5): 126-131.

An article based on the author's experience as a founder-owner of a cosmetics company, and his decision to go public.

Key points:

The author discusses the advantages and disadvantages of 'going public'. Some advantages are:

- Diversification of owners' assets,
- Ascertainable value for estate and inheritance taxes,
- Equity available as executive incentive,
- Equity available for acquisition and mergers,
- Personal satisfaction,
- Liquidity, and
- Increase in the possibility of realizing each of these advantages, while still holding absolute control.

Difficulties an owner-founder faces by going public are:

- Jealousy and bitterness among employees over the allocation of shares,
- Stock price becomes the chief concern and short-term results become important,
- Analysts, investors, and competitors start testing the business acumen of the owner-founder, and
- Pressure for maintaining the share prices and dividends constrains spending for long term growth of the company.

An entrepreneur should ask the following questions and weigh the advantages and disadvantages before making the decision to go public:

- Once the public becomes share-holding partners, can the owner resist their preoccupation with short-term results and/or fluctuations in the price of shares?
- Can the owner ignore the stock market's demand for consistent and constant increase in sales and earnings?
- Can the owner accept with grace and equanimity the public exposure of mistakes?

Key words: Going public.

SALOMON, S. & V LOCKHART (1980). **Land ownership and the position of elderly in farm families.** *Human Organization,* 39(4): 324-331.

Sample: 81 Germans and 91 Irish in rural Illinois
Data collection: Interviews, Observations
Data analysis: Z-test

Key points:

In a study of farming families in 2 communities (German and Irish), elders who maintain a future orientation and plan for transfer of holdings (German) tend to be able to maintain a rich and respectful family relationship.

Key words: Ethnicity, Farm families, German farm families, Irish in family business.

SCHAEFER, R. & J.A. DAVIS (1992). **Evaluation of auditor's going-concern risk in family business.** *Family Business Review,* 5(1): 63-75.

Advice for auditors of family businesses.

Key points:

The authors question the normal use of the "going-concern" concept when auditing a family business and believe that additional procedures are needed to ensure the financial statements' reliability. Below is a checklist of additional tests for auditors to evaluate the family firm's viability as a going-concern:

1. Has the company provided for leadership continuation? Have successors been chosen and trained?
2. Have ownership plans to move the business into the next generation been made?
3. Does the business have cash sources for what it may have to incur in case of death or illness?
4. Is the family prepared for the risks created by family investments?
5. To protect the business from failure, has the company set up checks and balances, such as a board nominated by outsiders to review major policy decisions?

Key words: Auditing, Succession planning, Outside board.

SCHEIN, E.H. (1983). **The role of the founder in creating organization culture.** *Organizational Dynamics,* 5(1): 13-28.

Three case studies

Key points:

Organization culture is the pattern of basic assumptions used to cope with the problems of external adaptation and internal integration. These basic assumptions are related to beliefs about human nature, the nature of human activity and human relationships, the nature of truth, and the organization's relationship to the environment. Assumptions that have worked in the past become part of the culture. The organization begins with the founder's assumptions and as it grows and learns from experience, the assumptions are modified. The founder or the leader uses various implicit and explicit ways to communicate these assumptions. Organization culture, in addition to political and power factors, are important in succession planning.

The key differences between owners and professional managers are that owners are more self-oriented, take long term view, consider the holistic organization, are more willing/able to take risks, are more intuitive and willing to pursue non-economic objectives, are more particularistic, are able to try new risky innovations, pay attention to the family ties, and are highly visible. Professionals, on the other hand, are more cautious, less loyal to the organization's original values, more concerned with short term performance, are often mistrusted, have a smaller stake in the company, have fewer privileges, can take risks but need the support of the owners, and are loyal to their professions.

Key words: Culture in family businesses, Succession planning, Founders versus managers.

SCHIPANI, C.A. & G.J. SIEDEL (1988). **Legal liability: The board of directors.** *Family Business Review,* 1(3): 279-285.

Legal advice regarding directors' liabilities.

Key points:

Directors have liabilities and should be aware of liability prevention techniques. These liabilities include:

1. *Duty of care*: Directors are required by statute to exercise care;
2. *Fiduciary duty*: Directors should not personally enter into a business transaction in which the corporation may be interested.

Liability prevention mechanisms include:

- Corporation must agree to indemnify directors for litigation expenses;
- Liability insurance;
- Use board of advisors instead of directors. However, advisors may be treated as directors for legal purposes;
- A director who concludes that the board is making an imprudent decision should dissent and make certain that the negative vote is recorded.

Key words: Directors' liabilities, Liability prevention mechanisms, Advisory boards.

SCHWARTZ, E.L. (1954). **Will your business die with you?** *Harvard Business Review,* 32(5): 110-122.

A conceptual article.

Key points:

Effective succession requires properly drafted documents, without which there may be undesirable consequences, such as liquidation, unnecessary estate or income taxes, etc. The author describes in great detail the technicalities of drafting succession documents.

Key words: Succession planning.

SCHWARTZ, M.A. & L.B. BARNES (1991). **Outside boards and family businesses: Another look.** *Family Business Review,* 4(3): 269-285.

Sample: 262 family business firms (Response rate - 30%)
Data collection: Questionnaires, follow up interviews

Key points:

This is a survey of CEOs regarding their attitudes toward inside and outside board members. The findings strongly support the inclusion of carefully selected outsiders. If outside members on the board are highly regarded by the first-generation entrepreneur, as well as by the next generation CEO, they will help to provide continuity in family businesses. Outside members are most helpful in providing unbiased views, forcing management accountability, and establishing networks of contacts. They are perceived as least helpful in day-to-day operations, resolving explicit family tensions, and working with very detailed company issues.

Key words: Board of directors - Outsiders, Insiders.

SCOTT, M. & R. BRUCE (1986). **Five stages of growth in small business.** *Long Range Planning,* 20(3): 45-52.

A conceptual article.

Key points:

A small business is one in which:

- Management is independent and usually comprised of the owners;
- Capital is supplied by an individual or a small group; and
- The area of operation is local, although the market may not be local.

The five stages of growth are:

1. *Inception*:

The main values driving the firm in this stage are those of the founder. The main skills will be those of the founder, and sources of fund are haphazard. Uncertainty is high and forward planning is low. The main concern is to develop a commercially acceptable product and establish it in the market. The most likely crisis is the demands that the business places on the energy, time, and finances of the owner/founder.

2. *Survival*:

The financing emphasis will shift to working capital and there will be an increased need for inventories. The owner's personal capital sources continue to bear the brunt, although credit financing may be available from suppliers. The firm earns marginal returns. The crises possible in this stage are uncontrolled growth, increased need and complexity of an expanded distribution system, threat of new entrants, and pressure for information.

3. *Growth*:

The firm is profitable at this stage, but all the profits are ploughed back into the business to finance the increased need for working capital. More formal organization structure and procedures will be set up. The most likely crises are the entry of large competitors and the demands of expansion into new markets and products.

4. *Expansion*:

Decentralized authority is introduced and administrative procedures are systematized. Long term funds will be necessary and long term loans will become available to the company. Company politics are likely to become a major issue and professional managers will be engaged. The most likely crises in this stage are the distance of top management from the action and the need for external focus.

5. *Maturity*:

In this model, the company continues to grow into a big business. The key issues facing management are expense control, finding growth opportunities, and finding a successor.

This model is intended to be a diagnostic tool for analyzing a firm's present situation and what strategies are suitable at each stages.

Key words: Organizational life-cycle stages.

SCRANTON, P. (1992). **Learning manufacture: Education and shop floor schooling in the family firm.** *Family Business Review*, 5(3): 323-342.

An article in the classic section of the journal and based on the diary of James Doak (1902-1906) in textile manufacturing firm.

Key points:

Sole proprietorships and partnerships were the most common form of private firms in 19th century America. The business was based on the shop floor and high value was placed on direct participation in and supervision of the production process. The proprietor had to know the details of the production process. Even when sons were sent to school to gain advanced skills in calculating and reading, they still went through the full apprenticeship term (5-8 years). Before WWI, customary apprenticeships, education through high school, and hands-on experience with merchandising were the 3 paths that dominated succession practices of proprietary manufacturing firms.

In the later decades, with the opening of new production-oriented schools, such as the Philadelphia Textile School (1884), the successors started combining education with a shortened apprenticeship period.

The apprenticeship served various ends:

- Besides technical skills, potential successors learned about the culture and relationships in the organization;
- Fathers were able to assess the prowess and potential of their sons.

With the passage of time, the earlier format of direct apprenticeship was replaced by a more complex format appropriate to new forms of manufacturing.

Key words: Successor training, Historical development.

SEYMOUR, K.C. (1993). **Inter-generational relationships in the family firm: The effect on leadership succession.** *Family Business Review,* 6(3): 263-281.

Sample: 105 firms (Response rate - 38%)
Data collection: Questionnaire
Data analysis: Cronbach alpha, t-test, regression analysis

Key points:

The author tests two hypotheses concerning the effects of family influences on leadership succession.

1. The quality of the work relationship between the owner-manager and the successor has a positive association with successor training. (Supported).
2. The quality of the work relationship between the owner-manager and the successor has a positive association with succession planning. (Not supported).

Significant differences are noted on the ratings that successors and owner-managers assign to the succession planning and training process; the owners' ratings are consistently higher. This inconsistency suggests that perhaps owners have implicit succession plans that they have not discussed with their successors.

Key words: Inter-generational relationships, Succession planning, Next generation.

SHANKER, M.C. & J. ASTRACHAN (1995). **Myths and realities: Family businesses' contribution to the U.S. economy.** *Annual proceedings of United States Association of Small Business and Entrepreneurship*: 21-31.

A conceptual article.

Key points:

Using three definitions of family business, the authors estimate family business numbers in the United States and their contribution to gross domestic product, and to employment.

1. *Broad definition of a family business*:

This definition requires that the family has some degree of effective control over strategic direction and that the business is at least intended to remain in the family. This includes businesses where no family member is in direct daily contact with the business but still has influence over the decisions made either by sitting on the board or owning a significant percentage of stock.

2. *Mid-range definition*:

This definition includes all the criteria in the broad definition and further requires the founder or a descendant to run the company. Businesses run by only one family member are considered family businesses in this category.

3. *Narrow definition*:

This definition requires multiple generations to be involved in the business, direct family involvement in daily operations, and more than one family member to have significant management responsibility.

Findings indicate that, depending on the definition used, the number of family businesses ranges from 4.1 to 20.3 million, employment ranges from 19.8 to 77.2 million, and between 15 and 59 percent of the U.S. workforce are employed in family businesses. Furthermore, family businesses account for between 19 and 78 percent of new jobs created between 1976 and 1990, as well as 12 to 49 percent of GDP.

Key words: Definitions of family businesses, Statistics.

SIEGEL, G., D.S. SHANNON, C.J. STAHL, & P.R. MELCHERT (1986). **Marketing consulting services to small businesses.** *Journal of Accountancy*, October: 160-170.

Sample: 65 Chicago area CEOs
Data collection: In-depth personal interviews
Data analysis: Percentages

Key points:

Crucial problems cited by CEOs of small businesses and the ones [marked with an *] most commonly requiring consulting services are:

- Marketing: inadequate sales, maintaining market shares, market research*, competition, manage/develop sales force*, and product development;
- Business/Financial information: computer systems, cash flow*, working capital, general financial data;
- Personnel: motivation, benefits*, training and development, recruitment and selection*;
- Operations: cost control and computerized accounting*, production efficiency, inventory control;
- Business Planning: long range strategic planning*.

Key words: Consulting.

SINGER, J. & C. DONOHU (1992). **Strategic management planning for the successful family business.** *Journal of Business and Entrepreneurship,* 4(3): 39-51.

Sample: Instructive and consultative efforts of Brain J.Lewis of Cos. Group Inc., Philadelphia. Number is not specified.
Data collection: Focus groups and advisory panels
Data analysis: Not specified

Key points:

The potential for survival of a family business is significantly increased if members of succeeding generations clearly understand the main issues related to organizational positioning and continuity in operational planning. Effective combinations of operational strategies and operational characteristics can be classified according to the business process technology and the family organizational values.

- Business process technology:
  - Strongly idea-centered: This business is research- and applications-centered. Projects are one-of-a-kind and the business depends on one person, a few experts, or stars in a family.
  - Strongly service-centered: The business is based on reliable service, especially on complex major assignments.
  - Strongly delivery-centered: This business involves routinized customer service, where customers demand a product more than a special service.
- Family organizational values:
  - Family centered business: This business stresses how family members feel about their work.
  - Business centered family: This business is seen as a means to provide livelihood and tangible rewards.

The firm's operating strategies should be consistent with its values. This model provides a clear picture why some firms succeed operating one way and others succeed by operating quite differently.

Key words: Strategic planning, Succession planning, Types of family businesses.

SONNENFELD, J.A. & P.L. SPENCE (1989). **The parting patriarch of a family firm.** *Family Business Review,* 2(4): 355-375.

Sample: 50 recently retired CEOs, 100 Fortune 500 CEOs (Response rate 67%), 100 retired Chief Operating Officers (Response rate 67%), 90 Chief Executives from Young Presidents Organization, 3 Harvard Business School 45th reunion classes
Data collection: Questionnaires, interviews, biographies, published accounts
Data analysis: Percentages, coding of open-ended questions

Key points:

A CEO's departure style has as much influence on an organization as the management style used during his/her tenure. The departure style adopted by the leader will vary according to the his/her 'heroic self concept'. The heroic self concept includes two features:

- *Heroic stature*: identification with leadership stature and a position above other employees;
- *Heroic mission*: a quest for an immortal contribution and a sense that he/she has a unique ability to fulfil the responsibility of the job.

The four combinations of heroic mission and heroic stature yield four departure styles. These are summarized in the table below:

Style	Heroic Mission	Heroic Stature
Monarchs	+	+
Generals	-	I
Governors	+	-
Ambassadors	-	-

Distinguishing features of different departure styles are:

- *Monarchs*:

Monarchs are in command in smaller firms, retain close control over key strategic decisions, and have long office terms. Supporters are confident about the monarch's abilities. These leaders achieve a high level of growth but face frustration in the latter part of their career, as they cannot outdo their past performances; monarchs struggle to remain in control for one last victory and do not leave the office unless forced to.

- Generals:

These leaders also have a close identification with their firms but are less successful in achieving their vision. They are, therefore, unable to retain control and spend their retirement planning a comeback as CEO.

- Governors:

  Governors serve the shortest terms in office and are found in larger companies. Their performances tend to be mostly lacklustre for most of the term, but striking in the last few years. They leave willingly at the end of their tenure and maintain virtually no contact after their departure.
- Ambassadors:

  These leaders also head larger firms and are not as captivated by their own strategic vision. They lead the firm to moderate increases in sales, assets, employment, and profits, and recognize the time to step down and serve as advisors. Their firms are most valued by investors.

On the whole, monarchs and generals feel more attached to the stature of their role and get the least fulfilment from it. Ambassadors and governors, however, are more satisfied with their achievements in the firm and less threatened by their loss of power. Although the CEOs of family businesses can follow any of the four departure styles, many aspects of the family business encourage the development of monarchs and generals. Some of these aspects are:

- The family identity is closely tied to the identity of the leader;
- Fear that the loss of title in the business will also signify loss of power in the family;
- Attachment to heroic stature as patriarchs;
- When leader is a founder too, he/she becomes completely absorbed in the firm and may feel they are losing a part of themselves;
- Fear of leaving the business to an incompetent successor.;
- Incongruent family life cycle stages of the founder and successor;
- Different genders of founder and successor;
- Intra-generational rivalries between potential successors; and
- Challenges to family leadership succession from non-family employees, customers, and suppliers.

The authors advise that a departing leader should plan an ambassador-like or governor-like exit. This typology of leadership provides a diagnostic tool for predicting behaviour and responding to specific challenges by each type of departing leader.

- The incumbent who is a monarch should learn the exit patterns of top leaders and be taught that successful leaders can detach themselves from the firm.
- In the case of a general, the criteria for evaluating the successors' performance must be standardized so that the general cannot rush back to the aid of the firm.
- Ambassadors often inherit the leadership as a long tradition of the family. They need to be challenged directly by the board so that they will continually add value to the business. After retirement, they remain involved with the firm, so the business does not lose their input.
- The governor must work with the successor to collectively embody the spirit of the founder so that the family does not become complacent in later generations.

Key words: Succession planning, Next generation, Departure style.

STALLINGS, S.L.A. (1992). **The emergence of American-Indian enterprise.** *Family Business Review,* 5(4): 413-416.

A research note.

Key points:

Although American-Indian-owned businesses have been growing over the past five years, they are still seriously under represented. The Bureau of Census estimates 21,380 such businesses in the U.S.A. For most of them, raising capital is a major problem. Some sources of raising capital and other facilities offered to these businesses are:

- Guaranteed loans from the Small Business Administration and the Bureau of Indian Affairs;
- Economic development grants, 25% up to 100,000, that do not have to be repaid;
- Income from reserve-based gambling operations; and
- No inheritance taxes on reservations and no federal income taxes.

Key words: American Indian family businesses, Ethnicity.

STIER, S. (1993). **Wellness in the family business.** Family Business Review, 6(2): 149-159.

A case study describing the efforts to bring in health consciousness in a printing and publishing firm.

Key points:

Poor employee health can lead to higher health and medical care expenditures and undesirable employee behaviour, such as tardiness, absenteeism, and turnover. Wellness programs in organizations can be promoted by owners and consultants, and are affected by family dynamics.

Key words: Health care in family firms.

STOKES, J.F. (1980). **Involving new directors in small company management.** *Harvard Business Review,* 58(4): 170-174.

A conceptual article.

Key points:

The mix of insiders and outsiders on the board should allow for enough insiders so that outsiders can obtain information on an ongoing basis. Insiders are valuable as two-way conduits, conveying the board's policy and direction to other managers throughout the organization, and providing the information required by the outside board members.

The firm's accountant, banker, and lawyer can help construct a list of candidates. These assistants themselves should not be included, as it could lead to conflicts of interest.

Outside directors can be integrated into a company by doing the following:

- Arrange plant visits and formal/informal meetings with the operating executives;
- Maintain regular communication through monthly newsletters, telephone conversations, etc.;
- Maintain a board book to retain information regarding previous meetings and discussions, agendas for the coming meetings, and another section that contains organization charts, corporate structure, directors' resumes, CEO's background, etc.;
- Send a copy of the board book to the directors at least one week before the scheduled meeting.

Key words: Board of directors - insiders, outsiders, Finding outside directors, Integrating outside directors into family firms.

SWAGGER Jr., G. (1991). **Assessing the successor generation in family businesses.** *Family Business Review,* 4(4): 397-411.

A conceptual article with case studies presented.

Key points:

The relationships within the successor generation can be understood using the concept of differentiation. Individuals can be characterized by their degree of differentiation along a spectrum, from fused and enmeshed to well differentiated. Well differentiated persons have a capacity for realistic self assessment, can assess others realistically, and are resistant to emotional pressures from others. Three dimensions of differentiation are valuable in assessing problems of inter-generational transitions and sibling relationships:

- Bonding versus rivalry,
- Autonomy versus dependency, and
- Leadership versus paralysis.

Based on the degree of differentiation within a family as a whole, and in its individual members, two criteria for consultants intervention are suggested:

- When estate planning is vague and incomplete, roles of family members do not match their interests and talents, criteria for career development is unclear, and leadership succession is vague, the focus of a consultant must be on both the parental and successor generation;
- When emotional individuation and differentiation have occurred in a family, and all members understand their roles, personal needs and goals, are capable of working realistically together, and are less prone to enact parental expectations, the consultant can focus on the successor generation.

Key words: Sibling relationship, Differentiation, Next generation, Succession planning.

SWARTZ, S. (1989). **The challenges of multi-disciplinary consulting to family-owned businesses.** *Family Business Review,* 2(4): 329-339.

An article based on the author's consulting experience.

Key points:

There is a high degree of reciprocal interdependence between the family and the business in a family business. Because of this interdependence, it is impossible to intervene in the business without affecting the family, and vice versa. One of the key functions of a consultant is to show the client constructive ways of managing the tensions that result from being in a dual system. Multi-disciplinary expertise in the form of a consulting team will be useful for the following reasons:

- Consultants need to have knowledge and experience both in family dynamics and business management;
- Presence of two consultants, each representing one of the arenas of the client's struggle, helps the client to develop a clearer vision of the overlapping systems, and legitimizes the importance of both systems;
- A consulting team itself represents a collaborative model for clients to observe and learn from;
- Business families are often highly reactive and complex. A team can effectively handle a high degree of emotionality without losing objectivity;

- Working as a team can provide consultants with a support group.

Bridging the differences in perspectives resulting from distinct professional backgrounds is one of the greatest challenges for effective multidisciplinary consulting. The goal in such a consulting effort is to recognize the differences and simultaneously develop a common perspective. Suggested ways of achieving this are through staff selection and training, process work, and external facilitation.

Key words: Team consulting, Multidisciplinary teams.

SWINTH, R.L. & K.L. VINTON (1993). **Do family owned businesses have a strategic advantage in international joint ventures?** *Family Business Review,* 6(1): 19-30.

A conceptual article.

Key points:

The likelihood of success of an international joint venture increases if both partners are family businesses. These firms have shared values that enable them to bridge the cultural barriers more effectively than publicly held companies.

Family firms seek long term profits, business continuity, support for current and future family, and new opportunities in terms of markets and technology. Non-family firms want short term profits, return to shareholders, minimized risks, new opportunities, and job creation.

Compatibility or incompatibility of the two firms can be worked out by comparing their objectives.

Key words: Family and non-family firms - joint ventures

TAGIURI, R. & J.A. DAVIS (1992). **On the goals of successful family companies.** *Family Business Review,* 5(1): 263-281.

Sample: 624 participants of the Smaller Company Management Program (SCMP) at the Harvard Business School.
Data collection: Seventy-four item questionnaire using a four-point scale.
Data analysis: Factor analysis.

Key Points:

This study about the goals and objectives of family owned and managed companies shows that they have multiple goals. Using factor analysis, the authors derived the following six goals considered most important by owner-managers in the sample:

1. Having a company whose image and commitment to excellence in its field makes its employees proud, and where employees can be happy and productive.
2. Provide the owner(s) with financial security and benefits.
3. Develop new and quality products.
4. Have the company be a means of personal growth, social advancement, and autonomy.
5. Have the company be a good corporate citizen.
6. Have a company that offers job security.

Key words: Goals and objectives of family firms.

TROSTEL, A.O. & M.L. NICHOLS (1982). **Privately held companies and publicly held companies: A comparison of strategic choices and management processes**. *Academy of Management Journal,* 25(1): 47-62.

Sample: 10 matched pairs of privately and publicly held firms
Data collection: Structured interview (approx. 90 minutes), questionnaire completed by subordinates regarding the CEOs, financial and employment data
Data analysis: For interviews - sign test using binomial distribution, paired t-test

Key points:

15 hypotheses about how ownership (private versus public) affects business strategies and management processes are tested. 11 of them are not supported.

Privately-held companies have a higher rate of sales growth over a five year period; however, these growth rates fluctuate more than those of publicly-held companies. The public companies' greater consistency in sales growth may be a reaction to the stock market's pressure for consistency. On the other hand, the privately-held companies' higher sales growth may be a reflection of longer term strategies.

Privately-held companies place more emphasis on asset utilization. They employ accounting policies that tend to reduce taxable income at the expense of reported earnings. This could be because privately-held businesses rely on internally generated cash and are free from stockholder pressure.

No significant differences are found between public and private companies with respect to the degree of formalization in planning, the usage of job descriptions, usage of explicit ROI calculations in decisions, education of managers reporting to the CEO, or ratio of administrative and professional personnel to sales. Therefore, differences in management processes or management styles are virtually non-existent.

Key Words: Strategic planning, Private versus publicly held companies.

TROW, D.B. (1961). **Executive succession in small companies.** *Administrative Science Quarterly*, 6: 228-239.

Sample: 108 small and medium firms
Data collection: Cases presented by **C.R. Christensen** in his book *Management succession in small and growing enterprises* (1953) is reanalyzed.
Data analysis: Fisher's exact test.

Key points:

Data originally collected by C.R. Christensen, using a sample of 108 small/medium manufacturing firms, are re-analyzed to determine the factors that influence the profitability of a firm after succession. The typical company in this sample is a family owned manufacturing firm. Succession planning is found to increase subsequent profitability. When the potential successor has a low level of competence, both succession planning and succession itself are delayed; when succession is unplanned, subsequent company profitability is dependent on the successor's abilities. The main factor influencing succession planning and subsequent profitability of the firm appear to be the availability of a competent successor.

Key words: Succession planning, Profitability.

UPTON, N., & D.L. SEXTON (1987). **Family business succession: The female perspective.** *Proceedings of 32nd annual world conference of the ICSB*: 313-318.

Sample: 29 family businesses
Data collection: "Firms were asked to respond to questions" (not stated whether this was using interviews or questionnaires).
Data analysis: Percentages

Key points:

Family business is defined as "one that includes two or more relatives and has at least two generations working together in an operating capacity." 58 percent of the respondents feel that men and women have the same opportunities for success. In a majority of the cases, daughters hold stereotypically female and other non-executive positions. In only 2 out of 29 firms are daughters considered for succession and, in both cases, no sons are available.

Key words: Daughters in family firms.

UPTON, N., K. VINTON, S. SEAMAN, & C. MOORE (1993). **Family business consultants - Who we are, what we do, and how we do it?** *Family Business Review,* 6(3): 301-311.

Sample: Two surveys: (1) 381 members of FFI (62% response rate), (2) 236 members of FFI (45% response rate)
Data collection: Questionnaires
Data analysis: Percentages

Key points:

The two surveys, administered to members of the Family Firm Institute, describe the state of research about family business. The respondents are predominantly white males, 40-49 years of age. The major issue internal to the firm is leadership succession, and those issues external to the firm are estate, financial, and legal planning. There seems to be a lack of theory/research/methods/techniques in the field. The respondents mention a few practitioners and theorists who have influenced the field, but very few names are repeated. Consultants for family businesses use personal interviews, group interviews, personality or psychological tests, ratio analysis, customer interviews, and video tapes.

Consulting in family firms is different from consulting in non-family firms due to the following reasons:

1. Family dynamics, emotions, and conflict resolution form an important part of family businesses;
2. Consulting is more personal in family businesses.
3. In family business consulting, the balance between family and business concerns needs to be maintained.

Common mistakes made by consultants in dealing with the family firms are:

1. Inability to understand family dynamics.
2. Focusing on symptoms rather than problems.
3. Inappropriate communication with members.

Some suggestions for improvement are:

- Peer review - Consultants should be encouraged to write cases;
- Team approach - Consulting teams can be more effective but they are not generally used because of economic considerations and lack of trust;
- Discussions among consultants through conferences, forums, etc., should be encouraged so that the experiences can be shared.

Key words: Consulting, Family firm institute survey, Review article.

VERDIN, J.A. (1986). **Improving sales performance in a family owned business.** *American Journal of Small Business,* 10(4): 49-61.

Sample: 58 respondents from a family owned chain of 7 retail shoe stores.
Data collection: Company records, two sets of questionnaires (one administered before and another after the spring/summer season) (Response rate of first questionnaire - 60%, response rate of second questionnaire - 54%)
Data analysis: ANOVA, Regression analysis

Key points:

In order to increase the sales performance in small business, regular feedback should be provided to the sales force. This feedback enables sales staff to set difficult and accurate goals, which lead to improved sales performance. Individuals with specific and challenging goals outperform individuals with specific and easy goals, "do-best goals", or ambiguously stated goals.

Key words: Sales performance, Planning.

VETTER, E.W. (1984). **Succession planning: Mastering the basics.** *Human Resource Planning,* 7(2): 99-104.

A conceptual article.

Key points:

Trying to link succession planning to strategy, integrated information systems, and development through organization movement, does not work. What needs to be done is a qualitative analysis using information provided in a usable form and regular review sessions. Effective succession planning depends on intelligent and diligent insights.

Key words: Succession planning - definition, Methodological issues.

WALKER, E.J. (1976). **'Til' business us do part.** *Harvard Business Review,* 54(1): 94-101.

A conceptual article.

Key points:

It is in everyone's best interest for executives' wives to understand their husband's career goals, for husbands to learn how to share their feelings, and for companies to understand that if the needs of the marriage are not met, the company, and not the marriage, may be the loser.

Key words: Work-family conflicts and spill-overs.

WALSCH, F. (1994). **Healthy family functioning: Conceptual and research developments.** *Family Business Review,* 7(2): 175-198.

A conceptual article.

Key points:

The very concept of family is undergoing redefinition in the wake of major social changes in recent decades. The idealized norm of nuclear family has given way to a multiplicity of family arrangements. The 1950s model of the white middle class nuclear family with a breadwinner father and a home-maker mother is currently found only in 8% of U.S. households.

The author identifies four views of a normal family:

- *Normal families as asymptomatic*: A family is normal if there are no symptoms of disorder in any family member.
- *Normal families as average*: Normal families are the ones that are common or prevalent from a statistical viewpoint.
- *Normal families as optimal*: A family is healthy if it possesses certain ideal characteristics.

- *Normal family processes*: Based on systems theory, the normal family engages itself in basic processes characteristic of human systems.

Well functioning families can be found in a variety of arrangements. Basic elements that help in healthy family functioning include:

- Connectedness and commitment of members as caring, mutually supportive individuals;
- Respect for individual differences, autonomy, and separate needs;
- For couples, a relationship between equal partners;
- Effective parental or executive leadership;
- Adequate resources for basic economic security and psychological support;
- Organizational stability characterised by clarity, consistency, and predicted patterns of interaction;
- Effective problem solving and conflict resolution processes; and
- Shared beliefs that enable mutual trust, ethical values, and connectedness with past and future generations.

Key words: Family dynamics.

WARD, J.L. (1988). **The special role of strategic planning for family businesses.** *Family Business Review,* 1(2): 105-117.

Sample: The article is based on findings of three studies: (1) 200 privately owned firms that were at least 5 years old in 1924, (2) 300 privately and 1500 publicly controlled firms, (3) 20 family firms.

Data collection: (1) Interviews conducted at firms that had survived till 1984. Not mentioned for (2) and (3).

Data analysis: Percentages

Key points:

Only 13 percent of the family firms continued to be owned by the same family after three generations. Those that survived and prospered (10% increase in employee base over 60 years) have renewed or regenerated their business strategies several times as market and competitive pressures changed. Often, the new business strategies were a result of changing family influences.

The six interdependent steps in the strategic planning process in family firms are:

1. Commitment to the future of the business;
2. Assessment of the health of the business;
3. Identification of the business alternatives;
4. Consideration of family and personal goals;
5. Selection of business strategy;

6. Assessment of the family's interests and capabilities;

Some reasons for the family business owner's reluctance to plan are:

- Owners do not like to share financial information with others;
- Some owners object to planning because the future is uncertain and feel that strategic planning is not helpful;
- Owners are unwilling to change the company;
- Owners have limited exposure to the formal planning process.

Benefits of strategic planning include:

- Strategic planning encourages commitment of family members;
- Company's rate of reinvestment in business can be assessed by managers and corrective action can be taken if needed;
- The very nature of planning involves a variety of individuals. This increases business knowledge and promotes common understanding;
- Strategic planning is a good way to prepare and involve potential successors in business.

Strategic planning is a valuable tool that helps business owners build such qualities as the ability to work toward consensus, team management, and shared decision-making. It identifies the fundamental business and family assumptions in a constructive way, and promotes healthy communication on critical family business issues.

Key words: Strategic planning, Renewal and regeneration of strategies, Steps in strategic planning, Benefits of planning.

WARD, J.L. (1990a). **The succession process: 15 guidelines.** *Small Business Forum,* 8(3): 57-62.

A conceptual article.

Key points:

Ward argues that 'succession is the most painful and critical time for family businesses'. Based on his experience of working with a large number of family businesses, he suggests 15 guidelines that may help in the transition process.

1. Succession is a process, not an event. In preparing the next generation members for the business, owners should make a conscious attempt to present a balanced perspective on business to next generation members.
2. Present the business as an option, not an obligation.
3. Successors should get outside experience.
4. Successors should hire into an existing job.
5. Encourage the development of complementary skills in the successor.

6. Teach successors the foundations.
7. Start the successor with mentors.
8. Designate an area of responsibility for the successor.
9. Develop a rationale or statement that specifies why all this is worth the pain.
10. Recognize that you are not alone.
11. Have family meetings.
12. Plan, plan, plan - Have a business plan, estate plan, and a succession plan simultaneously.
13. Create an advisory board.
14. Set a date for official retirement.
15. Let go.

Perpetuating a family business is the ultimate management challenge. However, the chances of success can be increased considerably by following the suggested guidelines and understanding that succession is a process that can take fifteen or twenty years to complete.

Key words: Succession process, Succession planning.

WARD, J.L. (1990b). **What is a family business? And how can we help?** *Small Business Forum,* 8(3): 63-71.

A conceptual article.

Key points:

There are three commonly held definitions of family business:

- A business is a family business if the family depends on the business for its livelihood;
- If the participants have a minimum of three roles (ownership, management, and family) which can be sources of conflict, the business is a family business.
- A family business is a business in which two or more family members influence the business.

The third definition is an academic definition that helps to quantify family businesses. Using this definition, 63 percent of all businesses are family businesses as they have two or more family members on their board of directors.

There are some fundamental differences between the strategic principles for businesses in general and those for family businesses.

- Change in top management is deemed useful for business in general, but family firms retain the same top management for decades;
- Reinvestment in the business is generally useful for developing new products, ideas, market, etc.; however, for family members, creating liquidity outside of the business is a high priority;

- Innovation and experimentation are considered important for business in general, but the last thing on the family business' agenda is experimentation;
- Businesses can generally benefit from accountability, but the entrepreneurial personality generally eschews accountability.

Family businesses have two unique characteristics:

1. The blurring and overlapping of family, ownership, and management issues;
2. Problems created by contradictions between the needs of the family and those of the business.

In order to deal effectively with these unique challenges, family businesses facing succession issues need to integrate business, estate, and succession plans all at once. These plans require three different types of expertise: accountant, lawyer, and family business consultant. These experts should meet with each other and with the business owner on a regular basis. Moreover, once the business has more than 50 employees, the author strongly recommends having a family forum and outsiders on the board.

Key words: Definitions, Consulting, Family and non-family firms.

WARD, J.L. & J.L. HANDY (1988). **A survey of board practices.** *Family Business Review*, 1(3): 289-308.

Sample: 147 privately controlled companies (Response rate - 42%)
Data collection: Mailed Questionnaires
Data analysis: Percentages, Median test

Key points:

48 percent of the sample have outside directors on their boards and CEOs who have experience with outside boards are more prone to include outsiders on their boards. CEOs in companies with outsiders on their boards use their board for advice, counsel, and accountability of management. On the other hand, CEOs with insiders on their boards report that they have a board because of the legal requirements. Only 2 percent of the CEOs report that the board is useful in succession planning. In general, non-family CEOs are more satisfied with their boards than entrepreneurs or family business successors.

Key words: Research framework on boards, Outside directors, Functions of board, Board structure.

WEISER, J., F. BRODY, & M. QUARREY (1988). **Family businesses and employee ownership.** *Family Business Review,* 1(1): 23-35.

Financial advice.

Key points:

Employee stock ownership plans (ESOPs) can yield financial and organizational benefits for family firms. The financial benefits include:

- Reduction in the cost of borrowing money because money borrowed through an ESOP is tax deductible (both principal and interest). Moreover, 50 percent of the interest income received from the ESOP is tax-free to the lending institution. As a result, the borrowing rate for ESOPs is especially low;
- Creation of a market for the closely-held firm's shares. The company's stock in the ESOP is appraised every year and the ESOP can buy shares during the year from individuals at the appraised value.

Properly structured employee ownership can lead to increased productivity, sales growth, and employment growth, by making employees owners thus involving owners in shop floor decision-making.

Pitfalls of ESOPs include:

- The ESOPs involve installation costs, administration costs, and dealing with complex pension and tax regulations.
- The installation of an ESOP can dilute the earnings per year of a company and depress stock value.

ESOPs are a particularly attractive option to family firms when there is no heir interested in continuing the business, and the owner is faced with the option of either selling the business to outsiders or liquidating it. An ESOP allows the retiring owner to leave a legacy, and allows the firm to continue as a healthy business. Moreover, ESOPs allow great flexibility in structuring a purchase of the retiring owners' stock, as a time frame can be laid for the transition in ownership.

Key words: Employee stock option plans (ESOPs) - benefits, pitfalls, steps in setting ESOPs; Succession planning.

WELSCH, J. (1991). **Family enterprises in the UK, the Federal Republic of Germany, and Spain: A transnational comparison.** *Family Business Review, 4*(2): 231-261.

Sample: This study integrates, analyzes, and compares the findings of three previous studies - one each in Spain, Germany, and United Kingdom. The sample size of each of these is - Spain - 750 (Gallo & Garcia Pont, 1988), Germany - 501 (Wieselhuber & Spannagl, 1988) (Response rate - 20%), United Kingdom - 8000 (Leach et al, 1990).

Data collection: Questionnaires for all three studies

Data analysis: Percentages, Bar charts

Key points:

In Spain and the U.K., family firms are responsible for more than 70% of the nation's GNP. Spanish firms are significantly younger than their counterparts in Germany and the U.K.. Large family firms are older than large non-family firms in Germany and the U.K.; family firms in the U.K. and Germany have operated under the same management for longer periods of time than family firms in Spain. The reluctance to sell shares in German family firms is greater than in British family firms. In the U.K., both family and non-family firms grow faster than family firms in Germany.

The three original studies use different measures and definitions of family businesses. This must be kept in mind when evaluating the results of this study.

Key words: Ethnicity, Family firms in the U.K., Spain, West Germany.

WELSCH, J.H.M. (1993). **The impact of family ownership and involvement on the process of management succession.** *Family Business Review,* 6(1): 31-54.

Sample: 183 (59 family firms and 124 non-family firms)(Response rate - 20%)

Data collection: Questionnaires

Data analysis: Mann Whitney U-test, Spearman correlation, Cronbach alpha

Key points:

After a thorough review of literature on management succession, the author presents four hypotheses related to management succession in family and non-family firms to test the rational, political, and bureaucratic content of the succession process.

1. Large industrial firms can be discriminated into family firms and non-family firms on the basis of the process of management succession.
2. Large industrial firms can be discriminated into family and non-family firms on the basis of the rational dimension of the management succession process.
3. Large industrial firms can be discriminated into family and non-family firms on the basis of the political dimension of the management succession process.
4. Large industrial firms can be discriminated into family and non-family firms on the basis of the bureaucratic dimension of the management succession process.

All four hypotheses are not confirmed. From the non-confirmation of these hypotheses, it is clear that the differences between the family and non-family firms are subtle. Some differences highlighted by the author are listed below. In family firms:

- More importance is given to academic education;
- Selection criteria for managers are less clearly defined;
- The individual's personality play an important role in selection;
- The immediate superior plays an important role;
- There is more reliance on in-house tests to avoid charges of nepotism;
- Human resource management experts are not used as much;
- Past performance and individual track record have less importance;
- Human relations issues are openly debated.

In this sample, the family firms are older than non-family firms. As a result, a greater amount of bureaucracy exists in the family firms.

Key words: Family and non-family firms - succession, Review of management succession.

WHISLER, T.L. (1988). **The role of the board in the threshold firm.** *Family Business Review*, 1(3): 309-321.

Sample: 73 companies (59 privately held, and 14 publicly held companies)
Data collection: Questionnaires, Interviews
Data analysis: Not mentioned

Key points:

As a closely held company grows, control must change from a closed to an open system. A "threshold company" is a firm in transition toward professionalization; outside directors can help a company cross the threshold.

A threshold firm is small, successful, and has arrived at a crisis point in its growth. If management does not make a number of important qualitative changes, the company will falter. At this stage, entrepreneurial management techniques must give way to more professional and analytical ones.

This transition places heroic demands on the entrepreneur who must develop new attitudes and perspectives to fit the fundamental changes in the company's strategy, staff, and requirements for the CEO. Outside directors can help by acting as coaches and observers. Within these contexts, outside directors play three important roles:

- Preceptor.
- Technical advisors.
- Arbitrator.

Outside directors can be found among business professionals, investment bankers, active functional managers from non-competing companies, business school professors, and retired executives from big companies. These individuals may be interested in serving as board members for any of the following reasons:

- Opportunity to learn by participating at the highest levels of a company,
- Opportunity to transmit knowledge,
- Opportunity to become better known in business community, and
- Chance to keep hand in the game.

The board plays an important role in larger and older companies. A proper match between the role of the board and the stage of a company's development can result in more effective corporate performance. In the smaller and newer companies, the board should play a minimal role. When a successful company approaches the threshold, it needs a working board, on which an outside director makes a difference. When the company moves beyond the threshold stage, a board becomes necessary; an increasing number of outsiders on the board can be helpful. In the company where insiders dominate the board, the distinction between governance and management will remain less clear than in other companies.

Key words: Threshold firm, Outside directors, Working board, Attributes of professionally managed firms, Attributes of entrepreneurial firm.

WHITESIDE, M.F. & F.H. BROWN (1991). **Drawbacks of a dual systems approach to family firms: Can we expand out thinking?** *Family Business Review,* 4(4): 383-395.

A conceptual article.

Key points:

Family firms have been viewed as being comprised of two systems: family and firm. This is commonly called the 'dual systems approach'. Drawbacks of the dual system are:

1. Subsystem stereotyping.
2. Inconsistent and inadequate analysis of interpersonal dynamics.

3. Exaggerated notions of subsystem boundaries.

Therefore, it is necessary to view the family firm as a single entity.

Key words: Family-business system.

WILLIAMS, R.O. (1992). **Successful ownership in business families.** *Family Business Review,* 5(2): 161-172.

A conceptual article.

Key points:

Business ownership, viewed from a broad perspective, encompasses knowledge, skill, integrity, responsibility, trust, and mutual consideration. The four key issues in effective ownership are:

1. Effective family communication requires trust. Sincerity, reliability, and competence are the three components that contribute to building trust in communication within the business families;
2. Leadership role modelling gives an opportunity to younger generations to learn by observation, and helps them to develop positive values;
3. Learning about money. To enable the younger family members to understand the value and importance of money, the author suggests the formation of an informal family investment partnership, beginning when children are in high school, college, or marriage;
4. Ownership roles. This focuses on what constitutes an effective owner, concentrating especially on issues of ownership and control.

Viewing ownership in a strictly legal sense is very limited and the spirit of ownership, if fully activated, can become a way to manage the business most effectively.

Key words: Ownership in family firms, Spirit of ownership.

WILLMOTT, P. (1971). **Family, work, and leisure conflicts among male employees.** *Human Relations,* 24(6): 575-584.

Sample: 79 men in two British companies
Data collection: Interviews at home and at work
Data analysis: Percentages

Key point:

Work affects family life in terms of working hours, taking work, worries, and/or strains home.

Key words: Work-family conflicts.

WINTER, M. & M. FITZGERALD (1993). **Continuing the family-owned home-based businesses: Evidence from a panel study.** *Family Business Review,* 6(4): 417-426.

Sample: 899 - First interview, 729 - Second interview
Data collection: 3 telephone interviews, 1989 - First (5 minutes), Second (30 minutes), 1992 - Third (5 minutes)
Data analysis: Descriptive statistics, Logistic regression

Key points:

Approximately one-third of businesses close down after three years. Reported reasons for quitting the business are:

1. Employment related issues (33 percent).
2. Family related issues (20 percent).
3. Economic issues (20 percent).
4. Growth issues (11 percent).
5. Health and retirement issues.

The probability of continuing to operate a business is affected by the owner's age, education, and enjoyment in the work. The older, more educated owners who like their work are more likely to continue regardless of the income generated by the business. Business owners in home-based businesses do it more for the enjoyment than for income generation.

Key words: Home-based businesses.

WONG, B., S. McREYNOLDS, & W. WONG (1992). **Chinese family firms in the San Francisco bay areas.** *Family Business Review,* 5(4): 355-372.

Sample: 100 first generation Chinese immigrants from 53 families
Data collection: Participant observation, Interviews, In-depth conversations
Data analysis: Not mentioned

Key points:

Ethnic resources and kinship ties are the key elements that promote entrepreneurship among first generation Chinese immigrants. Chinese family firms are grounded in traditional kinship systems, ancestor worship, and the values of: filial piety, reciprocity, and sentimentality. For the immigrant, a family business provides flexibility in terms of work hours, job description, and the salary drawn. The business also offers a relaxed work environment. These businesses are especially good for first generation Chinese immigrants who have no post-secondary education, have language difficulties, and who can find no other economic opportunities. For the generations brought up in the United States, however, the family business is not an attractive career option; they view the family business as too difficult and less rewarding. Moreover, they are often alienated by the management style of the first generation owners.

Several business owners plan to close their businesses when they retire, but others would like to continue it with the help of outside employees. The ones willing to continue are a minority. This plan will mean that Chinese family businesses started by the first generation immigrants may not last long in the U.S., a pattern similar to that in China, where family businesses have short life spans, though for different reasons. In China the practice of dividing the families assets equally among all male descendants makes growth difficult. Thus, they usually do not last more than three generations.

Key words: Ethnicity, Chinese family firms, First generation immigrants.

WONG, S.L. (1993). **The Chinese family: A model.** *Family Business Review,* 6(3): 327-340.

The original article was published in *British Journal of Sociology,* (1985). 36(1): 58-72.

Sample: 32 cotton spinning mills
Data collection: Not mentioned
Data analysis: Not mentioned

Key points:

The author states that the three distinguishing aspects of Chinese families are: nepotism, paternalism, and family ownership. Of the three, nepotism is an overblown concept and paternalism is often related to the nature of the labour market.

Family firms are prevalent among Chinese commercial and industrial enterprises. Such firms are not necessarily small, impermanent, and conservative, and tend to behave differently according to their stages of development. The stages of development described are outlined as follows:

1. *Emergent*: The common format of new businesses in China is the partnership. These partners are generally unrelated by ties of descent or marriage. However, partnerships are notably unstable. Most individuals enter this form of alliance for expediency, fully aware that one must fend for oneself. So partnerships generally remain undercapitalized. In the absence of mutual trust, cliques are formed. An asymmetry in the growth of shares develops as some partners place themselves in a more advantageous position. Ultimately, one partner attains majority ownership of the firm.
2. *Centralized*: The successful partner gains authority and is the uncontestable leader, running the business as he sees fit, often using a highly personalized leadership style. Profits are generally retained and reinvested, or transferred from one business to another. As his sons get older, the father generally, though often reluctantly, relinquishes control and the firm enters into the third stage.
3. *Segmented*: Traditionally, legitimate sons inherit the business, but in the Republic of China this inheritance pattern has been modified to an enlarged circle of heirs including a wife or wives and daughters of the head of the family. Generally, it is more advantageous for inheritors to keep their shares in the business for the following reasons:
   - Subdivision may not be feasible if the assets are integrated entities, such as property, processes, etc. ;
   - Even if subdivision is feasible, it may lead to lower efficiency, production, and economies of scale;
   - The value of the family firm is generally greater than its physical assets because of intangible assets that cannot be apportioned to individual heirs;
   - Most families have company regulations against selling shares to outsiders.
4. *Disintegrative*: Profits derived from the business is the first thing to be divided among inheritors. All sons are given an identical number of shares. Daughters generally get lesser allotments, given in the form of dowries when they marry. Once the brothers marry and have children, they may begin to feel that they get less than an equal share of the business. Since succession to the managerial positions is generally reserved for the sons, and the eldest son usually assumes the mantle of CEO, he has the earliest opportunity to work and is able to establish himself in the firm. A younger brother may acquire skills different from those of the older brother, or press for the creation of new ventures that can be run independently of the original business.

   The characteristic feature of this stage is the outward expansion of the enterprise, owing to segmentation, and a reduction in the flexibility of reinvestment and risk taking. The mutual watchfulness amongst the brothers in this phase is very similar to that of partners in the first phase. The same opportunity for asymmetrical growth is present and the stages are repeated. Although the relationship between the brothers are brittle, the most fragile bonds are between cousins. When cousins become co-owners, the economic considerations against the sale of the family firm become less inhibitive. The value of individual portions becomes much smaller due to subdivisions and this reduces the attraction of regular incomes derived from the shares. Generally, those in weaker bargaining positions decide to break off the economic ties with the firm.

Using the four stages of development discussed in the article, the author provides a table comparing the Chinese, Filipino, and Japanese family firms.

Key words: Ethnicity, Chinese family firms, Filipino family firms, Japanese family firms.

WORTMAN Jr., M.S. (1994). **Theoretical foundations for family-owned business: A conceptual and research based paradigm.** *Family Business Review,* 7(1): 3-27.

A review article.

Key points:

In 1994, Max Wortman took over as the editor of *Family Business Review.* On taking over, he presented a review of the existing literature and classified the literature according to:

- Theoretical components,
- Historical components,
- Environmental components;
- Organizational contexts,
- Content components, and
- Future of family-owned business.

He states that:

- In general, there have been few empirical studies in family business literature.
- Very little conceptual work has been conducted in the areas of historical, environmental, and organizational components.
- The focus of theoretical work has been on foundations, theories, law, and legal studies related to family businesses.
- The largest number of conceptual studies deal with the issue of succession.

Wortman suggests that there is a need for:

1. Development of a conceptual, measurable definition for the field;
2. Comprehensive frameworks that will provide a network for cause-effect relationships;
3. Studies related to the history of family-businesses, environmental studies, organizational studies, and different areas of strategy management.

Key words: Review article, Typology of research and conceptual work.

YLVISAKER, P.N. (1990). **Family foundations: High risk, high reward.** *Family Business Review*, 3(4): 331-335.

A conceptual article.

Key points:

The author discusses the risks and rewards of family foundations and suggests ways to make them effective. The identified risks and hazards of family foundations are:

- Differences that emerge among family members in determining the social needs and their priorities may lead to of family tensions, to feuds, and factions;
- A poor understanding of government regulations;
- Foundations lead to increased public recognition which some families may find difficult to manage.

The identified rewards of family foundations are:

- Foundations can help achieve a sense of higher purpose;
- Assessing public needs and evaluating grant proposals from the point of view of public interest is an incomparable and challenging educational experience;
- Society honours those who practice philanthropy.

An effective family foundation:

- Transmits the founding donors' sense of social commitment through successive generations;
- Agrees on an explicit set of goals and objectives;
- Has competent professional staff who are sensitive to and compatible with family members;
- Uses trustees when the number of family members is large;
- Includes credible outsiders;
- Is subject to conversion into public institutions in the future.

Key words: Family foundations.

4

BIBLIOGRAPHY OF ARTICLES NOT ANNOTATED

Abegglen, J.C. & W.L. Warner (1955). ***Big business leaders in America.*** New York: Harper and Brothers.

Alcorn, P.B. (1982). ***Success and survival of the family-owned business.*** New York: McGraw-Hill.

Aldrich, N.W. (1985). **Feuding families.** *Inc.*, January.

Balmori, D. (1985). **Trends in Latin American family history.** *Trends in History,* 3: 113-125.

Barnett, F. & S. Barnett (1988). ***Working together: Entrepreneurial couples.*** Berkeley: Ten Speed Press.

Barthel, D. (1985). **When husbands and wives try working together.** *Working Woman,* November.

Bass, B.M. (1985). ***Performance beyond expectations.*** *Orlando:* Academic Press.

Becker, E. (1973). ***The denial of death.*** New York: The Free Press.

Becker, B.M. & F.A. Tillman (1976). ***Management checklist for a family business.*** Washington, D.C.: U.S. Small business administration.

Becker, B.M. & F.A. Tillman (1978). ***The family-owned business.*** Chicago: Commerce Clearing House.

Benedict, B. (1968). **Family firms and economic development.** *Southwestern Journal of Anthropology,* 24: 1-19.

Benson, B., E.T. Crego, & R.H. Drucker (1990). ***Your family business: A success guide for growth and survival.*** Homewood: Dow Jones-Irwin.

Bernstein, P. (1985). **Family ties, corporate bonds.** *Working Woman,* May.

Bernstein, P. (1985). ***Family ties, corporate bonds.*** New York: Henry Holt.

Blotnick, S. (1984). **The case of reluctant heirs.** *Forbes,* July 134: 180.

Bonacich, E. (1973). **A theory of middleman minorities.** *American Sociological Review,* 38: 583-594.

Bork, D. (1986). ***Family business, risky business: How to make it work.*** New York: American Management Association.

Boswell, J. (1972). ***The rise and decline of small firms.*** London: George Allen and Unwin.

Bowen, M. (1978). ***Family therapy in clinical practice.*** New York: Jason Aronson.

Bray, J.H., D.S. Williamson, & P.E. Malone (1984). **Personal authority in the family system: Development of a questionnaire to measure personal authority in intergenerational family process.** *Journal of Marital and Family Therapy.* April: 167-178.

Brenner, M. (1988). ***House of Dreams: The collapse of an American dynasty.*** New York: Avon Books.

Brown, F.H. (1991). ***Reweaving the family tapestry: A multigenerational approach to family.*** New York: W.W. Norton.

Buchholz, B.B. & M. Crane (1989). ***Corporate bloodlines: The future of the family firm.*** New York: Carol Publishing Group.

Butrick, F.M. (1989). ***How to disinherit the IRS.*** Akron: Independent Business Institute Press Division.

Byron, R.F. (1976). **Economic functions of kinship values in family businesses: Fishing crews in North Atlantic communities.** *Sociology and Social Research,* 60: 147-160.

Calder, G. H. (1961). **The peculiar problems of a family business.** *Business Horizons.* 7(3): 93-102.

Cantor, G.M. (1982). **How to keep kids from suing each other.** *Inc.,* February.

Censer, J.T. (1991). **What ever happened to family history? A review article.** *Comparative Studies in Society and History,* 33: 528-538.

Chadeau, E. (1993). **The large family firm in twentieth-century France.** *Business History,* 35: 184-205.

Chan, W.K.K. (1992). **Chinese business networking and the Pacific Rim: The family firm's roles past and present.** *Journal of American-East Asian Relations,* 1: 171-190.

Christensen, C. (1953). ***Management succession in small and growing enterprises.*** Boston: Division of Research. Harvard Business School.

Church, R. (1986). **Family firms and managerial capitalism: The case of the international motor industry.** *Business History,* 28: 165-180.

Church, R. (1993). **The family firm in industrial capitalism: International perspectives on hypotheses and history.** *Business History,* 35: 17-43.

Cohn, M. (1992). ***Passing the torch: Succession, retirement, and estate planning in family-owned business.*** New York: McGraw-Hill.

Cole, P.M. (1993). **Women in family business: A systematic approach to inquiry.** Doctoral dissertation. Nova Southeastern University.

Collier, P. & D. Horowitz (1987). ***The Fords: An American epic.*** New York: Summit Books.

Commerce Clearing House. (1992). ***Federal estate and gift taxes explained.*** Chicago: CCH Tax Law Editors.

Cone, E.F. (1987). **Dad, I know I can handle it.** *Forbes,* October 26.

Crampton, C.D. (1994). **The entrepreneurial family.** Doctoral dissertation. Yale University.

Danco, L.A. (1967). **What do you do about 'tha ol'man' when you are the old man?** *Industrial Distribution.* July: 51-55.

Danco, L. A. (1981). ***Inside the family business: A guide for the family business owner and his family.*** Cleveland: University Press.

Danco, K. (1981). ***From the other side of the bed: A woman looks at life in the family business.*** Cleveland: University Press.

Danco, L.A. (1982). ***Beyond survival.*** Cleveland: University Press.

Danco, L.A. & D.J. Jonovic (1981). ***Outside directors in the family-owned business: Why, when, who and how.*** Cleveland: University Press.

Dannhaeuser, N. (1993). **The social limits of the family-operated firm in a German town.** *Journal of Developing Societies,* 9: 11-32.

Daunton, M.J. (1988). **Inheritance and succession in the City of London in the nineteenth century.** *Business History,* 30: 269-286.

Davis, J.A. (1982). **The influence of life stage on father-son work relationship in family companies**. Doctoral dissertation. Harvard University.

Davis, P. (1986). **Family business: Perspectives on change.** *Agency Sales Magazine.* June: 9-16.

Deeson, A.F.L. (1972). ***Great company crashes.*** London: W.Foulsham & Co. Ltd..

Diamond, M. (1991). ***Managing and operating a closely held corporation.*** New York: John Wiley & Sons, Inc.

Dodge, P.B. (1987). ***Tales of the Phelps-Dodge family: A chronicle of five generations.*** New York: New York Historical Society.

Drozdow, N. (1986). **Managing relationships in the family business.** *Agency Sales Magazine.* October: 35-39.

Dumas, C. (1988). **Daughters in family-owned businesses: An applied systems perspective**. Doctoral dissertation. Fielding Institute.

Dyer Jr., W.G. (1984). **Cultural evolution in organizations: The case of a family-owned firm**. Doctoral dissertation. Massachusetts Institute of Technology.

Dyer Jr., W.G. (1986). ***Cultural changes in family firms: Anticipating and managing business and family transitions.*** San Francisco: Jossey-Bass.

Dyer, Jr. W.G. (1992). ***The entrepreneurial experience: Confronting career dilemmas of the start-up executive.*** San-Francisco: Jossey-Bass.

Eckrich, C.J. (1993). **Effects of family business membership and psychological separation on the career development of late adolescents.** Doctoral dissertation. Purdue University.

Elder, G.H.,Jr. (1977). **Family history and the life course.** *Journal of Family History,* 2: 279-304.

English, A.R. (1958). ***Financial problems of the family company.*** London: Sweet & Maxwell Ltd.

Ferkany, S.T. (1992). **For the family: Building business in Monterrey, Mexico**. Doctoral dissertation. Wayne State University.

Flamhottz, E.G. (1986). ***How to make the transition from an entrepreneurship to a professionally managed firm.*** San Francisco: Jossey-Bass.

Fogarty, T.F. (1979). **The distancer and the pursuer.** *The Family.* 7: 11-16.

Frishkoff, P.A. & B.M. Brown (1991). ***Succession survival kit.*** Corvallis: Oregon State University Family Business Program.

Frun, W.M. (1983). ***Kikkoman: Company, clan and community.*** Cambridge: Harvard University Press.

Galagan. P. (1985). **Between family and firm.** *Training and Development Journal.* April: 68-71.

Gasson, R., G. Crow, A. Errington, J. Hutson, T. Marsden, & D.M. Winter (1988). **The farm as a family business: A review.** *Journal of Agricultural Economics,* 39: 1-41.

Goldberg, S.D. (1991). **Factors which impact effective success in small family-owned businesses: An empirical study.** Doctoral dissertation. University of Massachusetts.

Goldwasser, T. (1986). ***Family pride: Profiles of five of America's best run family businesses.*** Dodd, Mead & Co.

Gourvish, T.R. (1987). **British business and the transition to a corporate economy: Entrepreneurship and management structures.** *Business History,* 29: 18-45.

Groseclose, E. (1975). **You have problems? Consider the plight of Nation's SOBs.** *The Wall Street Journal,* March 20: 1.

Haid, R.L. (1994). **Stepping down and stepping out: A qualitative study of family business CEOs who have turned over management of the business to their families.** Doctoral dissertation. The Union Institute.

Hamilton, G.G. & K. Cheng-Shu (1990). **The institutional foundations of Chinese business: The family firm in Taiwan.** *Comparative Social Research,* 12: 135-151.

Handler, E. (1989). **Managing the family firm succession process: The next generation family member's experience.** Doctoral dissertation. School of Management: Boston University.

Hareven, T.K. (1977). **Family time and historical time.** *Daedalus,* 106: 57-70.

Harrison, B. (1974). **Ghetto economic development: A survey.** *Journal of Economic Literature,* 12: 1-37.

Hershon, S.A. (1975). **The problem of management succession in family businesses**. Doctoral dissertation. Harvard University.

Holland, P.J. (1981). **Strategic management in family business: An exploratory study of the development and strategic effects of the family-business relationship**. Doctoral dissertation. University of Georgia.

Hollander, B.S. (1983). **Family-owned business as a system: A case study of the interaction of family, task, and marketplace components**. Doctoral dissertation. University of Pittsburgh.

Hutson, J. (1987). **Fathers and sons: Family farms, family businesses, and the farming industry.** *Sociology,* 21(2).

Ianni, F.A.J. & E. Reuss-Ianni (1972). ***A family business.*** New York: Russell Sage Foundation.

Innarelli, C.L. (1992). **The socialization of leaders in family business**. Doctoral dissertation. University of Pittsburgh.

Jaffe, D. (1990). ***Working with the ones you love: Strategies for a successful family business.*** San Francisco: Conari Press.

Jithoo, S. (1985). **Success and struggle over one hundred and twenty years of Indian family firms in Durban.** *Eastern Anthropologist,* 38: 45-56.

Jonovic, D.J. (1982). ***The second generation boss: A successor's guide to becoming the next owner-manager of a successful family business.*** Cleveland: University Press.

Jonovic, D.J. (1984). ***Someday it'll all be yours...Or will it?*** Cleveland: Jamieson Press and University Press.

Jonovic, D.J. & W.D. Messick (1986). ***Passing down the farm.*** Cleveland: Jamieson Press.

Kasdan, L. (1965). **Family structure, migration, and the entrepreneur.** *Comparative Studies in Society and History,* 7: 343-357.

Kaslow, F. (1993). **The lore and lure of family business.** *The American Journal of Family Therapy,* 21: 3-16.

Katz, D. & R.L. Kahn (1978). ***The social psychology of organizations.*** New York: John Wiley.

Khalaf, S. & E. Shwayri (1966). **Family firms and industrial development: The Lebanese case.** *Economic Development and Cultural Change,* 15: 59-69.

Kicza, J.E. (1985). **The role of the family in economic development in nineteenth-century Latin America.** *Journal of Family History,* Fall: 235-246.

Klassen, H.C. (1991). **Entrepreneurship in the Canadian west: The enterprises of A.E. Cross, 1886-1920.** *The Western Historical Quarterly,* 22: 313-333.

Kohl, S.B. (1976). ***Working together: Women and family in South-western Saskatchewan.*** Toronto: Holt, Rinehart, and Winston.

Landis, R.G. (1990). **The family business: Problems of identity and authority in literature, theory, and the academy**. Doctoral dissertation. University of Pennsylvania.

Lea, J.W. (1991). ***Keeping it in the family: Successful succession of the family business***. New York: John Wiley.

Legler, J.R. (1989). **An integrated systems framework for analyzing family business planning**. Doctoral dissertation. Oregon State University.

Lentz, B.F. & D.N. Laband (1990). **Entrepreneurial success and occupational inheritance among proprietors.** *Canadian Journal of Economics,* 23: 563-579.

Liebowitz, B. (1986). **Resolving conflict in the family owned business.** *Consultation: An International Journal,* 5: 191-205.

Lomask, M. (1964). ***Seed money: The Guggenheim story***. New York: Farrar, Strauss & Co.

Lundberg, F. (1968). ***The rich and the super-rich.*** New York: Lyle Stuart.

Mace, M.L. (1971). ***Directors: Myth and reality***. Boston: Harvard Business School Press.

Malkin, R.S. (1992). **A guide for the practice of family business consulting**. Doctoral dissertation. The Union Institute.

Marcus, G.E. (1980). **Law in the development of dynastic families among American business elites: The domestication of capital and the capitalization of family.** *Law and Society Review,* 14: 859-903.

Margolick, D. (1993). ***The epic battle for the Johnson & Johnson fortune***. New York: William Morrow.

Marshack, K.J. (1995). **Love and work: How co-entrepreneurial couples manage the boundaries and transitions in personal relationship and business partnership.** Doctoral dissertation. The Fielding Institute.

MassMutual. (1993). ***Research Findings.*** Springfield, Mass.: Massachusetts Mutual Life Insurance company.

MassMutual. (1994). ***Research Findings.*** Springfield, Mass.: Massachusetts Mutual Life Insurance company.

Mattessich, P. & R. Hill (1976). **Family enterprise and societal development: A theoretical assessment.** *Journal of Comparative Family Studies,* 7: 147-158.

McGurrin, L. (1986). **The family company after going public.** *New England Business,* August 4.

McKnight, G. (1987). ***Gucci: A house divided.*** Donald J.Fine Inc.

Min, P.G. (1986-1987). **Filipino and Korean immigrants in small business: A comparative analysis.** *Amerasia Journal,* 13: 53-71.

Mosley, L. (1980). ***Blood relations: The rise and fall of the du Ponts of Delaware.*** New York: Atheneum.

Nelton, S. (1986). ***In love and in business: How entrepreneurial couples are changing the rules of business and marriage.*** New York: John Wiley.

Nonini, D.M. (1987). **Some reflections on "entrepreneurship" and the Chinese community of a West Malaysian market town.** *Ethnos,* 52: 350-367.

O'Donnell, E. (1985). ***Leading the way: An unauthorized guide to the Sobey empire.*** Halifax: GATT-Fly Atlantic.

Painter, W.H. (1971). ***Corporate and tax aspects of closely held corporations.*** Boston: Little, Brown, & Co.

Patrick, A. (1985). **Family Business: The offspring's perception of work satisfaction and their working relationships with their father.** Doctoral Dissertation. Fielding Institute.

Pave, I. (1985). **A lot of enterprise is staying in the family these days.** *Business Week.* July 1: 62-63.

Poe, R. (1980). **The SOBs.** *Across the Board.* May, 17: 33.

Pottker, J. (1992). ***Born to power: Heirs to America's leading businesses.*** Hauppauge: Barron's Educational Series.

Poza, E.J. (1989). ***Smart growth: Critical choices for business continuity and prosperity.*** San Francisco: Jossey-Bass.

Pratt, S.P. (1989). ***Valuing a business: The analysis and appraisal of closely held companies.*** Homewood: Dow Jones-Irwin.

Ram, M. & R. Holliday (1993). **Relative merits: Family culture and kinship in small firms.** *Sociology,* 27: 629-648.

Renshaw, J.R. (1976). **An exploration of the dynamics of the overlapping worlds of work and family.** *Family Process,* 15: 143-165.

Riordan, D.A. (1988). **The nature and effectiveness of management control in small family businesses**. Doctoral dissertation. Virginia Polytechnic Institute and State University.

Roddick, A. (1991). ***Body and soul.*** New York: Crown Publishers.

Rose, M.B. (1976). **The role of the family in providing capital and managerial talent in Samuel Greg and Company.** *Business History,* 18: 3754.

Rosenblatt, P. & S. Albert (1990). **Management and succession: intergenerational relationships in fact and metaphor.** *Marriage and Family Review,* 15: 161-170.

Rosenblatt, P.C., L. de Mik, R.M. Anderson, & P.A. Johnson (1985). ***The family in business.*** San Francisco: Jossey-Bass Publishers.

Savage, D. (1979). ***Founders, heirs, and managers: French industrial leadership in transition.*** Beverly Hills: Sage.

Schien, E.H. (1978). ***Career Dynamics: Matching individual and organizational needs.*** Redding: Addison-Wesley.

Scranton, P. (1986). **Learning manufacture: Education and shop-floor schooling in the family firm.** *Technology and Culture,* 27: 40-62.

Scranton, P. (1992). **Understanding the strategies and dynamics of long lived family firms.** *Business and Economic History,* 21: 219-227.

Seymour, K.C. (1992). **Inter-generational relationships in the family firm: The effect on leadership succession**. Doctoral dissertation. California School of Professional Psychology.

Shaw, R. (1959). **What about family owned corporations that have 'Gone Public'.** *The Magazine of Wall Street,* Jan 17: 411.

Sluyterman, K.E. & H.J.M. Winkelman (1993). **The Dutch family firm confronted with Chandler's dynamics of industrial capitalism, 1890-1940.** *Business History,* 35: 152-183.

Smith, S. (1993). **Fortune and failure: The survival of family firms in eighteenth-century India.** *Business History,* 35: 44-65.

Sonnenfeld, J. (1988). ***The hero's farewell: What happens when CEOs retire.*** Oxford: Oxford University Press.

Stempler, G.L. (1988). **A study of succession in family-owned businesses.** Doctoral dissertation. George Washington University.

Stern., M.H. (1986). ***Inside the family held business.*** New York: Harcourt Brace.

Stone, E. (1989). ***Black sheep and kissing cousins: How our family stories shape us.*** Bergenfield: Penguin.

Stryker, P. (1957). **Would you hire your son?** *Fortune,* March.

Symes, D.G. (1990). **Bridging the generations: Succession and inheritance in a changing world.** *Sociologia Ruralis,* 30: 280-291.

Syms, M. (1992). ***Mind your own business: And keep it in the family.*** New York: Mastermind Limited.

Tambunan, T. (1992). **The role of small firms in Indonesia.** *Small Business Economics,* 4: 59-72.

Tilles, S. (1970). **Survival strategies for family firms.** *European Business,* April: 9-17.

Titus, S., P.C. Rosenblatt, & R.M. Anderson (1979). **Family conflict over inheritance of property.** *The Family Coordinator,* July.

Toman, W. (1969). ***Family constellation.*** New York: Springer.

Topolnicki, D.M. (1983). **Family firms can leave the feuds behind.** *Money,* 12: 83-89.

Toy, S. (1988). **The new nepotism.** *Business Week,* April 4.

Vancil, R.F. (1987). ***Passing the Baton: Managing the process of CEO succession***. Boston: Harvard Business School Press.

Vesper, K.H. (1980). ***New Venture Strategies***. Englewood Cliffs: Prentice-Hall.

Vijverberg, W.P.M. (1990). **Nonfarm self-employment and the informal sector in Cote d'Ivoire: A test of categorical identity.** *The Journal of Developing Areas,* 24: 523-542.

Wagen, M. (1994). ***Annotated family business bibliography***. Lausanne: The Family Business Network (IMD).

Wall, J.F. (1990). ***Alfred I. du Pont: The man and his family***. New York: Oxford University Press.

Ward Jr., J. L. (1986). **Siblings and the family business.** *Loyola Business Forum,* 6: 1-3.

Ward, Jr., J.L. (1987). ***Keeping the family business healthy: How to plan for continuing growth, profitability, and family leadership***. San Francisco: Jossey-Bass.

Ward, Jr., J.L. (1991). ***Creating effective boards for private enterprises***. San Francisco: Jossey-Bass.

Watson, T.J. & P. Petre (1990). ***Father son & co.: My life at IBM and beyond***. New York: Bantam Books.

Weigel, D.J. (1992). **A model of interaction in the intergenerational family business**. Master's thesis. University of Nevada, Reno.

White III, F. (1983). **Widows who run the family business.** *Ebony,* November.

5

SUBJECT INDEX

MIX
Papier aus verantwortungsvollen Quellen
Paper from responsible sources
FSC® C105338

If you have any concerns about our products,
you can contact us on
ProductSafety@springernature.com

In case Publisher is established outside the EU,
the EU authorized representative is:
Springer Nature Customer Service Center GmbH
Europaplatz 3, 69115 Heidelberg, Germany

Printed by Libri Plureos GmbH
in Hamburg, Germany